THE COMPLETE GUIDE TO INTERNATIONAL JOBS AND CAREERS

Books by Drs. Ron and Caryl Krannich

The Almanac of American Government Jobs and Careers
The Almanac of International Jobs and Careers
Best Jobs For the 1990s and Into the 21st Century
Careering and Re-Careering For the 1990s
The Complete Guide To International Jobs and Careers
The Complete Guide To Public Employment
Discover the Best Jobs For You!
Discover the Right Job For You!
Dynamite Answers To Interview Questions
Dynamite Cover Letters
Dynamite Resumes
The Educator's Guide To Alternative Jobs and Careers
Find a Federal Job Fast!
High Impact Resumes and Letters
Interview For Success
Job Search Letters That Get Result
Jobs For People Who Love Travel
Mayors and Managers
Moving Out of Education
Moving Out of Government
Network Your Way To Job and Career Success
The Politics of Family Planning Policy
Re-Careering in Turbulent Times
Right SF-171 Writer
Salary Success
Shopping and Traveling in Exotic Asia
Shopping and Traveling in Exotic Hong Kong
Shopping and Traveling in Exotic India
Shopping and Traveling in Exotic Indonesia
Shopping and Traveling in Exotic Morocco
Shopping and Traveling in Exotic Singapore and Malaysia
Shopping and Traveling in Exotic Thailand
Shopping and Traveling in the Exotic Philippines
Shopping in Exciting Australia and Papua New Guinea
Shopping in Exotic Places
Shopping the Exotic Pacific

THE COMPLETE GUIDE TO INTERNATIONAL JOBS AND CAREERS

Second Edition

Ronald L. Krannich, Ph.D.
Caryl Rae Krannich, Ph.D.

IMPACT PUBLICATIONS
Manassas Park, VA

THE COMPLETE GUIDE TO INTERNATIONAL JOBS AND CAREERS: Your Passport to a World of Exciting and Exotic Employment

Second Edition

Library of Congress Cataloguing-in-Publication Data

Krannich, Ronald L.
    The complete guide to international jobs and careers / Ronald L.
Krannich, Caryl Rae Krannich.—2nd ed.
      p.   cm.
    Includes bibliography references and index.
    ISBN 0-942710-83-5 (cloth) : $24.95.—ISBN 0-942710-69-X (paper) :
$13.95.
      1. American—Employment—Foreign countries—Handbooks, manuals, etc.
2. Employment in foreign countries—Handbooks, manuals, etc. I. Krannich,
Caryl Rae. II. Title.
  HF5549.5.E45K73   1992
  650.14—dc20   92-10842
                                         CIP

For information on distribution or quantity discount rates, Tel. 703/361-7300, Fax 703/335-9486, or write to: Sales Department, IMPACT PUBLICATIONS, 9104-N Manassas Drive, Manassas Park, VA 22111. Distributed to the trade by National Book Network, 4720 Boston Way, Suite A, Lanham, MD 20706, Tel. 301/459-8696.

CONTENTS

PART I
UNDERSTANDING AND ACTION

PART II
EFFECTIVE JOB SEARCH
SKILLS AND STRATEGIES

PART III
FINDING YOUR BEST
WORK SETTING

PREFACE

The 1990s is truly a new decade for international affairs. Old adversarial political and military relationships are being turned upside down in a world where business and economics take center stage in a newly emerging political and economic order. The crumbling of the Russian Empire and communism, continuing indebtedness of the U.S., widespread poverty in the Third World, a strong Japan and Germany, the emergence of an economically unified Western Europe, the remarkably dynamic economies of the Newly Industrialized Countries (NICs) of Asia and the Pacific Rim, and the increase in regional political and military conflicts are redefining the basic relationships of nations in what is increasingly a global village. In their aftermath remains a great deal of uncertainty about what may well become a new world order or disorder.

The two or three major power centers that largely defined the post-World War II world order in both economic and military terms have given way to a highly competitive international arena where trade and economic development will largely define relations among nations in the decade ahead. If international political and economic developments in the early days of the 1990s are any indicators of things to come, the 1990s should prove to be one of the most exciting decades for international affairs—and especially for international jobs and careers. Military might no longer defines a nation's wealth and power. Indeed, the military remains an economic drain on nations that have learned that "many arms will make you poor and noncompetitive." Power in the 1990s is more appropriately defined in economic terms: the capacity of one country to consume the resources and wealth of other countries.

The momentous changes of the early 1990s have important implications for international jobs and careers. Government, once seen as the major employer of international specialists, is quickly getting out of the Cold War business and focusing more and more on the business of international trade and investment. As Western Europe finally puts its economic house in order by creating the world's largest consumer market at the foot of the collapsing Russian Empire, as Japan continues to aggressively invest in other countries, and as Newly

Industrialized Countries challenge the traditional developed countries in both manufacturing and service industries, a highly competitive race is on between countries and regions for increasing their share of international trade and economic development. National politics and military policies in the 1990s will more likely be influenced by what goes on in stock markets and the boardrooms of corporations than by what goes on in governments' foreign policy and military bureaucracies.

While many people want to work in the international arena, few people are prepared to enter today's rapidly changing international job market. Indeed, international jobs that once seemed to lead to exciting careers in government and with international organizations now appear to be "Cold War bureaucratic jobs and careers" that may no longer be attractive opportunities in a world without the Cold War. Many international skills appropriate for the decades of the 1960s, 1970s, and 1980s no longer seem appropriate for the 1990s. At the same time, few people understand the structure of the international job market as well as know appropriate job search strategies for finding jobs and advancing international careers. Indeed, much of the employment structure remains in the state of flux as new nations and economies emerge from the political rubble of the Cold War.

We wrote this book because there is a need to approach the subject of international jobs and careers from a different perspective than heretofore attempted. Most books on this subject are either rambling streams of consciousness or directories of organizations supposedly hiring in the international arena. Providing lists of names, addresses, telephone numbers, and brief annotated descriptions of organizations that can also be acquired through library research, most of these books leave out the most critical elements for finding international jobs—what to do, where to go, and how to market oneself to potential employers. In other words, they provide information on the organizations that largely define the international job market but little or nothing on the dynamics of getting into those organizations.

Our approach to this subject primarily focuses on international job search strategies and tactics. Rather than "boiler plate" general American career planning and job search approaches responsive to a particular cultural setting to the international job market, we examine the structure of the international job market and find that many of these approaches are inappropriate for international jobs. The brief one or two-page American resume, for example, is not appreciated by many employers who want to see a five to ten-page curriculum vita that gives them "the details" on candidates' qualifications. The motivations of many international job seekers are very different from those of job seekers back home. Many are primarily oriented toward adventure, challenges, travel, causes, and enjoying the international lifestyle than with getting ahead in terms of money, status, and position. Such motivations also challenge many career planning and job search strategies that are based on an implicit model of "success" within the American employment culture.

Our point throughout this book is that both the international job market and the international job seeker are different. Therefore, the strategies and tactics appropriate for linking individuals to the organizations that define the international job market also must differ.

By focusing on motivation and other major differences, this book treats the subject of international jobs and careers differently from other books. While we examine such traditional topics as skills identification, research, resumes, networking, and interviewing, we do so from the perspective of the international job seeker who functions within the international job market, a market quite different from the one encountered back home. As a result, we adapt the strategies and techniques to both the motivations of individuals and the requirements of organizations. Although by no means culturally neutral, our end result is at least a more culturally sensitive set of job search strategies and techniques appropriate for the international job market.

We also focus on important organizational alternatives or international work settings that are undergoing important changes in the 1990s—government, international organizations, contracting firms, nonprofit organizations, foundations, research organizations, educational institutions, businesses, and the travel industry. Our approach here is less oriented to describing each organization than to understanding how these organizations are linked together into networks that offer alternative opportunities for international job seekers.

Our bias toward understanding the **process** and formulating **how-to strategies** for linking one's motivation to the real world of jobs and careers is what makes this book different from others you may encounter. This in no way is meant to be critical of these other efforts which we find both necessary and important to finding an international job. In their present form, however, most are incomplete because they don't tell you what to do once you have a name, address, and telephone number in hand. Indeed, we have two separate volumes—*The Almanac of International Jobs and Careers* and *Jobs For People Who Love Travel*—that primarily focus on the organizational alternatives. This book is designed to make these other books work for you in more practical, how-to terms. It tells you how to best open the doors to meet the people behind the names, addresses, and phone numbers provided in numerous international job directories.

We also include a chapter on starting one's own international business—an important job alternative for many individuals who primarily view international jobs in terms of working for someone else's organization.

During the past 25 years we have pursued international jobs and careers both at home and abroad as well as counseled others in the process of finding international jobs. Like many others in the international arena, we very much enjoy what we do rather than have a burning desire to "make it" internationally or successfully climb someone's organizational hierarchy. We've found our own niche in the global community that enables us to do what we most enjoy doing.

If there were one factor explaining what we most enjoy about international jobs and careers, it really comes down to lifestyle. We have our "favorite" places that we return to again and again and other places we have no interest in ever seeing. We have friends and relationships spread throughout the world that make our international worklife especially rewarding. For us, it has been an extremely interesting, enriching, and rewarding worklife that we would not trade for any other type of job or career.

International job seekers are different. They can't really explain what pulls and pushes them into the international arena. It's often an addiction to travel, seeing new places, doing different things, being challenged, learning about the larger world around them, or being in the midst of exciting developments. Most are a particular type of entrepreneur who live fascinating lives.

Regardless of what motivates you to enter the international job market, we are certain of one thing: your timing could not be better. We believe the 1990s will prove to be one of the most exciting times for international jobs and careers. But be sure you have the right mix of skills to go along with your motivations. Don't make the mistake of many frustrated international job seekers who are high on motivation but low on marketable skills. Positive and wishful thinking are no substitutes for a sound curriculum vita and demonstrated international skills that communicate your qualifications to potential employers.

We wish you the very best and hope this book will give you that "extra edge" in navigating through an exciting and exotic sea of international jobs and careers. Join us as we take time to sail into this new decade of international opportunities!

Ronald L. Krannich
Caryl Rae Krannich

Chapter One

INTERNATIONAL JOBS AND CAREERS

Few employment arenas are as exciting, rewarding, entrepreneurial, intriguing, mysterious, and fraught with mischief and misfits than the international job market. Each year millions of anxious job seekers and curious on-lookers yearn to find employment in what appears to be the world's most "glamorous" job market. For some, it's a lifelong dream that may soon come true. For others, it's the continuation of an exciting yet unpredictable career begun many years before. And for others, who are just a step away from the armchair traveler, working abroad in some exotic setting is something they fantasize about; perhaps some day they will take an extended trip to the area they had hoped would yield employment in their younger years.

TURNING DREAMS INTO REALITIES

Let's talk truth about who we are and what we're doing here. You're different from the average job seeker; you're looking for an international job—a career track few people are adventuresome enough to pursue. You're deserting standard paths to career success. Others, including your family, may think you're an odd-ball. You appear unsettled in what you want to do with the rest of your life. After all, why didn't you pursue a "normal" career that would keep you close to home as well as lead to some form of apparent career success others could clearly understand? They really don't understand you and your international interests. And it's no use trying to explain your career interests and lifestyle anymore. In fact, the last time you returned home from abroad, few were really interested in what you did, even though it was very important to you!

It's time to get serious about finding an international job and pursuing an international career, regardless of what others may think about you. You want to do what you really enjoy doing—living and working abroad.

Maybe you're a dreamer. You want to live in some exciting and exotic places; meet intriguing people with international backgrounds; make big money; travel extensively; deal with pressing international issues; or live a thrilling lifestyle that only an international job can offer. Or perhaps you had an international experience that addicted you to the international arena. Chances are you will never shake that addiction as you continue to look for additional international experiences in the years to come—through education, travel, and employment.

Chances are you will never shake that addiction as you continue to look for additional international experiences.

Dreams often do come true for those who are determined to shape their future. But they especially come true for those who also know what they are doing and have the requisite skills for landing an international job.

While you may be highly motivated to get an international job, are you realistic about your future and prepared to tackle the international job market? Do you have the requisite knowledge and skills to make it in the international arena? Do you know who is hiring for international positions? What are the jobs, where are they found, and what do they pay? But most important of all, when will **you** land your international job? What will you have to do between now and then to make your career choice happen?

In the following pages we'll address these and many other concerns of international job seekers as well as answer some of the most important questions for getting an international job. We'll show you how to turn your dreams into realities by acquiring the necessary skills and developing appropriate strategies for landing a job in today's highly competitive international job market.

BEWARE OF CON ARTISTS

If you are a highly motivated international job dreamer, you may be susceptible to a great deal of wishful thinking. If you have little or no international experience and few international skills, you will probably experience numerous job search disappointments. Feeling frustrated, you may engage in random and sometimes mindless action in your effort to find an international job.

Worst of all, you may be especially vulnerable to numerous con artists who promise international jobs in exchange for exorbitant "placement fees." The lure of international jobs amongst naive and unrealistic job seekers has resulted in a flourishing industry of con men and rip-off artists who regularly advertise international placement services in newspapers and magazines, many of which may appear reputable. Disproportionately operating from Florida and Canada, these relatively unregulated scams take millions of dollars from thousands of highly motivated but frustrated international job seekers who believe international jobs must be controlled by such placement services. In over 90 percent of the cases, these operations result in fleecing individuals out of anywhere from $50 to $5,000. In fact, the situation has gotten worse during the past two years as more of these firms prey on gullible individuals, many of whom are unemployed construction workers or spouses lured into believing they can make big bucks working on construction projects in the Middle East or Australia. Few get such jobs. Instead, they normally lose about $1,000 to a fly-by-night "placement firm" that at best gives them a list of 100 employers and a travel video. This should not happen to you.

Beware of anyone who tries to charge you up-front fees for any services related to finding international jobs. Anyone who does is most likely about to treat themselves to your hard earned money in exchange for broken promises. As we will see in the following pages, no groups or individuals control international jobs or placements. Only **you** can find **your** international job. It's hard work, but it must be done by **you**. Be cautious dealing with anyone who says they can do it for you and accordingly charges an up-front fee for access to their "secrets."

The following pages will show you how to go about conducting your own international job search. You **will** find an international job if you have the requisite international skills, use appropriate job search strategies, and are persistent in connecting with the right employers.

However, don't expect to find an international job if you lack specific skills employers seek. While many skills used in the domestic U.S. job market may transfer to the international arena, employers also look for other skills based upon international knowledge and experience. Positive thinking, motivation, and persistence will play important roles in your job search, but they do not substitute for concrete international skills.

Whatever you do, make sure your international skills are at least equal to your high level of motivation.

A DIFFERENT WORKLIFE

The international job market does not attract the average type of job seeker who is primarily oriented toward the American concept of "career success" and who conveniently separates a professional life from a personal life, distinguishes between work and play, and views international travel as an incentive, reward, or vacation in relation to their present job. For international jobs generate important lifestyles where one's job and personal life merge into a unique form of worklife. It's a lifestyle where separating one's work and income from one's personal and family situation is often difficult to achieve. Resettling Cambodian and Haitian refugees, feeding the starving in Ethiopia, demonstrating a new irrigation pump in Indonesia, responding to political upheavals in Eastern Europe and the former Soviet Union, introducing new products into the Japanese and Chinese markets, or importing arts and crafts from India and Morocco are experiences unlike any found in jobs and careers back home. They are what push and pull many dedicated job seekers into the international job market. Addictive and cumulative, these experiences keep them moving in and around this job market for many years to comes.

> *International jobs generate important*
> *lifestyles where one's job and*
> *personal life merge into a*
> *unique form of worklife.*

UNIQUE JOB SEEKERS

Challenging, exciting, addictive, and sometimes dangerous, international jobs are particularly appealing for certain types of individuals. For many, these jobs are both personally and financially rewarding. Many would not trade their present international job and lifestyle for any job back home. Some become international nomads, obsessed with travel, new adventures, and living in exotic societies and cultures.

Indeed, for those who have lived and worked abroad, it is often difficult to communicate to others the uniqueness, excitement, challenge, and satisfaction of the international experience. A very personal, internalized experience for many people, working abroad is a unique form of entrepreneurship. After a few months of returning home, many of these individuals soon experience an unexplained yearning to get back into the international job market so they can once again travel the globe to be challenged and to experience something different. Even those who have returned home for five or ten years often get the urge to return to what was one of the most exciting times of their worklife. Many will take almost any job just to get back to living and working abroad. Not surprising, jobs back home seem boring compared to many jobs encountered abroad.

In many respects, the international employment arena is the last great frontier for striking out on one's own. It's filled with myths, martyrs, misfits, and missionaries—a particular breed of job seeker that is simultaneously fascinating and frustrated. We can think of few other employment arenas—other than perhaps Hollywood—that generate so many unrealistic job seekers who are high on fantasies and motivation but low on information and skills.

But being unrealistic is not necessarily negative for an international job search. Ironically, it is the dreams, fantasies, and unrealistic expectations—coupled with an unending drive, persistence, and entrepreneurial spirit—that successfully lead many such job seekers into the international job market. They often confound career counselors with their restlessness, sense of mission, and commitment to "go international" despite all odds and their general lack of goals, skills, and information. Setting goals based upon dreams rather than on an established pattern of motivations, skills, and experience, these people tend to defy standard career planning and job search methods.

The international employment arena is filled with myths, martyrs, misfits, and missionaries—a particular breed of job seeker that is simultaneously fascinating and frustrated.

THE INTERNATIONAL MYSTIQUE

Thinking of quitting your present seemingly boring job and pulling up stakes to move to Europe where you will find excitement and make good money? What about taking off for a few years to travel and work your way around the world? Maybe you want to join the Peace Corps? Perhaps you would like to land one of those high paying jobs in the Middle East that you've heard about? Or maybe you are committed to some important international causes, such as world hunger, population planning, health care, rural development, environmental issues, or refugee resettlement, that could use your energy, enthusiasm, commitment, and drive.

For more than 25 years we have pursued international jobs and careers. We've lived and worked abroad, counseled others on how to find international jobs, and assisted others in re-entering the U.S. domestic job market. We've fashioned an exciting career and lifestyle that enables us to regularly work abroad while maintaining our career base in the U.S. We've met our share of interesting and intelligent international entrepreneurs; social dropouts; those possessed with a cause; individuals obsessed with becoming culturally neutral and linguistically competent; and a wide range of expatriates, short-termers, tourists, and travelers who are all doing something interesting in the international arena. We've served as employees to others' organizations as well as freelanced and engaged in our own form of entrepreneurship. We've frequently wondered how others ever got involved with international jobs, and what continues to drive them in pursuing such careers. And we regularly hear from numerous individuals who seek to break into the international job market after having been struck with the travel bug, a case of wanderlust, a sense of mission, or a yearning to do something different, challenging, unique, or exotic.

They are the ultimate career risk-takers who are not obsessed with their careers. Many reject the conventional model of the "successful job seeker."

MOTIVATION AND LIFESTYLE

In contrast to most job seekers we encounter, the international job seeker is a very different type of individual in terms of motivation, goals, skills, and lifestyles. While the typical job seeker is usually motivated by money, career advancement, and "success" within some organizational structure, more often than not the international job seeker is motivated by a certain degree of restlessness to do something different; a need to change their work environment; a commitment to pursue an important cause or idea; or a desire to experience a different culture, society, and lifestyle.

International job seekers are the ultimate career risk-takers who are seldom obsessed with their careers. Many reject the conventional model of the "successful job seeker" that assumes you must have clear-cut goals and accumulate marketable skills that lead to career advancement and career success. Instead, such job seekers often take any job they can get, willingly compromise their career goals and skills to the requirements of particular jobs, and are always on the lookout for new job opportunities that may well become their next job jump within a highly unstable and unpredictable international job market.

While many international job seekers are looking for jobs and potentially satisfying international careers, they also seek to fashion a particular lifestyle that takes priority over any particular job or career. Indeed, the desire for an international lifestyle is often the driving force for seeking a job—any type of job—in order to "stay" abroad. Many are hopelessly addicted to international life. As a result, many international job seekers are less concerned with formulating clear job and career objectives and developing marketable skills than with finding a job in their favorite part of the world, be it Europe, Australia, Africa, Asia, or the Middle East. They are impatient with such basic **career planning questions** as *"What do you really want to do?"*, because they've already answered this question with a **lifestyle answer:** *"Get out of my present confining job and go work in England or, more specifically, in London."* Rather than deal with the fundamentals of career planning and the job search process—developing an objective, identifying skills, conducting research, writing resumes, networking for job leads, and interviewing for jobs—many of these people are preoccupied with locating job vacancies which they hope they can "fit" themselves into. They are more concerned with finding out *"where are the jobs"* than with *"what are the jobs"* and *"how to go about finding a job."*

Many job seekers approach the international job market high on motivation but low on knowledge and skills—a powerful mixture for job search failure and frustration.

Not surprisingly, many job seekers approach the international job market high on motivation but low on knowledge and skills—a powerful mixture for job search failure and frustration. Many are vulnerable to fly-by-night job search firms and hucksters that promise "international job placements" for up-front fees. Others are forever frustrated with their limited success in landing that perfect international job they have dreamed about for months and years.

THE CAREER COUNSELING DILEMMA

Many career counselors have difficulty applying conventional career planning and job search techniques to individuals with such motivations and behaviors. After all, conventional career planning and job search methods are based upon a model of "success" appropriate for the U.S. job market. They are culturally specific methods that assume individuals will be motivated by money, career advancement, and self-fulfillment.

What, then, happens when these methods are applied to individuals who fundamentally reject such a conventional "success" model in favor of seeking new experiences, following their intuition, pursuing a mission or dream, or satisfying lifestyle goals? Either individuals must alter their motivations and goals in order to make the methods work successfully, or the methods must be fundamentally altered to accommodate a very different set of motivations and goals.

Not surprising, international job seekers pose a basic dilemma for career counselors: How do you counsel someone whose primary concern is to find a job that will support an international lifestyle rather than to find a job they do well and enjoy doing and which leads to career advancement? How does one deal with the fundamentals of motivation and goal setting when such individuals do not fit into the conventional pattern of successful career planning? How helpful will the standard career planning and job search methods be in assisting someone who is unwilling to put money and career success first? How can we best assist people in finding jobs that may not necessarily use their strengths and often result in short-term and unstable employment? How can one go beyond pointing these people in the direction of job vacancy information and announcements in helping them find jobs and develop long-term careers in the international arena?

The very nature of the international job market challenges many conventional career planning and job search methods. Career planning approaches, for example, requiring job seekers to first assess their skills, abilities, and work values and then formulate a career objective that guides their job search toward satisfying long-term careers and progressive career advancement do not work well.

The international employment arena simply is not structured to permit the success of such models and methods. Rather, this is a highly fragmented and segmented job market; access is often difficult if not impossible for many types of jobs; employment is frequently short-term—with a three-year contract considered an excellent job opportunity; job-hopping among many disjointed jobs requiring different mixes of skills is a common pattern for those intent upon continuing employment abroad; and geographic location and cultural settings of employment blur the more traditional skill requirements for job performance. This structure forces international job seekers into a particular pattern for finding and maintaining jobs: they quickly learn the art of networking for developing professional relationships as well as for accessing job vacancy information. In short, those committed to seeking international jobs must be prepared to address both the lifestyle and career questions simultaneously.

FINDING AN INTERNATIONAL JOB

Finding an international job is not as difficult as it may initially appear. For those who already have international work experience, finding another international job requires a combination of technical skills, experience in particular segments of the job market, area and language capabilities, job networking activities, and tenacity. They find jobs by marketing their skills and abilities through a unique network of professional and personal "connections" they have developed over the years in the international arena.

If you lack the proper mix of international experience and connections for landing an international job, you can quickly acquire these keys for breaking into the international job market. You can do this by taking foreign language courses, traveling, joining study tours or semester abroad programs, acquiring an international internship, volunteering to work for an international firm or organization, getting an entry-level position with a nonprofit organization, or starting your own business. These and other opportunities for breaking into the international job market for those with or without higher education credentials and extensive international work experience are outlined in several chapters of Section III on "Finding Your Best Work Setting" which deal with nonprofit organizations, educational institutions, business, the travel industry, and entrepreneurship.

A DIFFERENT APPROACH

This is not the typical international jobs and careers book that is primarily an annotated listing of various organizations hiring international professionals. Several books, including our *Almanac of International Jobs and Careers* and *Jobs For People Who Love Travel*, already approach the subject in this manner. If you are primarily interested in getting a listing of such organizations, you should consult these other books.

On the other hand, if you are interested in understanding the structure of the international job market, learning about job search strategies and techniques appropriate for navigating this market, and exploring a few important job and career options not normally dealt with in other books, then this book is for you.

We approach our subject in terms of the major problem we see facing both international job seekers and career counselors—how to best deal with the issues of motivation and job/career objectives in a highly fragmented, segmented, decentralized, and chaotic international job market. In other words, how can we best advise those whose motivations and goals are not compatible with the standard career planning model as well as conventional job search methods?

Our solution to this problem is what occupies the remainder of this book. The solution is threefold. First, the chapters that follow take as a given the fact that many international job seekers are first and foremost oriented toward an international lifestyle which may or may not involve "making it" in the traditional sense of making money and achieving career success in the form of advancement up organizational or career development hierarchies. Therefore, the career planning and job search methods must be adapted to the motivations and goals of these individuals rather than require that international job seekers adapt their motivations and goals to the implicit goal-oriented and cultural requirements of the methods and techniques. They must accommodate individuals who by nature may be restless, adventuresome, entrepreneurial, and motivated by a sense of mission and seemingly unrealistic dreams.

Second, we attempt to bring some logic to the structure of the international job market, which by definition has few boundaries and which lacks a coherent structure for processing job information. We do this by addressing many myths and realities relevant to understanding international jobs and the international job market; discussing the structure of this market in terms of the types of jobs and organizations hiring international specialists; and pointing job seekers in the direction of key resources for locating job vacancies and organizations hiring for international positions.

Third, we address two areas—the travel industry and starting one's own international business—normally absent in other international books. These are important job and career options for individuals who desire an international lifestyle but who do not want many of the hassles involved in living abroad long-term, who continually face job instability and unpredictability, and who prefer working for themselves. If you are restless and are motivated by the desire to travel as well as live and work abroad, or wish to establish a domestic base from which to occasionally travel abroad as part of your job, the travel industry and owning your own international-related business—be it consulting or import-export—may be perfect career choices for someone with your particular mix of motivations, skills, and experience. These chapters are especially relevant to individuals who already have international experience but wish to permanently return home because of their age and family situations. Indeed, we find many people who have lived and worked abroad for 10 to 20 years want to continue working in the international arena but not in the same manner they have in the past. For many, it's time to settle down, own appreciating property, and ensure their children will be attending good schools back home. The travel industry and starting one's own business may be excellent international job and career options for such individuals since they enable them to continue working in the international arena but from a home base. In many respects, these two job and career options may be ideal solutions to the questions of motivation and objectives for many international job seekers.

THE INTERNATIONAL EXPERIENCE

Many international jobs and careers are exciting and cannot be duplicated in your domestic setting. For many individuals, there's nothing more exciting and personally fulfilling than completing a much needed irrigation project that will greatly improve the health and economic well-being of villagers in Indonesia, the Philippines, Bangladesh, Ghana, Egypt, or Peru; constructing roads and exploring for oil in the jungles of New Guinea, Borneo, or Sumatra; working for a multinational corporation in Hong Kong, Tokyo, Rome, or London to market new engineering products or promote banking services; practicing international law in Bangkok, Bombay, or Bonn; consulting on population planning programs in Africa and Asia; or importing arts and crafts from Morocco and Mexico.

Like travel in general, living and working abroad is a tremendous learning experience. While you may or may not get rich pursuing international jobs and careers, your life will be forever enriched by the people you meet, the stories you accumulate and tell others, and the cultures and societies you learn about. While the international lifestyle may appear exciting, exotic, glamorous, and devoid of problems to outsiders, to many insiders it's a very personal and fulfilling experience.

However, living and working abroad is required for only certain types of international jobs. Other international jobs are based in the United States. For example, many international agencies and organizations maintain both field and headquarter operations; headquarters are often located in Washington, DC, New York City, San Francisco, or Los Angeles. An international career with these organizations may involve rotation between field and headquarter locations or occasional travel to field sites abroad.

> *Living and working abroad is a tremendous learning experience. While you may not get rich pursuing international jobs and careers, your life will be forever enriched.*

In the pages that follow, we attempt to capture much of the excitement along with the problems and pitfalls of international careers. We're convinced that if we address the issues of motivation and goals head-on, you will be in a much better position to deal with various international job and career options. We will go beyond a mere listing of organizations which may or may not have a job for you nor provide you with the lifestyle you want. So join us as we take you on a journey into an exciting international job market as well as into your own motivations and goals for finding the job you want!

EXAMINE YOUR ICQ

But before we jump head-on into this subject, let's take a look at how you orient yourself for success in the international job market. Just how realistic, motivated, and prepared are you for finding an international job? What exactly are your qualifications? What about your educational level, training, and experience? What international job search skills do you process? Are you prepared to travel abroad for an interview as well as quickly move abroad if necessary?

While the chapters that follow will help you answer these questions in detail, you can start orienting yourself to these considerations by completing the following exercise for identifying your "International Career Quotient" or ICQ. Respond to each of the 50 statements according to the instructions and then compile your composite ICQ score at the end of the exercise.

INSTRUCTIONS: Respond to each statement by circling which number at the right best represents your level of knowledge, skill, attitude, experience, or behavior.

SCALE: 0 = not at all   3 = maybe, uncertain
            1 = strongly disagree   4 = agree
            2 = disagree   5 = strongly agree

1. I've traveled to 0, 1, 2, 3, 4, or 5 countries outside
   of North America, Mexico, and the Caribbean.
   (circle the number at the right)   0 1 2 3 4 5

2. I have a resume designed for a specific international
   job.   0 1 2 3 4 5

3. I have skills that are highly sought after in the
   international job market.   0 1 2 3 4 5

4. I know how to locate corporations which have field
   offices in specific countries.   0 1 2 3 4 5

5. I know how to get potential employers interested
   to contact me for a job interview.   0 1 2 3 4 5

6. I know at least 5 people who have international
   jobs and who are willing to give me job leads.   0 1 2 3 4 5

7. I know whom to contact abroad for information on
   international jobs.   0 1 2 3 4 5

8. I have set aside at least 20 hours per week to
   conduct my international job search.   0 1 2 3 4 5

9. I'm good at networking for information, advice,
   and job referrals.   0 1 2 3 4 5

10. I'm prepared to move abroad within 30 days.   0 1 2 3 4 5

11. I have a particular region and country in mind
    where I would like to work.   0 1 2 3 4 5

12. I'm willing to wait 6 to 18 months before landing
    an international job.   0 1 2 3 4 5

13. I can read, write, and speak fluently at least
    one foreign language.   0 1 2 3 4 5

14. I've taken 0, 1, 2, 3, 4, or 5+ college level courses in international business, finance, marketing, and economics. (circle number to right)   0 1 2 3 4 5

15. I have a high school diploma (1), B.A. (2), M.A. (3), Ph.D. (4), or Post-Doctorate (5). (circle number to right representing your highest education)   0 1 2 3 4 5

16. I've lived abroad for 0, 1, 2, 3, 4, or 5+ years. (circle number to right)   0 1 2 3 4 5

17. I have a clear idea of where I want to work in terms of countries, cities, and organizations.   0 1 2 3 4 5

18. I have a clear idea of what I want to do and have stated this at the beginning of my resume.   0 1 2 3 4 5

19. I already have held international jobs for 0, 1, 2, 3, 4, or 5+ years. (circle number to right)   0 1 2 3 4 5

20. Many of my friends and acquaintances are from other countries.   0 1 2 3 4 5

21. I keep abreast of international developments and thus consider myself knowledgeable about the international arena.   0 1 2 3 4 5

22. I know how the international hiring process works in most organizations.   0 1 2 3 4 5

23. I'm willing to travel abroad at my own expense to interview for a job.   0 1 2 3 4 5

24. I know how to conduct a long distance job search campaign.   0 1 2 3 4 5

25. I am a flexible person who can easily adapt to different situations and changing circumstances.   0 1 2 3 4 5

26. I'm generally tolerant of others and their ways of life.   0 1 2 3 4 5

27. I'm a good listener who empathizes with others.   0 1 2 3 4 5

28. I tend to get along well with people from other societies and cultures without going "native."   0 1 2 3 4 5

29. Ambiguities don't bother me much.   0 1 2 3 4 5

30. I'm generally a very patient person.   0 1 2 3 4 5

31. I'm also a very persistent and tenacious person.   0 1 2 3 4 5

32. I have a good sense of humor.   0 1 2 3 4 5

33. I don't take myself too seriously.

0 1 2 3 4 5

34. I'm interested in learning more about others.

0 1 2 3 4 5

35. I believe I'm a realistic person—I do my research, analyze situations in terms of pros and cons, and arrive at sensible and successful decisions.

0 1 2 3 4 5

36. I'm usually successful at what I do.

0 1 2 3 4 5

37. I welcome and thrive on adventure, challenges, and changing and unique situations.

0 1 2 3 4 5

38. I'm not like most other people I meet back home in terms of my motivations, goals, and career pattern.

0 1 2 3 4 5

39. I'm generally a very happy and contented person.

0 1 2 3 4 5

40. While money is important to me, it's not the driving force behind my desire to seek an international job.

0 1 2 3 4 5

41. I have a sense of commitment and responsibility to what I do.

0 1 2 3 4 5

42. I usually make a favorable impression on employers.

0 1 2 3 4 5

43. I try to keep my knowledge and skills as current as possible in my profession.

0 1 2 3 4 5

44. I'm strongly motivated to work hard at finding the right international job for me.

0 1 2 3 4 5

45. I know what I should and should not do when looking for an international job.

0 1 2 3 4 5

46. I know what is the best educational background for landing an international job.

0 1 2 3 4 5

47. I know what international skills employers are most looking for in today's international job market.

0 1 2 3 4 5

48. Within 30 minutes I can get 3 international job leads by phone.

0 1 2 3 4 5

49. I know how to get my first international job interview within 4 weeks and the first job offer within 60 days.

0 1 2 3 4 5

50. I know how to negotiate an international salary and benefits.

0 1 2 3 4 5

TOTALS FOR EACH COLUMN _____

GRAND TOTAL FOR ALL COLUMNS _____

If your composite score (Grand Total) is above 200, you may well be on your way to quickly finding an international job. If your score is between 150 and 199, you need to work on those items on which you scored between 0 and 3. If your score is below 150, you need to get yourself well organized for the international job market by following this book.

Now review each of the items on which you scored below 3 and note that you need to do something about moving your score on these items into the 4 and 5 columns. Many of the following chapters will help you do this. Other items may require additional education, experience, skills, and patterns of behavior—things that are beyond the scope of this book but within your own personal control.

Once you finish this book, complete this exercise again. You should increase your score by 20 percent. If you put this book into practice over the coming weeks by spending 20 hours each week on your international job search, you should improve your score by another 20 percent. Better still, you should eventually land a job you want!

ACQUIRE THE RIGHT RESOURCES

Each year millions of job hunters turn to career planning books for assistance. Normally they begin with a general book and next turn to resume and interview books. They may also find a few books, such as this one, that provide career information on specific employment fields.

If this book represents your first career planning book, you may want to supplement it with a few other key books. Many of these books are available in your local library and bookstore or they can be ordered directly from Impact Publications by completing the order form at the end of this book. Write for a free copy of the most comprehensive career catalog available today—*"Jobs and Careers for the 1990s."* To receive the latest edition of this catalog of over 1,000 annotated career resources, simply write:

IMPACT PUBLICATIONS
ATTN: Free Careers Catalog
9104-N Manassas Drive
Manassas Park, VA 22111

They will send you a copy upon request. Their catalog contains almost every important career and job finding resource available today, including many titles that are difficult if not impossible to find in bookstores and libraries. The catalog includes a comprehensive section on international jobs and careers.

Included in this catalog are our other career planning and job search titles that examine critical steps in the job search process as well as careers in special employment fields: *The Almanac of International Jobs and Careers, Jobs For People Who Love Travel, Best Jobs For the 1990s and Into the 21st Century,*

The Almanac of American Government Jobs and Careers, Find a Federal Job Fast, The Complete Guide To Public Employment, Careering and Re-Careering For the 1990s, High Impact Resumes and Letters, Dynamite Resumes, Dynamite Cover Letters, Dynamite Answers To Interview Questions, Job Search Letters That Get Results, Interview For Success, Network Your Way To Job and Career Success, Discover the Right Job For You, Salary Success, and *The Educator's Guide To Alternative Jobs and Careers.* If you are interested in our "Impact Guides" titles for travel or import-export purposes, ask for the latest trade catalog—*"Career and Travel Books"*—that includes 10 books encompassing Hong Kong, Thailand, Singapore, Malaysia, Indonesia, Morocco, India, Australia, New Zealand, Papua New Guinea, Fiji, Tahiti, and the Caribbean.

PART I

UNDERSTANDING
FOR ACTION

Chapter Two

TODAY'S
INTERNATIONAL ARENA

Finding an international job requires some basic understanding of how the international job market is structured as well as where international jobs will be found in the decade ahead. For at one level, almost anyone can find a job abroad—as an agricultural worker, waiter, waitress, or domestic worker. At another level, international jobs are few and far between, reserved primarily for individuals with specialized education, technical skills, and international experience. Knowing the structure as well as employment trends should help you better develop an effective approach for the international job market. This approach should align your motivations and goals with the realities of working in the international job market.

THE CHANGING
INTERNATIONAL ENVIRONMENT

Five major changes have taken place in the international arena during the past 20 years that have helped shape the present and future structure of the international job market:

1. The communication revolution has increasingly created a sense of world community and familiarized more people with other peoples, societies, and cultures.

2. Increased interdependency of national economies within the larger international economy results in the increased expansion of domestic business interests abroad and the development of multinational corporations.

3. Continuing poverty, overpopulation, and environmental degradation in the Third and Fourth World countries of Africa, Asia, Middle East, Eastern Europe, and Latin America requires renewed development efforts to resolve national and regional development problems.

4. The continuing expansion and contraction of the Cold War throughout the world; the collapse of the Soviet Union and other communist countries; and the diffusion of nuclear, chemical, and biological weapons to numerous countries, some of which are in the Third World, requires new military, intelligence, and foreign policy initiatives.

5. Internationalizing what used to be primarily domestic issues such as criminal activities attendant with the international production and distribution of illegal drugs and environmental problems such as global warming, acid rain, deforestation, water pollution, and hazardous waste disposal leads to new public policy initiatives closely tied to domestic policies.

Each of these developments has generated new job opportunities for individuals interested in communication, business, development, environmental, criminal justice, and war-related activities. As we move through the 1990s with a restructured world order attendant with the collapse of the Soviet Union and other communist nations in Eastern Europe and the rise of new populist regimes, business and development work will become even more important in the decade ahead as "Cold War careers" are replaced by new "post-Cold War careers" in the international arena.

Communication Revolution

The communication revolution has resulted in increased awareness of other societies and cultures and greater understanding of the interdependency of international political and economic events. Instant news reports from Moscow, Berlin, London, Mexico City, Bogota, and Cape Town underscore the ease of access to other parts of the world as well as a growing familiarity with other countries. Indeed, we live in an increasingly smaller world or "global village" due to the communication revolution.

This revolution has helped generate more interest in other societies especially in the areas of travel and education. More and more people travel abroad each year in search of new and exotic experiences. Popular destinations are often those that have received extensive media coverage. In 1990, for example, more and more tourists headed for the Soviet Union and Eastern Europe because of the highly publicized political changes taking place there. With the collapse of communism and the Soviet Union in 1991, fewer tourists ventured into what appeared to be chaotic political and economic situations in the former Soviet Union and Eastern Europe. Thailand, Indonesia, and Morocco became "in" destinations for travelers interested in visiting unique and exotic places.

Educational programs are increasingly becoming internationalized as they include more courses and programs on international affairs, languages, and business. Today, more than ever, students have opportunities to study and work abroad as part of international study, internship, and exchange programs. At the same time, English has increasingly become the language of international travel and business, and demand for native speaking English teachers in many countries remains high.

The communication revolution should continue throughout the 1990s in further internationalizing educational programs as well as generating interest in traveling abroad. Not surprising, education and travel should be major growth industries in the decade ahead.

Education and travel should be major growth industries in the decade ahead.

Economic Interdependency and Business Expansion

Throughout most of history great powers sought political and economic control abroad by acquiring the territories and peoples of other societies through a combination of colonialism and military subjugation. While military conflicts and ideologies continue as important means for determining political and territorial control of societies, they are becoming less important than the pragmatic role of business in developing the economic infrastructure of particular countries as well as in linking local economies to the larger global economy. In many countries the coup d'etat, military rule, and ideology have passed into history as bankers and foreign investors—those who service the national debt and extend credit for further economic expansion—have a major say in who runs the political affairs of a country. In this sense international business has become a powerful force for promoting democratic politics. Large multinational companies and an increasingly interdependent world economy are making old ideologies and traditional concepts of nation-states obsolete as more and more countries are recognizing the importance of transcending parochial interests in favor of increased foreign investment and regional economic cooperation.

The European Economic Community is one of the most important cases in point. As Great Britain and Western European nations prepare for the 1992 economic union by ending trade barriers and issuing a common currency, Europe is destined to become a powerful economic force with its block of more than 350 million producers and consumers. As foreign investors scramble to get a piece of the action before Europe ties the knot in 1992, more and more opportunities are opening for multinational corporations and small businesses in Europe.

The international business community is largely dominated by companies based in the United States, Japan, Germany, and Great Britain. Large industrial firms that played key roles in transforming the economies of the newly emerging industrial countries of South Korea and Taiwan are now active in investing abroad and increasingly compete with the multinational firms of the United States, Japan, Germany, and Great Britain in the developing world as well as in Europe, the United States, Hong Kong, and Singapore. Involved in trade, manufacturing, and infrastructure development (roads, dams, telecommunications, plant construction, housing), these firms employ thousands of sales representatives, engineers, architects, lawyers, accountants, and technicians.

At the same time, the transition of communist and socialist systems into more competitive political and free-market economic systems requires a greater emphasis on foreign business investment, entrepreneurship, and education. The economic reconstruction of Eastern Europe, Russia, newly independent states of the former Soviet Union, Central America, and Vietnam, Laos, and Cambodia will provide numerous opportunities for international businesses to expand their operations into these regions and countries. While many international lending institutions and multinational corporations are positioned well to respond to such changes by extending their field operations into new investment areas, small businesses as well as individuals are finding new opportunities to promote their products and services in these countries. With greater emphasis on entrepreneurship, we should see more small import-export and consulting businesses arising over the next decade.

Business—not government—will be the primary catalyst generating international jobs in the decade ahead.

In short, business—not government—will be the primary catalyst generating international jobs in the coming decade. These businesses will range in size from large multinational firms employing more than 100,000 people to small businesses and individual entrepreneurs who want to import and export products or offer specialized consulting services. Requirements for acquiring such jobs will range from highly specialized language and technical skills to basic entrepreneurism in the form of drive, tenacity, and networking skills accompanied by a valid passport, fax machine, and a list of international contacts.

The Developing World

The developing world, or what is commonly referred to as poor Third and Fourth World countries, have undergone numerous changes during the past three decades. Targets for government programs, non-governmental organizations, and lending institutions primarily aimed at rural development and population control, some of these countries have become remarkable success stories while others have become international basket cases worse off today than 40 years ago.

Asia boasts the largest number of success stories. Countries such as South Korea, Taiwan, Singapore, and the British colony of Hong Kong emerged in the early 1980s as surprising success stories as the economies recorded annual GNP growth rates in excess of 10 percent. These countries, in turn, became major investors in other developing countries during the late 1980s as they sought cheaper labor abroad as well as new markets for their products. Other Asian nations, such as Thailand, Malaysia, and Indonesia, are quickly following suit as they become the great success stories of the 1990s. Job opportunities in these countries have significantly shifted from governmental and nongovernmental organizations heavily involved in rural development and population policy to international businesses involved in the rapid industrialization and expansion of the urban service sectors. In some cases bilateral development assistance to these countries has nearly ended as international businesses play a central role in the economic expansion of these take-off economies. Individuals interested in rural development work will find few opportunities in these countries while opportunities for entrepreneurs will abound.

However, most of the developing world is not a success story. It remains mired in poverty, hunger, overpopulation, and political instability; environmental problems appear out of control. Either unable or unwilling to control runaway population growth and inflation as well as attract investors willing to take major risks, these countries require a great deal of development assistance from foreign governments and nongovernmental organizations to keep them economically afloat. In addition, many communist and ex-communist regimes, such as Russia, Vietnam, Cambodia, Laos, and former Eastern European block countries and the newly independent states of the former Soviet Union are economic "basket cases" requiring massive infusions of foreign capital and investment as well as bilateral aid. Many developing countries, especially in Africa, Latin America, and South Asia, are likely to continue with major development problems due to runaway population growth that effectively cancels what small economic development gains they make. In addition, many of these countries are likely to receive less bilateral aid as major donor nations reprogram assistance to Eastern Europe and the newly independent nations of the former Soviet Union. As a result, nongovernmental organizations will play an even more important role in the developing countries of Africa, Latin America, and South Asia.

Important political and economic changes that took place in the communist world from 1989 to 1991 will have far reaching consequences on the way government and business deals with the developing world over the next decade. Initially more and more government resources and business efforts will be concentrated on these developing economies. However, since the developing world now is home for 77 percent of the world's population and it's rapid population growth rates will put this percentage at 80 by the turn of the century, renewed efforts to solve the problems of developing countries will continue over the next decade. This means more job opportunities with nongovernmental organizations, multinational firms, and small businesses in Asia, Africa, and Latin America.

Whither "Cold War Careers"?

Shortly after World War II until the present many jobs and careers developed around the evolution of the Cold War. Perhaps best termed "Cold War careers," these are especially evident among thousands of jobs in such U.S. government organizations as the Department of Defense, the United States Information Agency, Central Intelligence Agency, Defense Intelligence Agency, and the Agency for International Development. These agencies, in turn, have been responsible for generating a huge number of defense, intelligence, and development careers and millions of jobs among government contractors and consultants who primarily depend on government contracts for their existence.

The future of many international jobs and careers are in danger with the ending of the Cold War attendant with the disintegration of the Soviet Union and Eastern European communist regimes and as economic development becomes the major goal of most societies in the decade ahead. Indeed, the assumptions underlying much of U.S. foreign policy are no longer valid given the collapse of the communist world. Major cutbacks will take place in defense spending, and foreign aid will be reallocated according to new priorities. Defense cutbacks will have a major impact on both Department of Defense hiring levels and the number of defense contractors and consulting firms involved in the department's procurement process. In the early months of 1990, for example, defense contracting had declined by 40 percent and the Department of Defense decided to cutback 40,000 procurement employees. The Department had definitely entered a period of major uncertainty about the future direction of defense policy. The impact of ending the Cold War appeared to be irreversible for the so-called "military-industrial complex" that had played a central role in shaping foreign and defense policies during the post-World War II period.

Many "Cold War careers" should adjust easily to the post-Cold War period of the 1990s. The Agency for International Development (USAID) and its relevant contractors and consultants, for example, whose Cold War purpose has been to strengthen non-communist regimes through development efforts, will begin shifting budgetary priorities into Eastern Europe and Central America. Indeed, during the 1980s USAID moved millions of dollars into nongovernmental organizations operating in Poland. USAID will most likely expand its scope of operations throughout Eastern Europe as well as possibly in the new states of the former Soviet Union, China, Vietnam, Cambodia, and Laos—some of which are now accepting the presence of U.S. Peace Corps Volunteers. On the other hand, careers in defense intelligence and military hardware and technology will undergo major changes rather than adjust well to the changing international environment.

Internationalizing Domestic Issues

The line between domestic and international issues is increasingly conceptual. It has become artificial given the growing economic and political interdependence of the domestic and international arenas. Oil crises in the Middle East, changes in the London and Tokyo stock markets, drug wars in Central and Latin America, environmental damage in Canada and Czechoslovakia, and political upheavals in the South Africa and China are felt immediately in New York City, Atlanta, San Antonio, and Sacramento. No longer can we deal with many domestic issues in isolation of their larger international setting.

The international drug problem will continue to act as a major catalyst in the growth of the American criminal justice system.

Indeed, America's horrendous drug and crime problems have international connections. Drug wars and terrorism in Central and Latin America affect the flow of illegal drugs and criminal activities in the streets of New York City, Washington, DC, Atlanta, Chicago, and Los Angeles. Drug lords in Hong Kong, Thailand, Burma, and Colombia help fuel America's drug culture which impacts on all aspects of the criminal justice system, from the hiring of more police officers to the overloading of the court systems and the expansion of prisons. The international drug problem will continue to act as a major catalyst in the growth of the American criminal justice system. As a result, more international job opportunities should be available within such government agencies as the

Department of Justice, Department of State, Drug Enforcement Agency, Central Intelligence Agency, and the Federal Bureau of Investigation. The Department of Defense may transform much of its Cold War role to that of an international police force involved in drug wars and combating terrorism. This could involve anything from ongoing intelligence operations to regular interdiction and major military operations to shut down the flow of drugs into the U.S. Some contractors and consultants will also benefit from the continuing expansion of the criminal justice system.

PREDICTING THE FUTURE

Similar to the end of World War II, 1989, 1990, and 1991 were major watershed years. The most momentous change was the disintegration of the Russian Empire which actually began more than a decade earlier; 1989 merely confirmed it was over. While communism did not end, it did undergo some radical transformations that may alter its ideology, structure, tactics, and following forever. More importantly, the political and economic changes taking place in the former Soviet Union, Eastern Europe, the Middle East, Central America, and China will result in a fundamentally restructured international environment for government and business. It will also result in new job opportunities in countries that were previously closed to non-communist societies.

Certain trends for international employment are evident based on knowledge of past patterns, current needs, and predictions of future developments in a restructured international arena. We see nine broad trends developing during the next decade:

1. **A changing world order attendant with new populist regimes in the former Soviet Union and Eastern Europe; the disintegration of the Soviet Union and the emergence of new nation-states; renewed economic rivalry between the U.S. and Asia; continuing poverty and political turmoil in Third and Fourth World countries; and the expansion of drug wars and terrorism in the Third World will result in new public policy initiatives and hiring emphases within government as well as among consultants, contractors, nonprofit organizations, and research groups.**

These trends have the most important consequences for developing new patterns of international employment in the coming decade. More and more students will be learning the languages and studying the economics, politics, and cultures of the new states within the former Soviet Union, Eastern European countries, China, and Japan. The break-up of communist regimes in Eastern Europe, the collapse of the Soviet Union, the emergence of new nation-states, continuing political turmoil in the Middle East and Central America, and the changing roles of China, Japan, and other major Asian economies will have major implications for international employment. The major casualties within the United States will be the Department of Defense and its hundreds of contractors and consultants that made lucrative careers out of providing the hardware for managing the Cold War. With the ending of the Cold War, the demilitarization of the Soviet Union in Eastern Europe, the transformation of NATO and the collapse of the Warsaw Pact, and the end of the Soviet Union and its military support for revolutionary causes in poor Third and Fourth World countries, the rationale for continuing high levels of military spending will be seriously challenged by new thinking on budgetary priorities. This rationale will be replaced with major arguments for making significant cuts in the defense budget. These cuts could mean very bad times for major defense contractors, retrenchment for both military and civilian personnel in the Department of Defense, and a reallocation of resources to domestic and foreign aid programs. The 1990s may be the worst of times for U.S. military and intelligence agencies but perhaps the best of times for the State Department, U.S. Peace Corps, Agency for International Development, and international-related agencies in the Departments of Commerce, Agriculture, Transportation, Treasury, and Health and Human Services and a new Department of Environment. Diplomacy will become a growth industry as more new nation-states emerge.

However, given the volatility of such changes, as well as the incremental nature of the Federal budgetary process, dramatic changes will be slow in coming. Ironically, Department of Defense adjustments to the changing world order will most likely lag by two to three years given constraints inherent in the annual budgetary process. Continuing rivalry between the U.S. and Asia will place greater emphasis on managing trade and monetary relationships. Problems with poverty and political turmoil in Third and Fourth World countries will place greater emphasis on improving the U.S. presence abroad through the activities of the State Department, the Agency for International Development, and the U.S. Peace Corps. Continuing problems with drug wars and terrorism will mean increased employment within the Defense, State, and Justice departments. Indeed, the role of the military may be transformed during the 1990s to better deal with the problems of terrorism and drugs.

2. **Eastern European as well as Third and Fourth World countries remain major political, military, and economic trouble spots during the next decade due to a combination of ethnic strife, factionalism, poverty, and the incapacity to develop because of ineffective bureaucracies, lack of organizational and political capacity, and economic turmoil.**

The end of the Cold War merely gives rise to new international challenges centered around Eastern Europe, the Middle East, and Third and Fourth World countries that remain steeped in poverty and political instability. Political fragmentation and military intervention along ethnic lines continues in Eastern Europe and the former Soviet Union as well as in China. Several Third and Fourth World countries acquire nuclear delivery, biological weapons, and high-tech terrorist capabilities to destabilize regions, threaten neighboring countries, and challenge major powers. Efforts to contain as well as promote the economic development of these countries will generate many new jobs in military intelligence, arms manufacturing and trade, economic development, and consulting. Indeed, the 1990s will offer a good job market for a new generation of missionaries and mercenaries.

3. **Government employment within the Defense Department declines substantially but remains steady and increases somewhat for other government agencies that extend their missions into newly opened countries.**

Contrary to many predictions that America may enter into a new period of isolationism due to the ending of the Cold War, the U.S. becomes increasingly international in its orientation because of increased economic competition from Japan, South Korea, Taiwan, Southeast Asian countries, and the newly restructured European Economic Community. Adjusting to the new international realities, several government agencies will be winners and losers as the U.S. government adjusts its programs and personnel to a changing international environment and new policy priorities. Expect major personnel declines in the military services, Department of Defense, the United States Information Agency, and military contractors. Major personnel increases should take place among international-oriented agencies within the Departments of Justice, Commerce, Education, Transportation, and Treasury as well as in such independent agencies as the Agency for International Development. The Central Intelligence Agency and the Defense Intelligence Agency will experience some personnel cuts while adjusting to the new international environment with greater emphasis on intelligence activities in Third and Fourth World counties—the major political, military, and economic trouble spots for the 1990s. The Federal government's international policy priorities will increasingly shift from military containment and intervention to issues of trade, economic development, technological transfer, environmental protection, political stability, and democracy. A new Department of Environment will become involved in international environment issues that threaten the future development of all countries.

4. **"Cold war careers" decline substantially while criminal justice and legal careers increase markedly in response to changing international realities.**

Jobs with the Defense Department, defense contractors, and the United States Information Agency as well as amongst traditional intelligence agencies decline as priorities shift to combating illegal drug trafficking and terrorism.

5. **A large number of international job opportunities open up in communist and ex-communist countries.**

As communism declines due to its organizational incapacity to deliver much beyond ideology and control over its populations, major development emphases will be on political and bureaucratic decentralization, foreign investment, international trade, and entrepreneurship. Most of the new international jobs will be related to business and entrepreneurship as Russia, Eastern European countries, China, India, and Vietnam attempt to emulate the thriving economies found in many Asian, Western Europe, and American countries.

6. **Developing Third and Fourth World countries require greater international assistance as the economic situation in many of these countries worsens.**

Runaway population growth continues to outstrip meager economic gains in many countries as more and more African, Latin American, and South Asian countries experience the vicious cycles of poverty, inflation, political instability, and military conflicts. Remaining unattractive areas for foreign business investment and entrepreneurship, these countries increasingly rely on bilateral aid, international loans, and nongovernmental organizations involved in traditional population planning and rural development programs. Nongovernmental organizations working in such developing countries remain as continuing and growing sources for international jobs.

7. **International jobs require more and more specialized and exotic skills, with a preference for individuals with technical and organizational skills.**

Except for English language teachers, the days when highly motivated generalists could find rewarding international jobs and careers are all but gone. The international job arena in developing, newly industrialized, and developed countries require individuals with specific marketable skills. With increased emphasis on business and development, many of these skills will be technical in content. While language and area studies skills will continue to play important roles in the international job market, they will be of secondary importance to technical skills.

8. **As more and more businesses expand their operations abroad and as many newly industrialized countries encourage continuing foreign investment and trade, the 1990s will become an explosive decade for multinational corporations, small businesses, and individual entrepreneurs seeking a piece of the rapidly expanding economic pie in Europe, Asia, the South Pacific, the Caribbean, and the new nations in the former Soviet Union.**

The 1990s should become an exciting and highly competitive decade for international businesses and entrepreneurs. Job opportunities will be plentiful for individuals who have the right mix of skills as well as know how to best find jobs in the chaotic international job market.

9. **International education and the travel industry will experience major growth throughout the 1990s in support of increased business expansion abroad as well as in response to a steady demand to visit new and exotic places.**

More and more educational programs will include languages, area studies, international business, and technology in their programs as well as offer programs for study abroad. The demand for teachers of English will increase in countries undergoing major educational and economic development. The single most rapidly developing international job market will be in the travel and hospitality industry as more people have the resources and desire to travel abroad. While the Caribbean and Europe will remain major travel destinations for Americans, the most rapid growth in the travel industry will take place in exotic and adventuresome locations, such as Thailand, Indonesia, the Philippines, China, India, Nepal, Turkey, and Morocco. International job opportunities will be plentiful with airlines, tour operators, hotels, and cruise lines.

These changes have important implications for those seeking international job and career opportunities. We see eleven major trends for the coming decade that will affect the way individuals approach the international job market:

1. More international job opportunities will be available for those who know where the jobs are and how to find them.

2. Greater competition will arise for international jobs as more and more individuals pursue international careers.

3. With few exceptions, most international jobs will require highly specialized and technical skills.

4. Educational preparation for international jobs should focus on combining language and area studies skills with marketable technical, business, and entrepreneurial skills. Some form of international experience prior to entering the international job market will also be helpful, be it in the form of an internship, study abroad program, or travel.

5. Large corporations based in the U.S. and operating abroad will have few international job openings for entry-level workers because international jobs with such companies are part of a promotion hierarchy in which only highly experienced personnel are sent abroad for assignments for which local nationals are not available. Expect few job opportunities with established international firms that already have talented local staffs running their operations.

6. The easiest and potentially most rewarding way to break into the international job market will be via nongovernmental and volunteer organizations working in developing countries or through educational institutions and the travel industry. Many jobs with these organizations require few technical and linguistic skills. The most important skills will be entrepreneurial in nature.

7. Fewer traditional job opportunities will be available in natural resource exploration, manufacturing, infrastructure, and development in such "favored" places as Hong Kong, Australia, New Zealand, Thailand, Indonesia, Saudi Arabia, and much of Western Europe. Jobs in these countries will increasingly require business, trade, and entrepreneurial skills. Such jobs, however, will be available in less desirable and remote locations in Africa, South Asia, Eastern Europe, and Latin America. Contractors and consultants specializing in rural and urban infrastructure—from dams, roads, and electrical and irrigation systems to public housing, water and sewer systems, mass transit, and waste disposal—as well as local government services will find numerous job opportunities as population pressures place continuing strains on underdeveloped infrastructure and public services. Engineering,

architect, construction, and public administration skills will be in demand.

8. The most effective international job searches will require networking skills for developing job leads and identifying vacancies. Responding to publicized job listings and using international "placement" services will be the least effective approach to finding an international job. The ubiquitous "connection" acquired through networking will prove most effective.

9. International career patterns will remain unstable and unpredictable as individuals frequently move between short-term jobs in different country settings.

10. Many international jobs, especially in Third and Fourth World countries which are home to nearly 80 percent of the world's population, are increasingly dangerous given increased political instability and terrorism in these countries.

11. New job opportunities in Eastern Europe and the new nations of the former Soviet Union will be disappointing as the economies in these areas continue to founder and become major losses for foreign investors. The greatest number of new job opportunities will be with businesses in the rapidly expanding Asia and Pacific Rim regions. Western Europe and Latin America will also offer many job opportunities for enterprising job seekers.

JOB MARKET STRUCTURE AND HIRING PRACTICES

Conducting an effective job search aimed at the international arena is often difficult to do given the overall structure of the international job market. The international employment arena is extremely decentralized and fragmented, and information on organizations and job vacancies is difficult to access. Nonetheless, with some basic information on the structure of the job market as well as a few leads on how to contact organizations and access job vacancy information, you will be well on your way to bringing some structure, coherence, and effectiveness to this job market. In other words, its best to first understand the **structure** of the international job market in order to best handle the **process** of finding a job within the structure.

Job searches in general tend to follow the structure of particular job markets. In the United States, the domestic job market is also highly decentralized, fragmented, and chaotic. While information on organizations and job vacancies in the U.S. is at best incomplete, you do find numerous directories on organizations and many services are available to assist you with a domestic job search. These range from executive search firms to public employment agencies, from classified ads in newspapers and trade journals to job listing services, job banks, and resume marketing services. Furthermore, it is a relatively open job market for enterprising job seekers who can easily network for job leads and apply directly for jobs within a single community. Within a short period of time you can position yourself well within this decentralized yet fairly open job market. The biggest difficulty comes when trying to conduct a long-distance job search campaign which may involve traveling, for example, between Chicago and Los Angeles to develop job leads and interview for jobs. The logistics of conducting a part-time job search by telephone, letters, and periodic travel to another community lessens one's overall job search effectiveness when compared to a full-time job search involving frequent face-to-face informational interviews in a single community.

The international employment arena is extremely decentralized and fragmented, and information on organizations and job vacancies is difficult to access.

The structure of the international job market is even more decentralized and fragmented than the domestic U.S. job market. More importantly, it tends to be closed to outsiders. The implications of this decentralized and closed job market are many for international job seekers. It argues for job search strategies that will best organize international job vacancy information and help penetrate what appears to be essentially a closed system to outsiders.

The following characteristics of the international job market should be kept in mind when formulating the most effective job search strategies that will be responsive to the decentralized and closed nature of the market:

1. **Unless promoted from within an organization and transferred abroad with little or no international skills and experience, most international jobs require specific types of international skills and experience beyond basic travel and language competency.**

   While you can easily break into the domestic job market through entry-level positions which require few skills and little experience, not so for most jobs in the international job market. What entry-level positions exist are most likely found with headquarters staff and involve basic organizational management functions. They may involve little or no international travel and thus have questionable international content. Multinational corporations and large businesses operating abroad seldom hire individuals for international positions other than for consulting positions. For example, full-time IBM employees working abroad tend to be local nationals and management personnel transferred from headquarters in the United States. They may also hire others as consultants or short-term employees, especially if these individuals have specialized technical and language skills that would assist their operations. However, these individuals will most likely remain short-term employees rather than individuals who will advance up IBM's corporate ladder. What international positions exist in such companies are filled from within the organizational ranks through a clearly defined hierarchy of promotions. Experienced employees, who have little or no international experience, including no language skills, are often promoted to overseas posts because of their intimate knowledge of the organization and its products, services, and internal decision-making structure. From the perspective of the organization, hiring someone from outside the organization for such important overseas postings would be foolish. Specific organizational experience is much preferred over international experience. After all, international experience can be quickly acquired by being posted abroad and by working through the local national staff. Therefore, to get an overseas job with such organizations means either working from within the ranks for promotions abroad or being hired by a firm because of extensive experience that can be directly transferred to their organizational products and services. While such promotion and foreign assignment practices are largely responsible for the high turnover and adjustment problems of corporate executives who are unprepared for living and working abroad, nonetheless, it is the practice and it will likely continue in the foreseeable future.

Even nongovernmental organizations working on development projects in Third and Fourth World countries recruit individuals with technical skills, language competency, and international experience. Health workers, such as doctors and nurses, are more likely to break into the international job market than most other types of job seekers primarily because their skills are in demand. Even U.S. Peace Corps Volunteers, who at one time were primarily inexperienced generalists, are increasingly recruited on the basis of their technical skills. For many Volunteers, their Peace Corps experience becomes the first step in getting international experience for other international jobs and life-long international careers. Indeed, ex-Peace Corps Volunteers are now found in abundance within the U.S. State Department and the Agency for International Development and among most contracting and consulting firms as well as nongovernmental organizations operating in Third and Fourth World countries. In fact, in 1990 for the first time in history all heads of U.S. civilian agencies in Nepal—the Ambassador, USAID mission director, U.S. Information Service director, and Peace Corps director—were ex-Peace Corps Volunteers. Most had started their international careers as young inexperienced generalists who acquired international skills and experience through their two to three year Peace Corps service. This milestone will most likely be repeated in other countries during the next decade as the growing "Peace Corps network" demonstrates its commitment to international careers and its continuing success in landing one international job after another in a highly decentralized and chaotic job market that continues to be closed to outsiders.

Travel experience and language competency are not special qualifications for international employment. These are "givens" anyone seeking an overseas job should possess. Without these you do not appear to be a serious job candidate nor have you taken the first steps toward the international job market. While many people do get hired for international jobs without travel experience and language competency, they possess special skills and qualifications that are in demand and thus these override other basic considerations.

Travel experience and language competency are not special qualifications for international employment. These are "givens".

---

2. **Job changes, career advancement, and patterns of employment within the international arena tend to involve movement between many jobs as well as a great deal of job-hopping, uncertainty, anxiety, and frustration.**

Especially with international development work, where jobs are tied to specific government contracts and grants, international careers tend to follow an unpredictable pattern involving frequent moves between jobs, projects, organizations, and countries. One pattern may be to work abroad for a government agency, move on to several contracting firms and nongovernmental organizations that receive government contracts and grants, become a recipient of a personal services contract, and then start one's own contracting and consulting firm either from abroad or based in the U.S. Another pattern might be to start working for a nongovernmental organization, then move into an overseas government position and later start one's own import-export business. This element of job uncertainty and fluidity between jobs, projects, organizations, and even international lifestyles often means individuals are constantly looking toward their next contract, job, assignment, or career opportunity. Even among overseas staff of the State Department and the Agency for International Development, the typical three-year tour begins with planning one's next move to hopefully an even better assignment. This will involve maintaining a good record in one's present job as well as attempting to manipulate the reassignment process in Washington, DC. Few people want their next assignment to be Ouagadougou, Calcutta, Beirut, or Bucharest, but Tokyo, Beijing, Bangkok, Manila, Istanbul, Cairo, Moscow, Madrid, Rome, Paris, Vienna, London, Toronto, or Rio would be nice.

Since many international jobs and careers evolve unpredictably and through word-of-mouth transmission, and many jobs tend to isolate one from the larger international job community, it's important to develop contacts and be in many places at many times so you can learn about impending vacancies. Indeed, international job seekers are noted for using ubiquitous "connections," "dropping names" of people they know or at one time met, or boasting to others about their roles in previous jobs or assignments. In fact, they develop such an international personality in order to quickly connect themselves to current developments and job vacancy information in the international job market. Because of their unstable international job and career situations—often spending no more than two to three years on a particular project or in a specific country, these people are used to making numerous new acquaintances, retaining few long-term friendships, and always having to say "good-bye" to those they have just begun to know and develop close friendships with. As a result, by necessity they must learn to quickly make new acquaintances, effectively network with other international workers, send out numerous resumes, and join organizations that will better put them into contact with other organizations hiring individuals with their interests, skills and experience. In this sense, they are used to developing many superficial friendships, few of which ever develop into close long-term relationships.

Few international careers follow a traditional career path of moving up a single organizational hierarchy for the simple reasons that most of these organizations are small; their organizational structures tend to be flat and exhibit a short hierarchy of management positions; and they are primarily oriented toward delivering services at the field level through jobs that are very technical in orientation. Therefore, given the motivations of many international job seekers to work at the field level where much of the excitement and action is found, and given the flat structure of organizations, many international jobs and careers involve moving from one field position to another in what quickly becomes a seemingly never-ending pattern of delivering field services in different project and country settings. Only in government agencies, such as the State Department, USAID, the United States Information Service, and the United Nations, does one find a hierarchical bureaucratic structure that involves advancement up a career ladder. In such organizations, individuals who are primarily oriented toward getting things done at the field level increasing become disconnected from the field as they advance their careers. In some cases international careers become less interesting as individuals move up the career ladder where they become more involved in managing the organization and monitoring its pro- curement process than with doing what was initially the real fun and prime motivating factor for pursuing international work—getting things done in the field, or literally getting their hands dirty in development work. Monitoring a contractor's project to provide irrigation services in Egypt, for example, is much different than being in the field putting together the project with government officials and villagers and then seeing the results of one's labors—improved health, increased agricultural production, and new job opportunities.

3. **The best international jobs are found at home rather than abroad.**

This may appear to be a contradiction in logic, but it is the case more often than not. Job vacancies tend to be announced and the recruitment process initiated at the headquarters level. The field, which is where the job is performed abroad, is where qualified candidates will be assigned, but not necessarily from where they will be hired. As a result, most hiring for international positions is done in New York City, Washington, DC, Los Angeles, and San Francisco. Your job search will primarily involve networking for contacts with the headquarters staff as well as traveling to these U.S. cities rather than making a trip abroad in search of job vacancies with field offices.

4. **Many international firms also have a bias toward hiring from headquarters rather than finding qualified candidates in the field.**

Indeed, this becomes a major problem for international job seekers who are already living and working abroad. Many mistakenly feel they are the best qualified for local jobs because of their physical presence, knowledge of the local situation, and their superior language capabili- ties and extensive contacts within the local business and government communities. Such logic, however, is countered with another more compelling logic as well as the ironic reality of often having to return home to find their next job rather than conduct their job search from their present expatriate base abroad. In many cases this hiring bias is justified, because some candidates may have "too much" field experience—they've been abroad **too** long. Some international experience is essential, but living and working abroad for several years without recharging one's skills and intellect back home for extended periods of time is not necessarily a positive qualification when applying for an international job. These expatriates may lack current knowledge and skills necessary for success in the field. In fact, many consulting firms prefer hiring US-based consultants rather than locals and expatriates who lack a "fresh" and comparative perspective. Furthermore, expatriates are sometimes too politically involved in the local bureaucracy, too well adjusted to the local culture, and too willing to avoid risks that might jeopardize their next "local" job. Many employers believe risk-taking, rather than acquiescence to local conditions, is essential for the success of international projects.

Living and working abroad for several years without recharging one's skills and intellect is not necessarily a positive qualification.

---

5. **International job vacancy information is poorly communicated through traditional information sources, such as publications and job listing services.**

Many international jobs that appear in newspapers, magazines, and newsletters are already filled by the time they are advertised. It's best to apply directly to organizations that normally have international job openings. Many of these firms maintain an in-house resume bank which they do refer to when they have impending vacancies. You should get your resume into their banks as well as send an updated resume to these organizations every year. At the same time, many of these firms welcome individuals who network with their organization. Many are looking for individuals with specific technical and exotic skills as well as the willingness to quickly relocate. Depending on what type of skills you have and the specific job you are looking for, you should also advertise your experience and qualifications among firms that are hired by employers to recruit qualified candidates for specific types of positions. Known as "headhunters" and "executive search firms," these companies are paid by employers. Many of these firms specialize in recruiting in one or two areas, such as computer specialists, communication technicians, or petroleum engineers and oil riggers. Some newsletters and data banks are useful, and we will identify these later.

6. **Given the poor dissemination of international job information as well as the high demand for ostensibly glamorous international jobs, some fly-by-night and fraudulent international or overseas job finding services that require up-front fees still operate and prey on naive individuals who don't know any better.**

The international job finding business is big business involving millions of dollars being paid by both employers and candidates to firms specializing in linking individuals to job vacancies. As with any business involving lots of money, you'll find the good, the bad, and the ugly operating in the same arena. Some job search firms give a false impression that the international job market is highly centralized and that they have some secret to information on and access to this job market. The only problem is that many can't do much better—probably less so—than you can do in conducting a job search on your own. Worst of all, many of these firms require fees—$150 to $5,000—from the job applicant. The sure sign that you may be taken on an expensive journey in finding an international job through such a firm is when they want up-front money from you. Reputable and effective firms get paid by the employer who seeks out their services to locate qualified candidates. They normally contact you rather than you contact them. They seek out individuals who have sufficient international skills and experience to be "in demand" by international organizations and firms. Without naming names, let us just say that many of the best firms don't have to advertise in tabloids and sleazy magazines, although some also advertise in ostensibly reputable publications, because they have already established strong word-of-mouth reputations for delivering reputable services.

7. **The most interesting, well paid, and easiest international jobs to find and perform tend to be with organizations that operate within the larger international arena rather than with domestic organizations that only operate in a single country.**

Many international job seekers still believe they can travel directly to a country to look for employment with local organizations. Such trips and job search efforts are often a waste of time and money. The reality is that foreign workers are usually discriminated against in most countries. Indeed, it is very difficult to get directly hired by a local firm because of major legal restrictions on employing foreign workers in jobs that compete with the local labor. These restrictions include complicated and expensive visas, stringent residency requirements, and hefty local taxes. In some countries you may be able to get a work permit to perform only certain types of jobs over a limited number of months, but the process may take up to one year to get the permit! In other countries, such as the United States, it's virtually impossible to get a work permit unless you have the proper residency documentation. Furthermore, even if you are successful in becoming a "local hire," you may quickly discover other problems, such as low wages, high tax rates (30-50%), and travel restrictions. For example, you may be prohibited from traveling outside the country unless you have a tax clearance and pay an expensive "departure fee" whenever you wish to exit the country. Entry back into the country may invalidate your work permit and visa and require you to initiate the whole time consuming and expensive process over again. While you may find exceptions to this general rule, your best choice of employment will be with multinational firms that have already negotiated the status of their employees with the host country. This often means you can be hired from outside the country and moved there at the company's expense and provided with housing, travel, shipping, and educational benefits. You may be given special visa status that may exempt you from most local taxes, permit you to enter and exit the country with few restrictions, and import and export your household goods duty-free. In other words, living and working abroad with such an organization will be much easier as you avoid the hassles of the local legal system that is largely designed to discourage foreign workers by making "working in our country" simply difficult.

STRUCTURE OF OPPORTUNITIES

Understanding the structure of the international job market and devising job search strategies responsive to what is essentially a decentralized and closed job market must ultimately be linked to specific organizations and jobs that exist in the international arena. Most of the jobs are found with the following categories of organizations:

1. Government
2. International Organizations
3. Contracting and Consulting Firms
4. Nongovernmental, Nonprofit, and Private Voluntary Organizations

5. Multinational Corporations
6. Businesses and the Travel Industry
7. Educational Organizations
8. Trade and Professional Associations
9. Foundations
10. Research Organizations

In addition, thousands of entrepreneurs operate on their own, without the benefit of organizations and bureaucracies, in conducting all types of business in the international arena.

The chapters that follow examine the structure, the process, the organizations, and the entrepreneurs that define the international job market. Each chapter should further open what is basically a closed structure as well as help organize and centralize information on the "what," "where," and "how" of finding an international job that may also lead to an international career. In so doing, we outline international job search strategies that should be both realistic and effective for the coming decade.

If you are looking for specific names and addresses of international employers to contact, you should examine our book, *The Almanac of International Jobs and Careers*. Designed as a companion volume to this book, *The Almanac of International Jobs and Careers* is keyed to the organizational chapters in Part III of this book. It summarizes hundreds of major international employers, many of which may be relevant to your interests and skills. If your primary motivation for international employment is travel, you may want to examine our other volume, *Jobs For People Who Love Travel*, which covers both domestic and international employment.

Chapter Three

MYTHS, MOTIVATIONS, AND ACHIEVING SUCCESS

Over the years we have met and worked with hundreds of individuals in the international arena. We've encountered our share of journalists, corporate executives, bankers, missionaries, educators, researchers, lawyers, artists, writers, development workers, medical personnel, government bureaucrats, politicians, tour operators, military, soldiers of fortune, volunteers, contractors, consultants, and entrepreneurs to write a separate book on interesting international personalities! We regularly hear from hundreds of other individuals who are interested in breaking into the international job market, re-entering it after an lengthy absence, or changing international jobs and careers. We also have conducted job search seminars abroad for those interested in re-entering the U.S. job market or finding other international employment.

THEY'RE A DIFFERENT TYPE

We've always been fascinated with the international arena and the many interesting people who work abroad. We wonder how and why they got involved with international work rather than stay home to follow traditional careers up someone's corporate ladder or pursue a standard American lifestyle complete with a home mortgage and stable community life.

What we've learned over the years is that these people are different from the people we know back home in terms of motivations, personalities, and lifestyles. While some go international for the money, most are simply restless, curious, or stricken with that unexplained addiction to travel and a desire to pursue an idea, cause, or lifestyle that cannot be satisfied in some job back home. Some are international junkies who thrive in the international arena. Others literally dropped out of their own societies and work-driven lifestyles back home for more easy-going and personally rewarding lives abroad. For many of these people, their ideas of getting ahead and achieving career success are to move on to another interesting, challenging, and satisfying international job. Someday they may have to return home to "settle down," but in the meantime many believe they are having the time of their lives; they want to continue this lifestyle indefinitely—as long as they can remain employed abroad in some type of job. Many work in jobs that are not particularly glamorous nor interesting, but their jobs enable them to do what they most enjoy—living abroad. Most are successful in changing jobs to continue their international lifestyles.

> *These people are different from the people we know back home in terms of motivations, personalities, and lifestyles.*

What concerns us most are the motivations and job search behavior exhibited by individuals who have never worked abroad but who want to "break into" the field. Many of these people are students who have some foreign language competency, traveled or studied abroad, or pursued an international course of study. Others are ex-military personnel who have lived abroad but now want to become international consultants or literally "make big bucks" abroad to compensate them for their many lean years working for Uncle Sam. Many are ex-Peace Corps volunteers and medical personnel who have worked in health care and rural development for a few years and now want to find another interesting and personally rewarding international job. Some are frustrated State Department and USAID employees who work in organizations most recently noted for low morale and blocked career advancement opportunities. And some are construction workers—heavy equipment operators, electricians, carpenters—who have never worked abroad but who heard they can make big money in a hurry working abroad. We also hear from numerous entrepreneurs who seek our advice on developing contacts for importing products from the Asian and Pacific regions—unexpected contacts with individuals who have become attracted to our travel book series—"Impact Guides".

What motivates these people to pursue international jobs and careers or strike out on their own into an unfamiliar employment frontier? What is it they really want to do? How do they differ from the ordinary job seeker? The career and motivation patterns for experienced international workers are fairly evident.

Many, for example, got started by accident rather than by design. They lived abroad as children of international workers. Some signed up for the military or Peace Corps and received interesting assignments that convinced them that they should pursue an international career. Many began as students who took a course, joined a study program abroad, or just traveled abroad during their summer break. They found the international experience and lifestyle interesting, so much so that they wanted to do it full-time. Many journalists, corporate executives, and business people also got involved accidentally; many were transferred abroad as part of the corporate promotion process. Missionaries, Peace Corps Volunteers, development workers, and many government personnel seem to initially pursue international jobs and careers by design.

Many have totally unrealistic expectations and questionable motivations.

We also see patterns among those who are interested in "breaking into" the international jobs market. Many have totally unrealistic expectations and questionable motivations. Like perceptions of Hollywood, they see international jobs as being glamorous and high profile jobs that are well paid and result in major changes in peoples' lives and relations between nations. And like Hollywood, there are a few such international jobs, but they are few and far between the many other types of less glamorous, low profile, and low to average paying jobs most commonly found abroad.

Let's take a look at some of the most common myths that motivate individuals to pursue international jobs as well as prevent them from achieving success in the international job market. By examining these myths and corresponding realities, we should get a clearer picture of our motivations and how to best organize ourselves for finding an international job.

MYTHS AND REALITIES

International work has a certain lure and mysticism which was once reserved for itinerant missionaries, anthropologists, and soldiers of fortune of decades ago. Indeed, there are probably more myths about international jobs than of any other type of work.

Most job seekers are unprepared and naive in approaching the international job market; some might be best termed "job dumb." They play around the periphery of this job market with little success in penetrating it successfully. They muddle-through the job market with questionable perceptions of how it works. Combining facts, stereotypes, myths, and folklore—gained from a mixture of logic, experience, movies, nightly news reports, and advice from well-meaning friends and relatives—these perceptions lead job seekers down several unproductive paths. They are often responsible for the self-fulfilling prophecy and lament of the unsuccessful international job seeker: *"There are no jobs available for me."*

Some of the more important myths preventing individuals from achieving success in the international job market include:

MYTH 1:   **International employment pays extremely well compared to salaries in the States.**

REALITY   The financial rewards of international employment vary greatly. Some jobs—especially international consulting—can pay very well. Jobs with many nonprofit organizations pay poorly. For those living abroad, special financial benefits are often offset by additional expenses incurred in trying to maintain a certain lifestyle as well as lost opportunities for supplementing income, such as appreciation on property in the States or job opportunities for one's spouse.

Many international jobs are exciting, but many are dull and boring.

MYTH 2:   **International jobs are very challenging and interesting.**

REALITY   Some international jobs are exciting, but many are dull and boring. The excitement tends to come from the lifestyle which involves traveling and learning about other cultures, eating different foods, meeting new and different people, and encountering unique events. Foreign Service Officers often end up stamping travel documents in some dreadful, hot and dirty capital city where the most exciting things to happen are to receive a letter from home, take a trip outside the country, acquire a new videotape, or check into a first-class hotel which has hot water and air conditioning. These are the events that make working and living abroad interesting for many people. They are often the subjects of peoples' "war stories" about *"how it was when we lived and worked abroad."*

MYTH 3:   **International work involves exciting and sometimes exotic travel.**

REALITY: Travel is definitely a benefit for many individuals who have international jobs. However, the excitement of travel often wears off after age 40, after children reach high school age, after the third move in five years, after the tenth flight in a single year, and after the third lost suitcase and another terrifying taxicab ride from another chaotic airport. On the other hand, young, inexperienced, and single people tend to disproportionately enjoy the novelty of international travel. Like all novelties, this one can wear off after a while.

MYTH 4:   **International development work is personally rewarding because of the positive changes one is able to make in the lives of others.**

REALITY: International development work is personally rewarding for individuals who can make a difference in the lives of others. But development work also is one of the most frustrating areas of international work. Few changes actually take place; the process tends to be very political; and development work fails more often than it succeeds. Individuals working for the USAID missions in Third World countries, for example, are more likely to be preoccupied with obligating funds and putting out brush fires on problematic USAID projects than in making progress in development. For many people, development work becomes more of a personal ego trip than one of concrete long-term accomplishments. Satisfaction comes more from "mingling with the locals"—speaking the local language, eating the local foods, laughing at the local jokes, and receiving the exaggerated status accorded to well-educated foreign development workers.

MYTH 5:   **International lifestyles are better than back home.**

REALITY: International lifestyles vary considerably. Living abroad can mean a large and comfortable home with servants and a good international school for one's children. But such comforts are often offset by daily inconveniences of transportation and communication, by poor health and recreation facilities, by cultures which are best remembered rather than lived, and by the unemployed spouse situation. In many countries one spends a great deal of time on the basics of living, such as shopping for food and getting from point A to point B. Local health facilities may be rudimentary or downright dangerous. And one's spouse is likely to be unemployed—a recurring and serious problem for two-career couples who have chosen to live abroad and then find international living a tremendous strain on their marriage, often ending in divorce. Local cultures may place constraints on women. Consequently, adverse living conditions may result in a low level of work output and little professional development. For families with teenage children, the international lifestyle often becomes a serious liability because excellent international high schools are only found in a few countries. At this point in life, many people are anxious to return home or be transferred to a country which has a good international school. Others get tired of international living. Added to these adverse conditions are safety considerations attendant with the continuing rise of international terrorism and anti-Americanism. Consequently, the international lifestyle is not for everyone nor is it for some people at particular stages in their lives.

The international lifestyle is not for everyone nor is it for some people at particular stages in their lives.

MYTH 6: It's easier to find an international job while traveling or living abroad than by networking or applying from the U.S.

REALITY: From where one should best look for an international job depends on several factors. Expatriates living in-country often have an advantage in landing short-term contract jobs because of their location. Many companies prefer hiring someone already in the field for small jobs that may only involve $10,000 to $30,000 in labor expenses. It's cheaper to recruit such people than to transport someone from abroad to do these jobs. Consequently, expatriates will be in a good position to find many of these short-term jobs. On the other hand, many government agencies and companies prefer hiring their long-term field personnel from the States because they find a larger pool of qualified candidates based there. They have a bias for hiring individuals who are one-step removed from the local situation and who are more involved in the professional mainstream which is based back home rather than in some isolated location abroad.

Recruitment and hiring decisions tend to be centralized with headquarters staff.

Most important of all, recruitment and hiring decisions tend to be centralized with headquarters staff. They publicize vacancies, interview candidates, and select the finalists. Living and working abroad tends to place one outside this centralized recruitment process. Ironically, expatriates living abroad are well advised to make regular trips back home in order to better position themselves in the international job market.

MYTH 7:   **One must have a great deal of international experience to get an international job.**

REALITY: It depends on the situation and the job. Many jobs require little or no international experience—only a specific or exotic skill that is difficult to find.

MYTH 8:   **Travel experience and language competency are essential to finding an international job.**

REALITY: This is one of the great myths of finding an international job. While travel, foreign languages, and international education may help you find a job, they are not necessarily prerequisites for entering the international job market. Indeed, many people break into this job market without such backgrounds. They possess other more important skills

which are in demand. In many countries, English is the
working language of international jobs. Knowing a foreign
language may be crucial to one's job in some countries,
such as Japan, China, Indonesia, and France, but not so for
many jobs in other countries, such as Germany, Hong
Kong, Singapore, the Philippines, or India.

MYTH 9: **An international-related educational background is
essential for finding an international job.**

REALITY: An international education may be helpful in better understanding the international arena, but it is no guarantee of
gaining entrance to the job market. At best such an education will better help you network with others you meet in
the international job market. The most important international courses to take will be business, especially in
accounting and marketing, and foreign languages. History,
art, culture, sociology, education, interdisciplinary Third
World courses, and even international business may be
interesting to take and will definitely enrich your stay
abroad. But few such courses will directly help you find an
international job since they have little skill content other
than teaching the same courses to others either at home or
abroad. At the same time, education in general is important
for many international jobs, especially in cultures where
"qualifications" are equated with higher educational degrees
—regardless of the particular field of study. Education and
qualifications have different meanings in different cultures.
Thus, the higher one's educational level—measured as the
possession of a B.A., M.A., or Ph.D.—the better your
chances of landing an international job. In fact, international jobs are more sensitive to educational credentials and
how they translate into status in other countries than to
specific performance skills. All things being nearly equal,
a candidate with an M.A. is more likely to be hired than
someone with only a B.A. Therefore, the more educational
credentials you can accumulate, the better positioned you
should be in the international job market. Even a B.A.
degree does not mean a great deal abroad these days.

MYTH 10: **Living and working abroad is dangerous.**

REALITY: It can be dangerous, but it seldom is. Living and working
abroad may actually increase your safety quotient. It's
much safer to work abroad than in many places in the U.S.

where your chances of being in an accident, mugged, or killed are some of the highest in the world. However, some countries in the Middle East and Latin America have reputations as being dangerous for foreigners and particularly for Americans. If you work in one of these countries, you should take sensible precautions to ensure your safety, such as hiring guards and a driver, locking your doors, changing your daily routines, avoiding strange places, and never walking alone at night.

MYTH 11:   **There are few international jobs available today.**

REALITY: There are numerous international jobs available today for those who know where they are and how to find them. In fact, we expect to see the number of international job opportunities increase steadily over the next decade as the world economy becomes even more interdependent, national boundaries become more open, and populations move more easily between countries. The basic problem is breaking into what often appears to be a relatively closed job market. If you shed many of your preconceptions of the international job market, examine your motivations, develop an intelligent plan of action, and simply persist with a well organized and focused international job search, you should be able to join millions of others who work in this fascinating job and career arena.

MYTH 12:   **It's best to use an international job placement service to get an international job.**

REALITY: You should be able to do just as well in finding an international job on your own than by hiring someone to help you. In fact, many of these so-called placement firms have bad reputations for exploiting clients and engaging in fraudulent practices. Some misrepresent their services by convincing vulnerable job seekers that they have some special access to international job vacancies and employers. Many require up-front fees for the promise of helping you find a job. Few do much more than mail your resume to different organizations that have overseas operations. This you can easily do on your own by spending a few hours in your local library surveying international directories and with the same results—few if any invitations for interviews. The most reliable firms are the "headhunters" and "executive search" firms that are paid by employers to hire specific types of individuals. If you follow the advice of this book, you should have no problem penetrating the international job market and finding the job that best fits your interests, skills, and motivations. You will do much better than many firms that try to get you to buy into their questionable placement services. In the meantime, if you decide to use such a firm, be sure you carefully examine their perform-ance record rather than accept their promises of perform-ance. Paying up-front fees is a sure sign you are buying promises rather than playing for performance.

MYTH 13: **One has to have "connections" in order to break into the international job market. Whom you know is more important than what you can do.**

REALITY: While "connections" and knowing people are important to finding any job, and especially important when seeking an international job where information on job vacancies and opportunities is difficult to access, they are by no means essential. Your most important asset will be your market-able skills in a job market that places high value on unique job skills. How well you communicate your skills, experi-ence, and motivations to employers—be it through resumes, letters, application forms, word-of-mouth, headhunters, executive search firms, classified ads, or contacts and "con-nections"—will largely determine your success in getting the job. You should use contacts and "connections" not because they are **the** way to get an international job. They are some of the most efficient and effective ways of communicating your availability and qualifications in a job market noted for being highly decentralized, fragmented, and chaotic. The system, or lack thereof, is not organized well for efficiently and effectively communicating job vacancy information nor linking qualified candidates with job vacancies. Therefore, your job is to organize your own system for best communicating your qualifications to potential international employers. Contacts, "connections," and networking strategies should become a few of your many methods for organizing this job market around your qualifications.

MYTH 14: **Most international jobs involve a great deal of travel. An international job will enable me to see and experi-ence the world.**

REALITY: Many international jobs involve very little travel. The most traveling you may ever do is when you move from your home base to the job site abroad, and then return for a home visit once or twice in a two to three year period. Some international jobs involve working in one location, sometimes isolated, for one to two years at a time. If you are looking for an international job because you particularly like to travel, you may be better off looking for a job that involves a great deal of travel. These jobs are most likely found with headquarters staff, in international sales, or in the travel industry. This is one of the major mistakes some individuals make when choosing to "go international" with their career. Their major motivation for wanting an international job is travel. They assume that international jobs involve a great deal of travel to many interesting places or such a job will give them an opportunity to do more travel. They quickly learn they may have greater opportunities for international travel had they stayed home and found a good paying job with generous vacation time or one that involved periodic travel abroad. Whatever you do, don't assume an international job will give you more opportunities to travel. It may or may not. If you really want to travel abroad to many places, make international travel your career or start your own international business. An international job may result in getting stuck is some undesirable location that neither gives you the income nor time to do the travel you dreamed of doing while living and working abroad. Always start by examining your motivations for seeking an international job.

MYTH 15: **Most international jobs require moving and living abroad.**

REALITY: Many do but many others don't. Many international jobs are based in the United States and involve periodic travel to work sites abroad. International consultants and contractors, for example, may spend one to two months at a time on projects abroad, but their work base is back home. Educators, researchers, foundation employees, and business people often spend only a few weeks a year working abroad. Even employees of the State Department and US-AID will spend much of their career in Washington, DC. City and state government employees involved in promoting tourism and trade are based in their home communities from where they conduct international business. In fact, many people enjoy their international jobs, careers, and lifestyles precisely because they have the best of both worlds—based at home and regularly travel and work abroad. They can still remain a part of their own society and communities while maintaining an exciting international career. In so doing, they avoid many of the hassles involved in full-time living and working abroad. Ironically, some of these people might change careers if their international jobs required lengthy residence abroad!

MYTH 16:   If one wants to work in the international arena, it's best to work for government or a multinational corporation.

REALITY: Government agencies and multinational corporations do offer numerous international job opportunities, but they are only a few of the many players in the international job market. In fact, you may find some of the most interesting and rewarding jobs are found with nonprofit organizations or nongovernmental organizations (NGOs) and small or medium-size businesses in the travel and hospitality industries. On the other hand, you may discover being an international entrepreneur—either as some type of free-lancer, independent consultant, or importer-exporter—to be much more interesting than working for others who will largely determine your work agenda and your future in the international arena.

MYTH 17:   The best international jobs are found within the U.S. State Department and USAID or with the United Nations.

REALITY: These may be great jobs for some people, but they aren't for others, including many present employees who are looking for other more rewarding alternatives. While these high-profile organizations appear to offer many international glamour jobs, in reality competition is keen for these jobs and many are disappointing, boring jobs. Morale is especially low in the State Department and USAID because of recent changes in the personnel systems that do not reward international expertise and experience; career rewards are given to those who can demonstrate managerial expertise—a skill that requires little or no demonstrated international or area expertise. Benefits continue to erode as these agencies cutback on traditional perks. Furthermore, many of the jobs primarily involve the procurement process—from obligating funds to monitoring contracts. Individuals who go into these organizations with the expectation of doing significant international work often are disappointed in discovering they are primarily pushing paper, stamping passports, monitoring problematic projects, and financing contractors. The real exciting international work is often contracted-out to consultants, contractors, nonprofit organizations, and universities. United Nations work, while well paid, is often boring and very political. Competition for jobs and promotions tends to follow nationalistic lines since a certain percentage of jobs are reserved for particular nationals. Many jobs are simply boring—involve little work content, numerous unproductive meetings, and a great deal of bureaucratic routines. If you are interested in getting things done, seeing the results of your international labors, and productivity and responsiveness, these organizations may not be appropriate for you. Indeed, many employees with these organizations often wonder whatever happened to the really interesting international jobs and exciting lifestyles they expected when joining the organizations. Few recommend their jobs to their friends or relatives. Needless to say, there are many other more interesting and rewarding international jobs than those found with these high-profile organizations.

MYTH 18:   **The international hiring process seems to take forever. It takes longer to find an international job than to land a job back home.**

REALITY: This also depends on the situation. Some organizations, especially government and the United Nations, may take an extraordinary amount of time to fill a vacancy because of the large number of candidates applying for a position, numerous decision-making levels, and the need for security clearances. Other organizations may take a long time because they are looking for someone with a highly specialized or technical skill that is difficult to find even with the hiring of an executive search firm. But other organizations may do just the opposite—hire in a very short period of time. Since many of the organizations have few legal restrictions on their hiring practices—especially time consuming affirmative action and equal opportunity requirements—they have a great deal of flexibility in determining how they will hire. In short, they will do what they want and need to do. As soon as an impending vacancy becomes apparent, for example, hiring officials will literally "spread the word" within their old boy/girl networks to identify candidates who have the proper mix of skills, experience, and motivation for the job. This network may be very efficient in identifying the three top candidates within a matter of hours without having to hire a firm to recruit someone or list the vacancy in some publication or data bank. If you make yourself known by plugging into these networks, you may discover finding an international job takes less time than landing a domestic job. Therefore, it's extremely important that you learn how to effectively network for international job information, advice, and referrals—an essential skill for continuing international job and career success.

MYTH 19: **It's difficult to start one's own international business.**

REALITY: Depending on what you want to do as well as your entrepreneurial skills, it's relatively easy to get started and operational within a short period of time. All you need is some basic information, a business plan, contacts, and the resources to finance the initial stages of your venture. In fact, the coming decade should be an unparalleled period for international entrepreneurship as "development" of countries increasingly becomes defined in terms of encouraging greater foreign investment, joint ventures, and import-export arrangements. Government agencies are becoming increasingly oriented toward encouraging and promoting private business involvement abroad, from large multinationals to small businesses and individual entrepreneurs. If you love to travel, and also want to have an international dimension to your career, starting your own business may be an ideal solution to the "international career" question.

MYTH 20: **The job search techniques that work for finding a domestic job also work well for finding an international job.**

REALITY: Some do but many don't because they are based upon a culturally-biased model of achieving career success in the American job market. They assume that job applicants are primarily motivated to get jobs they do well and enjoy doing and then make job moves that demonstrate career growth and advancement. Such skilled and motivated people are supposed to be oriented toward career success. However, many international job applicants could care less about such career success. Many of them are primarily oriented toward experiencing adventure and unique experiences as well as pursuing ideas, causes, challenges, and lifestyles. If an international career somehow develops from these experiences and pursuits, so be it. But success measured in terms of positions, money, and advancement up someone's organizational hierarchy is a cultural bias implicit in the standard career planning and job search models used by most career counselors.

MYTH 21: **It's best to learn about other cultures and adjust one's behavior to meet the local expectations. The more I act like the locals, the easier it will be for me and my job.**

REALITY: Yes, you should understand and be sensitive to other cultures. But it's not necessary to go to extremes by always behaving like the locals. Indeed, many people become overly sensitive to other cultures and engage in silly behaviors that are even embarrassing to the locals who aren't sure who such foreigners think they are! Other cultures have expectations for both foreigners and expatriates which are not the same as for the locals. As such, you are permitted to be different as long as you are not offensive. If you try to "go bush" you may not be respected as much as when you maintain your own identity. In addition, today's "global village" is changing rapidly and thus it's difficult to know exactly what the local expectations are for foreigners and expatriates. Furthermore, the international business, government and development cultures have increasingly become Americanized. Except for a few local cultural peculiarities, you should be able to adjust well to an international employment culture without having to "go native." Your identity should always be an asset when functioning in the international job market. Just don't become obnoxious and offensive.

MOTIVATION

The myths and realities provide a glimpse into some of the perceived advantages and disadvantages which motivate individuals to pursue international

work. They may raise important questions about your own motivations and desire
to pursue an international career. The major motivations most international job
seekers exhibit appear to be:

1. **Money:** Everybody wants it but only a few people really make big
    money in international jobs and careers. The biggest money is
    usually made by people who manage other peoples' money—the
    investors, bankers, and venture capitalists who operate on percentages
    and at high risk levels. Many international jobs pay excellent salaries
    which may also be exempt from Federal, state, and local taxes back
    home (first $80,000 is exempt from Federal taxes if one lives abroad
    for at least 11 consecutive months). This tax break applies to private
    sector employees living and working abroad. Federal government
    employees working abroad are not exempt from Federal taxes, and
    many private sector employees must pay taxes to their countries of
    residence. But given additional housing and living adjustment
    benefits, as well as lower costs of living in many countries, many
    individuals working abroad do well financially. Comparable jobs
    back home may pay less and have fewer benefits.

2. **Adventure:** Especially for young, restless, inexperienced, and single
    individuals, international work can be very exciting. Working in
    Latin America, Africa, Europe, the Middle East, or Asia is for some
    people the last great frontier. New places and different cultures be-
    come extremely life enriching experiences.

3. **Curiosity:** The international arena is an object of curiosity for many
    people who always thought about living and working abroad. They
    may feel it is now time to do something different in their lives, so
    they decide to try an international job to see what it's all about.

4. **Pursue a cause:** Several public causes can be pursued through
    international employment. Many individuals want to promote
    U.S. foreign policy, international peace, population planning, environ-
    mental control, and rural development. Numerous government agen-
    cies, private development organizations, religious groups, and
    nonprofit organizations are organized to pursue such causes.

5. **New challenges:** International work does offer new and unusual
    challenges, from basic living to getting a job done. Individuals often
    find such work challenges their basic assumptions about people as
    well as work itself.

6. **Lifestyle:** Many individuals are motivated to work in the interna-
    tional arena because of the lifestyle. The work itself brings them into

contact with new and interesting cultures; the work may change constantly; and they are given an extraordinary amount of status and authority—the "big fish in a small pond" phenomenon—not commonly found with many jobs in the United States. Indeed, exaggerated status and bloated egos are widespread among many international workers.

7. **Travel:** Many people are hopelessly addicted to travel. Like clockwork, every three, six, or twelve months they have a burning desire to take to the road to discover new and exciting places. Many of these people believe it may be best to incorporate their travel addiction into a job or career that involves frequent international travel.

8. **Escape and revitalization:** Some people wish to escape from their present jobs and careers which are basically boring, deadend, and unrewarding. Some are even unemployed individuals seeking overseas jobs. They believe an international job will be the antidote to revitalizing their careers and achieving renewed career success and personal happiness.

Those who work long-term in the international arena often find the advantages outweigh the disadvantages in defining their motivations to continue pursuing international jobs and careers. In addition, many long-term international workers don't know what else they could or would do if they left this employment arena. Therefore, they see no other alternatives to their international career and lifestyle.

ORIENTATION TOWARD SUCCESS

International work is not for everyone. Most organizations working in this arena identify a particular type of individual who is best suited for international work. These people tend to have the following characteristics:

1. **Adaptability and flexibility:** Willing to adapt to changing circumstances and adjust to the norms of the situation.

2. **Tolerance and empathy:** Listen to others, understand their behavior, accept different behaviors as legitimate, tolerate ambiguities, be open-minded, and respect others' beliefs.

3. **Sensitivity to cultural differences:** Adjust to cultural differences without going "native"; maintain one's own identity.

4. **Patience and perseverance:** Balance the American work ethics of punctuality, productivity, and getting things done now with work cultures that place higher value on maintaining and expanding power, developing harmonious interpersonal relations, avoiding face-to-face confrontations, and solving problems through consensus rather than through other rational decision-making techniques.

5. **Humor:** Maintain a sense of humor especially in situations which are sometimes frustrating; don't take oneself too seriously. Many cultures respond well to people who always wear a friendly smile and an attitude of fun and humor.

6. **Curiosity:** Be open to new experiences, willing to learn, and accepting of new and unfamiliar patterns.

7. **Self-confidence and initiative:** Be willing to take initiative without being offensive or threatening the power of others. Entrepreneurs who are also sensitive to local decision-making practices are highly valued in the international arena.

8. **Facility in foreign languages:** Especially for individuals living and working in countries where the local language is important to day-to-day business, they should have some ability to learn a second or third language.

While these characteristics are common among many individuals who work in the international arena, there is also a negative side to them. Indeed, there is a fine line between being tolerant, sensitive, and patient, and being useless on the job. Some individuals adjust **too** well and thus accomplish little or nothing other than "enjoy" their international lifestyles. For many professionals who are very job-oriented, international employment can take a serious toll on their professional development.

PREREQUISITES FOR SUCCESS

How successful you will be in landing an international job as well as continuing in the international employment arena depends on several factors that relate to you as an individual as well as the organizations offering job opportunities. Like any job, international jobs have their advantages and disadvantages, positives and negatives, ups and downs. Some people are fortunate enough to find jobs they really love. Many become obsessed with their work to the exclusion of all other interests and pursuits. Most people, however, find jobs that are okay but nothing particularly special or exciting. They are not unhappy with their jobs nor are they particularly happy with them. To many, a job is a job is a job; its advantages outweigh possible disadvantages of not having the job at all.

However, we do know what leads to job search success both at home and abroad. Success is determined by more than just a good plan getting implemented. It is not predetermined nor is it primarily achieved by intelligence, thinking big, time management, or luck. Based upon experience, theory, research, and common sense, we believe you will achieve career planning success by following many of these 20 principles:

1. **You should work hard at finding an international job:** Make this a daily endeavor and involve your family. Spend the necessary time conducting research on organizations offering international opportunities as well as networking among those who operate within the international job arena.

2. **You should not be discouraged with setbacks:** You are playing the odds, so expect disappointments and handle them in stride. You will get many *"no's"* before finding the one *"yes"* which is right for you. Expect to receive twice as many rejections for international jobs than for domestic jobs simply because of the more competitive nature of international jobs. This means you may have to work twice as hard in overcoming the rejections. If you are unable to deal with rejections as part of the game, you will be headed for trouble. Try to turn negatives into positives. Learn from them, leave them, but remember them as stepping stones to future acceptances.

3. **You should be patient and persevere:** Expect three to six months of hard work before you connect with the international job that's right for you.

4. **You should be honest with yourself and others:** Honesty is always the best policy, but don't be naive and stupid by confessing your negatives and shortcomings to others.

5. **You should develop a positive attitude toward yourself and others:** Nobody wants to employ guilt-ridden people with inferiority complexes. At the same time, neither do they want to hire self-centered individuals. Focus on your positive characteristics as well as the employer's needs.

6. **You should associate with positive and successful people:** Finding an international job largely depends on how well you relate to others and how effectively you engage your networking skills. Avoid associating with negative and depressing people who complain and

have a *"you-can't-do-it"* attitude. Run with winners who have a positive *"can-do"* outlook on life.

7. **You should set goals:** You should have a clear idea of what you want and where you are going. Without these, you will present a confusing and indecisive image to others. Clear goals help direct your job search into productive channels. Moreover, setting high goals will help make you work hard in getting what you want.

8. **You should plan:** Convert your goals into action steps that are organized as short, intermediate, and long-range plans.

9. **You should get organized:** Translate your plans into activities, targets, names, addresses, telephone numbers, and materials. Develop an efficient and effective filing system and use a large calendar for setting time targets and recording appointments and useful information.

10. **You should be a good communicator:** Take stock of your oral, written, and verbal and nonverbal communication skills. How well do you communicate? Since most aspects of your job search involve communicating with others, and communication skills are one of the most sought-after skills, always present yourself well both verbally and nonverbally.

11. **You should be energetic and enthusiastic:** Employers are attracted to positive people. They don't like negative and depressing people who toil at their work. Generate enthusiasm both verbally and nonverbally. Check on your telephone voice—it may be less enthusiastic than your voice in face-to-face situations.

12. **You should ask questions:** Your best information comes from asking questions. Learn to develop intelligent questions that are non-aggressive, polite, and interesting to others. But don't ask too many questions.

13. **You should be a good listener:** Being a good listener is often more important than being a good questioner and talker. Learn to improve your face-to-face listening behavior (nonverbal cues) as well as remember and use information gained from others. Make others feel they enjoyed talking with you, because you are one of the few people who actually **listens** to what they say.

14. **You should be polite, courteous, and thoughtful:** Treat gatekeepers, especially receptionists and secretaries, like human beings. Avoid being aggressive or too assertive. Try to be polite, courteous, and gracious. Your social graces are being observed. Remember to send thank-you letters—a very thoughtful thing to do in a job search. Even if rejected, thank employers for the "opportunity" given to you. After all, they may later have additional opportunities, and they will remember you.

15. **You should be tactful:** Watch what you say to others about other people and your background. Don't be a gossip, back-stabber, or confessor.

16. **You should maintain a professional stance:** Be neat in what you do and wear, and speak with the confidence, authority, and maturity of a professional.

17. **You should demonstrate your intelligence and competence:** Present yourself as someone who gets things done and achieves results—a **producer**. Employers generally seek people who are bright, hard working, responsible, can communicate well, have positive personalities, maintain good interpersonal relations, are likeable, observe dress and social codes, take initiative, are talented, possess expertise in particular areas, use good judgment, are cooperative, trustworthy, and loyal, generate confidence and credibility, and are conventional. In other words, they like people who score in the "excellent" to "outstanding" categories of the annual performance evaluation. Many want God!

18. **You should not overdo your job search:** Don't engage in overkill and bore everyone with your "job search" stories. Achieve balance in everything you do. Occasionally take a few days off to do nothing related to your job search. Develop a system of incentives and rewards—such as two free days a week, if you accomplish targets A, B, C, and D.

19. **You should be open-minded and keep an eye open for "luck":** Too much planning can blind you to unexpected and fruitful opportunities. You should welcome serendipity. Learn to re-evaluate your goals and strategies. Seize new opportunities if they appear appropriate.

20. **You should evaluate your progress and adjust:** Take two hours once every two weeks and evaluate what you are doing and accom-

plishing. If necessary, tinker with your plans and reorganize your activities and priorities. Don't become too routinized and thereby kill creativity and innovation.

These principles should provide you with an initial orientation for starting your international job search. As you become more experienced, you will develop your own set of operating principles that should work for you in particular employment situations.

TAKE TIME TO SAIL

Let's assume you have the necessary skills to open the doors to employers for the international job you want. Your next step is to organize an effective job search. Organization, however, does not mean a detailed plan, blueprint, or road map for taking action. If you strictly adhere to such a plan, you will most likely be disappointed with the outcomes. Instead, your job search should approximate the art of sailing—you know where you want to go and the general direction for getting there. But the specific path, as well as the time of reaching your destination, will be determined by your environment, situation, and skills. Like the sailor dependent upon his or her sailing skills and environmental conditions, you tack back and forth, progressing within what is considered to be an acceptable time period for successful completion of the task.

The plan should not become the end—
it should be a flexible means
for achieving your goals.

While we recommend planning your job search, we hope you will avoid the excesses of too much planning. The plan should not become the **end**—it should be a flexible **means** for achieving your stated job and career goals. Planning makes sense, because it requires you to set goals and develop strategies for achieving the goals. However, too much planning can blind you to unexpected occurrences and opportunities, or that wonderful experience called **serendipity**.

We outline on page 64 a hypothetical plan for conducting an effective job search. This plan incorporates seven distinct but interrelated job search activities over a six month period. If you phase in the first four job search steps during the initial three to four weeks, and continue the final four steps in subsequent weeks and months, you should begin receiving job offers within two to three months

ORGANIZATION OF JOB SEARCH ACTIVITIES

Activity	Weeks															
	1	2	3	4	5	6	7	8	9	10	11	12	13	14	15	16
■ Thinking, questions, listening, evaluating, adjusting	━	━	━	━	━	━	━	━	━	━	━	━	━	━	━	━
■ Identifying abilities and skills	━															
■ Setting objectives		━														
■ Writing resume			━													
■ Conducting research			━	━	━	━	━	━	━	━	━	━	━	━	━	━
■ Prospecting, referrals, networking								━	━	━	━	━	━	━	━	━
■ Interviewing							╌	╌	╌	╌	╌	╌	╌	╌	╌	╌
■ Negotiating job offers												╌	╌	╌	╌	╌

after initiating your job search. Interviews and job offers can come at any time—often unexpectedly—during your job search. An average time is three months, but it can occur within a week or take as long as five months. During the recession of 1991-1992, international job seekers reported taking a longer time to complete their job searches than in the previous two-year period. Recessions can easily add two to three months to a job search. Indeed, 1993 and 1994 may be such a period as more and more countries experience recessions. If you plan, prepare, and persist at the job search, the pay-off will be interviews and offers.

While three months may seem a long time, especially if you need to work immediately, you can shorten your job search time by increasing the frequency of each job search activity. If you are job hunting on a full-time basis, you may be able to cut your job search time in half. But don't expect to get a professional level job quickly. It requires time, hard work, and persistence.

This hypothetical time frame is generally applicable to most domestic jobs. The time frame for international jobs, however, may be longer given the logistics of recruiting and hiring. In some cases, the selection process will take a long time because the organization will need to narrow down a large number of candidates in order to interview only a few in the field location abroad. Other jobs may require length security clearances. And in still other cases the time between when a vacancy is announced and filled may be very short, because an organization relies heavily on the informal word-of-mouth networking process for recruiting candidates.

Part II

EFFECTIVE JOB SEARCH
SKILLS AND STRATEGIES

EFFECTIVE JOB SEARCH
SKILLS AND STRATEGIES

Knowledge expressed in the form of job search skills is power when conducting an international job search. The type of knowledge you possess and act upon will largely determine how successful you will be in landing the international job you want.

Knowing **where** the jobs are is important to your international job search. But knowing **how to find a job** in a job market noted for being relatively chaotic and closed is even more important. Such knowledge helps answer some of the most important questions of your job search:

- What strategies and tactics should I use for uncovering job leads and communicating my special qualifications to international employers?

- Where do I get a list of government agencies and corporations that have operations and branch offices abroad?

- Where can I locate the ten top contracting and consulting firms working on development projects in Third World countries?

- What type of resume and letter should I write when applying for an international job?

- Should my resume be the standard one to two-page resume recommended for the American employment culture or should it be much longer?

- Should I include an objective as well as a list of references on my resume?

- How and where should I disseminate my resume and job search letters? Should I broadcast them to hundreds of employers or target only a few employers?

- What is networking and how should I use it when looking for an international job?

- What should I do about my outdated wardrobe which wasn't much to begin with when I moved abroad three years ago for a job that required only casual and somewhat "local" dress? Indeed, how do interviewees best dress these days for an interview? What type of clothes, accessories, and colors seem appropriate?

- What type of interview questions should I be prepared to answer as well as ask?

- What exactly should I negotiate when I get to the final stage of responding to a job offer?

- How much flexibility is there with international salaries and benefits? When and how should I address the compensation question?

All of these job search questions are important in determining your effectiveness in the international job market. In contrast to the basic *"What are the jobs?"* and *"Where are the jobs"* questions, which primarily include job titles, lists of job leads, contact information on potential employers, and job vacancies, our job search questions and answers in the next three chapters focus on the methods, approaches, strategies, tactics, and how-tos of getting a job. They invariably address certain types of tactical questions job seekers need advice on, such as *"What should I do about _____"* or *"What's the best way to approach _____?"* They better organize you for getting an international job by helping you best communicate your qualifications to employers. They take as a "given" your motivation, educational background, qualifications, and experience. These questions focus on targeting your job search on specific employers through an effective job search campaign involving a series of specific job search activities—assessing skills, specifying objectives, conducting research, writing resumes and letters, networking, conducting interviews, and negotiating salary.

Before you acquire names, addresses, and phone numbers of potential international employers, you should possess the necessary job search skills and strategies for gathering and using job information effectively. In the next four chapters we outline the most important skills and strategies for conducting an effective international job search. While these skills and strategies are appropriate for most employment situations, we have adapted them to the issues and special needs of international job seekers.

YOUR FOUNDATION SKILLS

The skills and strategies outlined in Chapters Five, Six, and Seven are directly transferable to most international job situations. They constitute the **foundation skills and strategies** from which you must custom-design effective approaches for various international jobs and careers.

Each have their own hiring cultures, consisting of both formal and informal personnel practices.

However, one important word of caution is in order before you plunge into this skills section and become a true-believer in such concepts as functional skills, combination resumes, referral letters, prospecting, networking, and informational interviewing. Government agencies, nongovernmental organizations, multinational corporations, educational organizations, small businesses, associations, consulting firms, foundations, and research organizations each have their own hiring cultures, consisting of both formal and informal personnel practices. Even within each group, individual organizations will differ in how they recruit, evaluate, and select individuals. Some organizations will have highly formalized application and testing procedures. Others maintain computerized talent banks which they regularly use for recruiting new personnel. Many work strictly on an informal, word-of-mouth basis. Others have developed important formal and informal networking mechanisms. And still others frequently use professional recruiting services—"headhunters" and "executive search firms"—to identify and select job candidates, especially for locating highly skilled and hard to find individuals.

If you fail to adapt the skills and strategies outlined in the next four chapters to specific employment situations, you will encounter difficulties with your job search. Based upon your research activities, you must adapt, adapt, adapt, adapt. In the end, you will learn there is no one best approach which can be used universally for all organizations and employment situations.

Chapter Four

CAREERING COMPETENCIES AND JOB SEARCH ASSISTANCE

Preparation for an international job search involves a combination of knowledge, skills, and abilities relevant to both the international job market and particular jobs. To be successful, you must understand where you are going and how you will get there.

DEVELOP NEW CAREERING COMPETENCIES

How well can you plan and implement a job search that will lead to several interviews and an international job offer that is right for you? The answer to this question is found by examining your present level of job search knowledge and skills. Successful job seekers, for example, use a great deal of information as well as specific skills and strategies for getting the jobs they want.

Let's begin by testing your current level of job search information and skills as well as specify a level you need to attain. You can easily identify your job search competencies by completing the following exercise:

INSTRUCTIONS: Respond to each statement by circling which number at the right best represents your situation.

SCALE: 1 = strongly agree   4 = disagree
           2 = agree   5 = strongly disagree
           3 = maybe, not certain

1. I know what skills I can offer employers in different occupations.

    1   2   3   4   5

2. I know what skills employers most seek in candidates.

    1   2   3   4   5

3. I can clearly explain to employers what I do well and enjoy doing.

    1   2   3   4   5

4. I can specify why an employer should hire me.

    1   2   3   4   5

5. I can gain support of family and friends for making a job or career change.

    1   2   3   4   5

6. I can find 10 to 20 hours a week to conduct a part-time job search.

    1   2   3   4   5

7. I have the financial ability to sustain a three to six month job search.

    1   2   3   4   5

8. I can conduct library and interview research on different occupations, employers, organizations, and communities.

    1   2   3   4   5

9. I can write different types of effective resumes, job search letters, and thank-you notes.

    1   2   3   4   5

10. I can produce and distribute resumes and letters to the right people.

    1   2   3   4   5

11. I can list my major accomplishments in action terms.

    1   2   3   4   5

12. I can identify and target employers I want to interview.

    1   2   3   4   5

13. I can develop a job referral network.

    1   2   3   4   5

14. I can persuade others to join in forming a job search support group.

    1   2   3   4   5

15. I can prospect for job leads.

    1   2   3   4   5

16. I can use the telephone to develop prospects and get referrals and interviews.

    1   2   3   4   5

17. I can plan and implement an effective direct-mail job search campaign.

    1   2   3   4   5

18. I can generate one job interview for every 10 job search contacts I make.

    1   2   3   4   5

19. I can follow-up on job interviews.   1   2   3   4   5

20. I can negotiate a salary 10-20% above
     what an employer initially offers.   1   2   3   4   5

21. I can persuade an employer to renegotiate
     my salary after six months on the job.   1   2   3   4   5

22. I can create a position for myself in an
     organization.   1   2   3   4   5

     TOTALS FOR EACH COLUMN   _____

     GRAND TOTAL FOR ALL COLUMNS   _____

You can calculate your overall careering competencies by adding the numbers you circled for a composite score. If your grand total is more than 60 points, you need to work on developing your careering skills. How you scored each item will indicate to what degree you need to work on improving specific job search skills. If your score is under 40 points, you may wish to skip this and the next four chapters; go directly to the chapters in Part III on "Finding Your Best Work Setting." The remainder of this section will focus on developing your careering competencies. After completing this section, you should be well prepared to conduct your own international job search.

CONSIDER USEFUL
JOB SERVICES

You have two options in organizing your job search. First, you can follow the principles and advice outlined in this self-directed book. Just read the chapters and then put them into practice by following the step-by-step instructions. Second, you may wish to seek professional help to either supplement or replace this book. Indeed, many people will read parts of this book—perhaps all of it—and do nothing. Unwilling to take initiative, lacking sufficient time or motivation, or failing to follow-through, some people will eventually seek professional help to organize and implement their job search. They will pay good money to get someone else to tell them to follow the advice found in this book. Some people need this type of expensive motivation.

At the same time, we recognize the value of professional assistance. Especially with the critical skills identification and objective setting steps (Chapter Five), some individuals may need more assistance than our advice and exercises provide. If this pertains to you, by all means seek professional help.

You also should beware of pitfalls in seeking professional advice. While many services are excellent, other services are useless and fraudulent. Remember, career planning and job assistance are big businesses involving millions of dollars each year. Many people enter these businesses with little or no expertise.

Indeed, many get into the business because they are unemployed. In other words, they major in their own problem! Others are frauds and hucksters who prey on vulnerable and naive people who feel they need a "specialist" or "expert" to get them a job.

You will find several types of services promising to assist you in finding employment overseas. You should know something about these professional services before you venture beyond this book.

While many services are excellent, other services are useless and fraudulent.

If you are interested in exploring the services of job specialists, begin by looking in the Yellow Pages of your telephone directory under these headings: Management Consultants, Employment, Resumes, Career Planning, and Social Services. Several career planning and employment services are available, ranging from highly generalized to very specific services. Most services claim they can help you. If you read this book, you will be in a better position to seek out specific services as well as ask the right questions for screening the services. You may even discover you know more about finding an international job than many of the so-called professionals!

At least ten different career planning and employment services are available to assist you with your job search. Each has certain advantages and disadvantages. Approach them with caution as well as with a set of intelligent questions for screening out those that are least likely to help you. Never sign a contract before you read the fine print, get a second opinion, and talk to former clients about the **results** they achieved through the service. With these words of caution in mind, let's take a look at the variety of services available.

1. **Public employment services:** Public employment services usually consist of a state agency which provides employment assistance as well as dispenses unemployment compensation benefits. Employment assistance largely consists of job listings and counseling services. However, counseling services often are a front to screen individuals for employers who list with the public employment agency. If you are looking for entry-level jobs in the $10,000 to $16,000 range, contact this service. Most employers do not list with this service, especially for positions paying more than $18,000 a year. If you walk through one of these offices, you will find that most people are unemployed and look poor; they will likely remain so for some time. In fact, some

experts believe we should abolish these offices altogether because they exacerbate unemployment; they take people away from more productive channels for employment—personal contacts—and put them in a line to waste time and meet few helpful and positive people. We recommend avoiding these offices, unless you are really down on your luck and want some company. Indeed, few of these offices ever list international or overseas jobs or are prepared to deal with the special needs of international job seekers.

2. **Private employment agencies:** Private employment agencies work for money, either from applicants or employers. Approximately 8,000 such agencies operate nationwide. Many are highly specialized in technical, scientific, or financial fields. Some also specialize in international and overseas jobs. The majority of these firms serve the employers since employers—not applicants—represent repeat business. While employers normally pay the placement fee, many agencies charge applicants 10 to 15 percent of their first year salary. These firms have one major advantage: job leads which you may have difficulty uncovering elsewhere. Especially for highly specialized fields, a good firm can be extremely helpful. The major disadvantages are that they can be costly and the quality of the firms varies. Be careful when the money question arises. Many firms promising overseas jobs require up-front fees—a sure sign to be cautious. Make sure you understand the fee structure and what they will do for you before you sign anything.

3. **College/university placement offices:**   College and university placement offices provide in-house career planning services for graduating students. While some give assistance to alumni, don't expect too much help if you have already graduated. Many of these offices are understaffed or provide only rudimentary services, such as maintaining a career planning library, coordinating on-campus interviews for graduating seniors, and conducting workshops on how to write resumes and interview. Others provide a full range of well supported services including testing and one-on-one counseling. Aside from providing general career planning advice, few of these offices are organized to provide specialized assistance for individuals interested in international jobs and careers. However, they may be able to give you some good referrals to faculty members or organizations that are familiar with the international job arena. Check with your local campus to see what services you might use.

4. **Private career and job search firms:** Private career and job search firms help individuals acquire job search skills. They do not find you

a job. In other words, they teach you much—maybe more but possibly less—of what is outlined in this book. Expect to pay anywhere from $1,500 to $10,000 for this service. If you need a monetary incentive to conduct your job search, contract with one of these firms. One of the most popular firms is Haldane Associates. Many of their pioneering career planning and job search methods are incorporated in this book.

5. **Executive search firms:** Executive search firms work for employers in finding employees to fill critical positions in the $60,000 plus salary range. They also are called "headhunters," "management consultants," and "executive recruiters". These firms play an important role in linking high level technical and managerial talent to organizations. Don't expect to contract for these services. Executive recruiters work for employers—not applicants. If a friend or relative is in this business or you have relevant skills of interest to these firms, let them know you are available—and ask for their advice. If you are interested in getting in contact with such firms, you should refer to a few of the following how-to books and directories for strategies and contact information: *The Directory of Executive Recruiters, Stalking the Headhunter, The Headhunter Strategy, How To Select and Use an Executive Search Firm*, and *How To Get a Headhunter To Call*.

6. **Marketing services:** Marketing services represent an interesting combination of job search and executive search activities. They can cost $2,500 or more, and they work with individuals anticipating a starting salary of at least $50,000 but preferably over $60,000. These firms try to minimize the time and risk of applying for jobs. A typical operation begins with a client paying a $150 fee for developing psychological, skills, and interests profiles. Next, a marketing plan is outlined and a contract signed for specific services. Using word processing equipment, the firm normally develops a slick "professional" resume and mails it along with a cover letter, to hundreds—maybe thousands—of firms. Clients are then briefed and sent to interview with interested employers. While you can save money and achieve the same results on your own, these firms do have one major advantage. They save you **time** by doing most of the work for you. Again, approach these services with caution.

7. **Women's Centers and special career services:** Women's Centers and special career services have been established to respond to the employment needs of special population and employment groups. Women's Centers are particularly active in sponsoring career planning workshops and job information networks. These centers tend to be

geared toward elementary job search activities because their clientele largely consists of housewives who are entering or re-entering the workforce with little knowledge of the job market. Special career services arise at times for different categories of employees. Unemployed aerospace engineers, teachers, veterans, air traffic controllers, and government employees have formed special groups for developing job search skills and sharing job leads. Most of these centers dispense general career planning and job search advice for their particular groups. Few are familiar with the uniqueness of the international job market. Therefore, don't expect to receive much assistance from them in finding an international job or career.

8. **Testing and assessment centers:** Testing and assessment centers provide assistance for identifying vocational skills, interests, and objectives. Usually staffed by trained professionals, these centers administer several types of tests and charge from $500 to $800 per person. You may wish to use some of these services if you feel our activities in Chapter Five generate insufficient information on your skills and interests to formulate your job objective. Try our exercises before you hire a psychologist.

9. **Job fairs or career conferences:** Job fairs or career conferences are organized by employment agencies, executive search firms, corporations, and government agencies to better link hard-to-find candidates to employers. Usually consisting of one to two-day meetings in a hotel, employers meet with applicants as a group and on a one-to-one basis. Employers give presentations on their companies, resumes are circulated, and candidates are interviewed. Many of these conferences are organized around particular skill areas, such as engineering and computers. These are excellent sources for job leads and information—if you get invited to the meeting. Employers pay for this service—not applicants. More and more government agencies are using job fairs to recruit hard-to-find clerical and technical personnel, some of which involve international positions.

10. **Professional associations:** Professional associations often provide placement assistance. This usually consists of listing job vacancies or organizing job information exchanges and job search seminars at annual conferences. These meetings are good sources for making job contacts in different geographic locations within a particular professional field. But don't expect too much. Talking to people at professional conferences will probably yield better results than reading job listings and interviewing at conference placement centers. Nonetheless, many international associations do offer such services. International

health workers, for example, should consider membership in the National Council for International Health (1701 K St., NW, Suite 600, Washington, DC 20036, Tel. 202/833-5900). The cost of membership in such an association may more than pay for itself with the contacts one makes for job and career purposes. If you are living abroad, it may be a good idea to attend such conferences in order to keep in contact with your professional network. You never know when a professional contact may later development into an important job lead.

Other types of career planning and employment services are growing and specializing in particular occupational fields. Many claim to have special access to the international job market. You may wish to use these services as a supplement to this book. Whatever you do, proceed with caution and know exactly what you are getting into. Remember, there is no such thing as a free lunch, and you often get less than what you pay for. After reading the next three chapters, you should be able to make intelligent decisions about what, when, where, and with what results you can use professional assistance. Shop around, compare services and costs, ask questions, talk to former clients, and read the fine print with your lawyer before giving an employment expert a job using your hard earned money!

Chapter Five

IDENTIFY SKILLS, STATE OBJECTIVES, AND ACQUIRE USEFUL KNOWLEDGE

Self knowledge is power in today's job market. When it is focused around skills, objectives, and the needs of employers, such knowledge should result in effective resumes, letters, and interviews that lead to job offers and satisfying jobs. When focused on the international job market, this knowledge helps open the doors to potential employers.

ESSENTIAL SKILLS

Let's begin by asking two questions about your past activities and future goals:

- What do you do well and enjoy doing?

- What do you want to do in the future that best reflects what you both do well and enjoy doing?

The first question probes your past and present history of skills, abilities, motivations, interests, and preferences. The second question projects these past considerations into the future. These questions are central to acquiring the self-knowledge necessary for conducting an effective job search. They help link your past work and lifestyle patterns to future job, career, and lifestyle goals which may or may not be a central part of your experience.

The international job market of today and tomorrow increasingly requires higher levels of work-content skills which may also be unique and highly technical skills. We take these as "givens" since we assume you already have the necessary work-content skills to qualify for a job interview, receive a job offer, and perform the job. If not, you may need to acquire additional education, training, and work experience—individual qualifications that are beyond the scope of this book.

In this chapter we turn to a second set of critical skills for getting the job you want—**job search skills**. Focusing primarily on job finding strategies and tactics, these skills are as important as work-content skills for getting a job interview and receiving a job offer. They also help advance your career once you are on the job. In this sense, they are **basic job market survival skills** you must acquire and practice on a continuous basis. In Chapter Four you identified the degree to which you possessed several of these skills by completing an exercise for identifying your careering competencies. Here we examine several important job search skills necessary for finding a job.

Form and presentation should never be confused with nor replace substance. You must be able to perform the job you are being hired to do.

One word of caution before we proceed further. The soft job search skills outlined in this and subsequent chapters do not substitute for concrete work-content skills. Most job search skills focus on form and presentation. They should never be confused with nor be expected to replace substantive skills. While you may be invited to job interviews and offered jobs based on the quality of your resume, letters, networking abilities, and interview behavior, you must also be able to perform the job you are being hired to do and deliver what you say you can deliver. The bottom line is that you probably won't fool enough people to get the job. However, should you fool enough people and get the job based on your impressive job search skills, you may not keep the job long. For it doesn't take long before an employer learns he or she has made a mistake by hiring someone who misrepresented credentials and qualifications—they simply don't deliver with quality performance. They are good at getting jobs but not at keeping them for long.

DEVELOP AN
EFFECTIVE JOB SEARCH

Several job search skills help you prepare for face-to-face meetings with potential international employers. They stress how you must (1) organize yourself for this job market, and (2) communicate your qualifications and value to employers. These skills also are important **sequential steps** required for planning and implementing an effective job search. These skills and steps include:

- Identifying your strengths
- Stating your job objective
- Conducting job research
- Writing resumes and job search letters
- Dressing appropriately to meet people who have input into the hiring process
- Prospecting, networking, and informational interviewing
- Interviewing for the job
- Negotiating salary

The figure on page 83 illustrates the relationship of these steps to one another in the overall job search. Each step has a well defined set of rules—based upon employers' expectations and job searchers' successful experiences—you should learn and practice.

In this chapter we examine the first three job search steps—identifying strengths, stating objectives, and conducting job research. These steps focus on becoming better acquainted with yourself and your environment. They must be completed **prior to** the three image management steps in Chapter Six—writing resumes and letters and dressing appropriately—and the three action steps in Chapter Seven—networking, interviewing, and negotiating salary.

The job search skills and steps examined in this and subsequent chapters are generally valid for acquiring most international jobs both in the public and private sectors. However, additional job search activities are required when seeking employment with governments and international agencies. The Federal government, for example, requires most applicants to complete a standard application form—the SF-171. The United Nations has its own special application forms and hiring procedures. We will address unique job search skill requirements and activities for particular organizations in the appropriate chapters of Part III. This chapter as well as Chapters Six and Seven outline the **foundation skills** for conducting an effective job search regardless of particular settings or circumstances.

JOB SEARCH STEPS

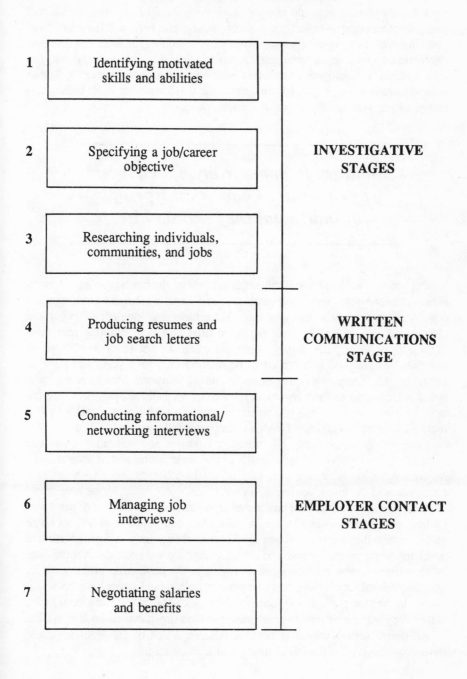

1	Identifying motivated skills and abilities	
2	Specifying a job/career objective	**INVESTIGATIVE STAGES**
3	Researching individuals, communities, and jobs	
4	Producing resumes and job search letters	**WRITTEN COMMUNICATIONS STAGE**
5	Conducting informational/ networking interviews	
6	Managing job interviews	**EMPLOYER CONTACT STAGES**
7	Negotiating salaries and benefits	

COMMUNICATE YOUR STRENGTHS

What do you do well and enjoy doing? Why should I hire you? What will you give me in exchange for this position, salary, and benefits? How long will you stay with this organization or project? Will you adjust well to your new international worklife environment? Although they may not directly ask you these questions, employers nonetheless want answers to these questions. It is to your advantage to prepare thoughtful answers to these basic questions **before** you communicate your qualifications to employers.

Contrary to popular myth, employers often do not know what type of of individual they should hire.

Put yourself in the shoes of the employer. He or she has a problem—how to select someone who will solve problems and be a winner for the organization. Winners are not born every day. They have a unique set of skills and abilities employers readily seek but have difficulty both defining and finding. Contrary to popular myth, employers often do not know what type of individual they should hire nor what the requirements for a particular position should be. Most employers make imperfect hiring decisions. Many fear they will spend a great deal of time and money selecting a candidate, yet still make the wrong hiring decision. This is a particular concern with international jobs that require relocating employees abroad for extended periods of time. If the employee doesn't stay long, additional recruitment and relocation costs can become very expensive and the stability of the organization and projects may be in jeopardy. Only after a few months of on-the-job experience with the new employee will the employer begin to confirm or reject initial hiring anxieties.

Indeed, many international businesses report an alarming number of personnel problems with employees who are transferred abroad but have to be sent home early because they do not function well abroad. Many have serious adjustment problems which cannot be resolved through language and cross-cultural training. While many of these problems can be traced to the inadequate preparation for the international experience, many of these people should never have been sent abroad in the first place simply because they lack important international living skills. They may be outstanding performers in their organizations back home, but in a different setting they may become failures. Much of the problems could have been resolved at the initial hiring and transfer stages.

Knowing this, you should try to lower employers' hiring anxieties as well as position yourself well within the job market in relation to (1) other job seekers, and (2) your own career goals. The best way to do this is to focus on your **strengths and accomplishments**. You should communicate to employers that it is you they want to hire, because you are a winner with the necessary strengths to accomplish their goals. In addition, you will adjust and perform well in cross-cultural settings because you have the necessary attitudes, personality, disposition, and communication skills for success. Unlike many other job seekers who try to **meet** the expectations of employers, you want to **raise** their expectations to your level of strengths and accomplishments. Most important, you want to help employers define their hiring needs as **your** skills and abilities. Let them know that you have a unique mix of international skills and experience that is **more** than they expected. Since many international jobs require entrepreneurial individuals who are creative and take initiative, you should let employers know you are such a person—if indeed you are!

How can you best communicate your strengths and accomplishments to employers? Start by understanding what employers want. Most seek individuals who are competent, intelligent, honest, and likeable. Add to this a major concern with "adjusting well" to other cultural settings and getting along well with nationals while also getting the job done. They also want someone who takes initiative, is a self-starter, and is capable of devising creative solutions to unique problems and situations.

Above all, employers want to know your strengths and weaknesses. While they tend to look for indicators of your weaknesses, your task is to ensure they know your strengths.

> *You want to help employers define their hiring needs as your skills and abilities.*

Always organize your communication in direct reference to the needs and concerns of your target audience. Avoid discussions of your weaknesses, or turn them into discussions of your strengths. Focus the employer's attention on what you do well—your strengths. This two-part self-assessment question will help orient you in the proper direction:

"What do I do well, and what do I enjoy doing?"

This question both identifies and helps communicate what you do best (strengths and accomplishments) and what you most enjoy doing (motivations, attitudes, values, and preferences). By linking your strengths to things you enjoy doing, you should be able to present a powerful picture of enthusiasm, purpose, and potential performance to employers. This question also should come **prior to** deciding on alternative international jobs and careers. Your answer to this question should direct your job search into fruitful channels. If properly answered, it will identify and clearly communicate your job objective as well as your best skills, abilities, and talents to potential employers who, in turn, will invite you to a job interview.

By linking your strengths to things you enjoy doing, you should be able to present a powerful picture of enthusiasm, purpose, and potential performance to employers.

Unfortunately, many people work against their own best interests. Unaware of their strengths, they end up marketing their weaknesses by first identifying job vacancies and then trying to fit their "qualifications" into job descriptions. Indeed, this is a common approach of many international job seekers who become obsessed with trying to find out "where the jobs are" rather than focus on communicating to potential employers what they really do well and enjoy doing in the international arena. They are willing to compromise their interests and skills by taking any job in order to live and work abroad or to remain in the international job market. This approach often frustrates applicants by presenting a picture of a job market which is not interested in them. As a result, many people attempt to acquire new work-content skills in hope of finding a job in a "growing" field, even though they do not enjoy using such skills.

Two types of skills relate to your strengths and accomplishments. **Work-content skills** tend to be technical and job-specific in nature. Proficiency in typing, programming computers, operating a crane, or welding are work-content skills. They require formal training, are associated with specific trades or professions, are used only in certain job and career settings, and use a separate skills vocabulary, jargon, and subject matter for specifying technical qualifications for individuals entering and advancing in an occupation. While these hard skills do not transfer well from one occupation to another, they are critical for entering certain occupations. For many international jobs, especially in such technical fields as communication, engineering, construction, and natural resource exploration, these types of skills are in great demand.

A second skills category is called **functional or transferable skills.** These skills are associated with numerous job settings, are usually acquired through experience rather than formal training, and can be communicated through a highly generalized and somewhat abstract vocabulary.

While most people can identify only a few work-content skills, they have numerous—perhaps as many as 300—transferable skills. These skills enable them to change jobs and careers without acquiring additional specialized education and training. These are very important skills for individuals hoping to break into the international job market but who possess little or no demonstrated international work experience.

Transferable or functional skills can be classified into two general categories—organizational/interpersonal skills and personality/work-style traits:

Organizational and Interpersonal Skills

___ communicating	___ trouble shooting
___ problem solving	___ implementing
___ analyzing/assessing	___ self-understanding
___ planning	___ understanding
___ decision-making	___ goal setting
___ innovating	___ conceptualizing
___ logical thinking	___ generalizing
___ evaluating	___ managing time
___ identifying problems	___ creating
___ synthesizing	___ judging
___ forecasting	___ controlling
___ tolerating ambiguity	___ organizing
___ motivating	___ persuading
___ leading	___ encouraging
___ selling	___ improving
___ performing	___ designing
___ reviewing	___ consulting
___ attaining	___ teaching
___ team building	___ cultivating
___ updating	___ advising
___ coaching	___ training
___ supervising	___ interpreting
___ estimating	___ achieving
___ negotiating	___ reporting
___ administering	___ managing

Personality and Work-Style Traits

___ diligent	___ honest
___ patient	___ reliable
___ innovative	___ perceptive
___ persistent	___ assertive
___ tactful	___ sensitive
___ loyal	___ astute
___ successful	___ risk taker
___ versatile	___ easy going
___ enthusiastic	___ calm
___ out-going	___ flexible
___ expressive	___ competent
___ adaptable	___ punctual
___ democratic	___ receptive
___ resourceful	___ diplomatic
___ determining	___ self-confident
___ creative	___ tenacious
___ open	___ discrete
___ objective	___ talented
___ warm	___ empathic
___ orderly	___ tidy
___ tolerant	___ candid
___ frank	___ adventuresome
___ cooperative	___ firm
___ dynamic	___ sincere
___ self-starter	___ initiator
___ precise	___ competent
___ sophisticated	___ diplomatic
___ effective	___ efficient

Several self-assessment techniques are available for identifying your work—content and transferable skills. These techniques stress your positives or strengths rather than identify your negatives or weaknesses. Best of all, they help you develop a rich vocabulary for communicating your "qualifications" to employers. Each exercise requires different investments of your time and effort as well as varying degrees of assistance from other people. We recommend that you use the most complete and extensive activity—the Motivated Skills Exercise—to gain the most thorough understanding of your strengths. Nonetheless, examine each of these self-assessment devices with a critical eye toward using one or more that may best work for you.

We are by no means true believers nor advocates of all of these self-assessment devices. Each has certain advantages and disadvantages; all have biases and limitations. You should be aware of these limitations before blindly jumping to conclusions about your past, present, and future skills and strengths as well as the implications of such self-knowledge for formulating a job and career objective.

Each has certain advantages and disadvantages . . . Most are based upon a simple deterministic theory of behavior.

Please approach these exercises with caution. There is nothing magical nor particularly profound about them. Most are based upon a simple **deterministic theory of behavior**—understanding your past patterns of behavior are good predictors of your future behavior. Not a bad theory for most individuals, but it is rather simplistic and disheartening for individuals who wish to—and can—break out of past patterns as they embark on a new future. This is especially important for individuals interested in pursuing international jobs and careers but who do not have an international track record from which to analyze their so-called international-relevant patterns of behavior. Furthermore, most exercises are historical devices. They provide you with a clear picture of your past, which may or may not be particularly useful for charting your future.

Nonetheless, most of these self-assessment exercises do help you accomplish the following:

1. Organize data on yourself.

2. Target your job search around clear objectives and skills.

3. Generate a rich vocabulary of skills and accomplishments
   for communicating your strengths to potential employers.

If you wish to go beyond these historical and deterministic self-assessment devices, you will need to use other less predictive but more ego enhancing and futuristic approaches: positive thinking, creative imagery, breakthrough thinking, market research, and force field analysis—techniques that do help many people break out of past patterns that prevent them from realizing their lifelong dreams. Such techniques are often responsible for the significant transformation of many individuals' patterns of behavior. These are **change techniques** rather than **pattern maintenance techniques**.

If you feel our exercises are inadequate for your needs, by all means seek professional assistance from a testing or assessment center staffed by a licensed psychologist, as outlined in Chapter Four. These centers do in-depth testing which goes much further than our self-directed, historical motivated skill exercises. They, too, have their own limitations, but they may give you more information and direction than we can provide here.

Checklist Method

This is the simplest method for identifying your strengths. Review the two lists of transferable skills outlined on pages 87-88. Place a "1" in front of the skills that **strongly** characterize you; assign a "2" to those skills that describe you to a **large extent**; put a "3" before those that describe you to **some extent**. After completing this exercise, review the lists and rank order the 10 characteristics that best describe you on each list.

Skills Map

Richard N. Bolles has produced two well-known exercises for identifying transferable skills based upon John Holland's typology of work environments. In his book, *The Three Boxes of Life*, he develops a checklist of 100 transferable skills. They are organized into 12 categories or types of skills: using hands, body, words, senses, numbers, intuition, analytical thinking, creativity, helpfulness, artistic abilities, leadership, and follow-through.

Bolles' second exercise, *"The Quick Job Hunting Map,"* expands upon this first one. The *"Map"* is a checklist of 222 skills. This exercise requires you to identify seven of your most satisfying accomplishments, achievements, jobs, or roles. After writing a page about each experience, you relate each to the checklist of 222 skills. The *"Map"* should give you a comprehensive picture of what skills you (1) use most frequently, and (2) enjoy using in satisfying and successful settings. While this exercise may take six hours to complete, it yields an enormous amount of data on past strengths. Furthermore, the *"Map"* generates a rich skills vocabulary for communicating your strengths to others. The *"Map"* is found in the appendix of Bolles' *What Color Is Your Parachute?* or it can be purchased separately in beginning, advanced, or "new" versions from Ten Speed Press or Impact Publications. Order information on these assessment instruments is included in the resource section of this book.

Autobiography of Accomplishments

Write a lengthy essay about your life accomplishments. This could range from 20 to 100 pages. After completing the essay, go through it page by page to identify what you most enjoyed doing (working with different kinds of information, people, and things) and what skills you used most frequently as well as enjoyed using. Finally, identify those skills you wish to continue using. After analyzing and synthesizing this data, you should have a relatively clear picture of your strongest skills.

Motivated Skills Exercise

The Motivated Skills Exercise is one of the most complex and time consuming self-assessment exercises. However, it yields some of the best data on skills, and it is especially useful for those who feel they need a more thorough analysis of their skills. Developed by Haldane Associates, this particular exercise is variously referred to as "Success Factor Analysis" or "System to Identify Motivated Skills". While you can use this technique on your own, it is best to work with someone else. Be prepared to devote from six to eight hours to this exercise. It is divided into five steps. The steps follow the basic pattern of generating raw data, identifying patterns, analyzing the data through reduction techniques, and synthesizing the patterns into a transferable skills vocabulary. You need strong analytical skills to complete this exercise on your own. The five steps are as follows:

STEP 1: Take 15 to 20 sheets of paper and at the top of each sheet write one achievement. Your **achievements** are those things you enjoyed doing and felt a sense of accomplishment in doing. These include childhood experiences as well as educational, military, recreational, home, or work-related achievements. For example, at the top of the paper you might state:

> *"I learned to play the guitar and joined a rock group while in high school."*

> *"I received an 'A' in physics from the toughest teacher in school."*

> *"As a Peace Corps Volunteer, I helped my village organize a revolving fund that resulted in the development of several small village enterprises and 9 new jobs."*

> *"I reorganized the files of our office which improved the efficiency of operations."*

> *"I presented a paper at a conference on community-based irrigation associations in the Philippines that*

resulted in increased government involvement in supporting local cooperative efforts."

"I competed in the marathon and finished in the upper third."

"I wrote a proposal for developing a pilot population planning program in Kenya that resulted in a three-year, $2.3 million USAID contract."

"I organized a committee to investigate reducing the number of customer complaints."

"I sang a solo in our church choir."

"I wrote an essay in Spanish which received first prize in the annual foreign language competition."

"I traveled to Burma on my own—and had a marvel-ous time despite all the discouraging stories I heard before leaving on this trip."

STEP 2:   Select from among your achievements the seven most important ones and prioritize them. Identify the factors that explain your success in each achievement. Examples of these success factors might include various aspects of managing, communicating, creating, analyzing, designing, supervising, coordinating, and problem solving. On each page detail your achievements—how you got involved, what you did, how you did it, and what the outcome was.

STEP 3:   Further detail the "what" and "how" of your achievements by having your spouse or a friend interview you for a 60-minute period. Have them ask you to elaborate on each of your achievements and note the terminology you use to elaborate on your skills and abilities. Record your answers for each achievement on separate pieces of paper.

STEP 4:   Combine the self-generated and interview data on your achievements into a single master list of success factors. Group the factors into related categories beginning with the most important factor. For example, if "supervising" is your strongest achievement, "decision-making" and "delegating" may be related to this factor. Therefore, the factors would cluster as follows:

supervising decision-making delegating	selling promoting demonstrating
creating designing initiating	decision-making managing strategizing

STEP 5:   Synthesize the clusters into new combinations for projecting your past skills into the future. For example, the clusters "supervising—decision-making—delegating" and "creating—designing—initiating" may combine into a new skill category called "creative management". This is the key step in this exercise, because it begins to relate your past strengths to your future goals. It functions as a **bridge** between your skills and your stated objective.

A similar "pattern" approach, dubbed "Motivated Abilities," trademarked as "SIMA," and religious and messianic in tone, is found in Arthur Miller and Ralph Mattson's, *The Truth About You*.

Try to find a job "fit for you" rather than try to "fit into a job" you think looks interesting.

SPECIFY YOUR OBJECTIVE

When you identify your strengths, you also create the necessary data base and vocabulary for developing your job objective. Using this vocabulary, you should be able to communicate to employers that you are a talented and purposeful individual who achieves **results**.

If you fail to do the preliminary self-assessment work necessary for developing a clear objective, you will probably wander aimlessly in the job market looking for interesting jobs you might fit into. Your goal, instead, should be to find a job or career that is compatible with your interests, motivations, skills, and talents. In other words, try to find a job fit for you rather than try to fit into a job you think looks interesting.

Job hunters with clearly stated objectives have several advantages over those who do not. Their job search is much easier and enjoyable, because they approach it with confidence and optimism. They gain greater control over the job market, because they structure the job market around their goals. They communicate a reassuring sense of purpose and self-confidence to employers who worry about hiring individuals who don't know what they want. They write well designed resumes and letters that help employers make clear choices. For employers lacking basic hiring criteria, such applicants help them better define their "needs" as the applicant's job objective.

Therefore, if you want to achieve the best results, you must have an objective **before** conducting your job search. With a clear objective, you can target your job search at specific high pay-offs in the job market. A clear objective will help organize your job search into a coherent and manageable whole.

Objectives can be stated in many different forms. Most people think of an objective as a statement of what they would **like to do**. However, such an objective is self-centered. Employers, on the other hand, want to know what **you will do for them**. The best job objective is an employer-centered one: state **what you can and will do for employers**.

Some people know precisely what they want to do and can state their objective in employer-centered terms. Others find identifying and stating a job objective to be the most difficult and frustrating aspect of the whole job search process. Many international job seekers, for example, are unclear what type of work they want to do. Finding international work to be a highly ego-involved activity, they invariably see their job and career future in self-centered rather than employer-centered terms. While many have marketable skills and extensive international experience, they don't communicate these well to employers. As a result, they present an unclear and muddled picture of themselves to employers who are looking for specific talents that will contribute to their operations. If you feel you don't have a strong employer-centered work objective, here are some approaches you can use to help formulate a clear and effective objective.

Develop Your Data Base

Several practical self-directed exercises can alleviate the frustrating aspects of this task. The exercises require you to generate and analyze information about yourself. Begin thinking of your objective as being composed of several ingredients relating to your work values, skills, and knowledge of work environments. Five activities or steps will help you generate a complete set of data for stating your objective.

The first step is to **identify your work and career values** by completing several exercises:

1. List 10 things you would like to achieve before you die. Alternatively, write your obituary for the year 2020 stressing highlights or achievements of your career and life.

2. Think of at least 10 answers to this question: *"If I had $1,000,000 I would..."*

3. List 10 things you prefer and enjoy doing. Prioritize each item.

4. Identify 10 working conditions which you view as negative. Prioritize each condition.

5. List 10 working conditions which you view as positive. Prioritize each item.

6. Check as many of the following work values you feel are desirable in your employment:

__	contribute to society	__	be creative
__	have contact with people	__	supervise others
__	work alone	__	work with details
__	work with a team	__	gain recognition
__	compete with others	__	acquire security
__	make lots of money	__	make decisions
__	work under pressure	__	help others
__	use power and authority	__	solve problems
__	acquire new knowledge	__	take risks
__	be a recognized expert	__	work at own pace

7. Write an essay on your ideal job. Include a weekly calendar of daily activities divided into one hour segments. Specify your duties, responsibilities, authority, salary, working conditions, and opportunities.

The second step is to **gather information on how others see you and your goals.** Ask your spouse or two or three close friends to frankly critique both your strengths and weaknesses. You want them to respond to these questions:

- What are my strengths and weaknesses?
- How can they be improved?
- What working conditions do I enjoy?
- What are my career goals?

The third step is to examine the data you generated in the previous section of this chapter on your strengths. Include it with the information you just generated yourself and received from your spouse and friends. **Rank order which skills you most and least prefer to use in your job or career.**

The fourth step is optional, depending on whether you feel you need more information on your work values, interests, and skills. **Take one or two psychological, aptitude, or vocational tests.** Your options include:

- *Strong-Campbell Interest Inventory*
- *Myers-Briggs Type Indicator*
- *Edwards Personal Preference Schedule*
- *Kuder Occupational Interest Survey*
- *APTICOM*
- *Jackson Vocational Interest Survey*
- *Ramak Inventory*
- *Vocational Interest Inventory*
- *Career Assessment Inventory*
- *Temperament and Values Inventory*

Information from these tests should reinforce and validate the information you gathered from the self-assessment exercises. See a career counselor or a licensed psychologist for identifying and administering the proper tests.

The fifth step is to **test the information concerning your objective against reality and the future** by asking yourself these questions:

- Is my objective realistic?
- Can it be achieved within the next year, 5 years, or 10 years?
- Who needs my skills?
- What factors might help me or hinder me in achieving my objective?

You will further clarify your objective as you expose yourself to more job market information while conducting library research and talking to people about your skills, different jobs, and career opportunities. Procedures for gathering such information are outlined in this chapter.

State Skills as Outcomes

You now should be prepared to develop a one sentence statement of your job objective. Begin by stating your objective at a general level. Next, restate it at a more specific level on your resume so that it has an international job focus.

We recommend developing a **functional job objective.** Outlined by Germann and Arnold in *Bernard Haldane Associates Job and Career Building*, this very basic objective stresses linking your **skills** to employers' expected **outcomes.** At a general level it would appear in the following skills-outcomes framework:

> *"I would like a job where I can use my ability to (<u>one of my primary</u> <u>skills or strengths</u>) which will result in (<u>an important organizational</u> <u>or expected employer outcome</u>)."*

However, international job seekers need to go one step further when stating an objective in this format. Given their international orientation, they should also link their skills and expected employer outcomes to **where** they want to work. By doing this, they are able to incorporate their geographic and lifestyle preferences into their targeted job objective.

If, for example, you wish to write international grant and research proposals, you might state the general objective in these terms:

> *"I would like a job where my international technical research and writing experience will result in new and expanded health care programs in Africa."*

The same objective should be re-written at a more specific level for your resume:

> *"An international management consulting position where strong grantsmanship, research, and writing abilities will be used for developing and expanding innovative community-based health care programs in Western Africa."*

Including both skills and outcomes along with a geographic preference, this objective is **targeted** toward particular employers. This objective is tailored for an international job, because it identifies **where** you want to work—in Western Africa. If your geographic preferences are broader than just Western Africa, you might substitute for "Western Africa" any of the following: Africa, Asia, Latin America, developing countries, Third World countries. On the other hand, you may have a preference for a specific country and thus want to target your resume just for jobs in that country. The more specific you can be, the clearer you will communicate your goals to employers. At the same time, you must be careful not to be too narrow and thus eliminate yourself from consideration for other jobs. For example, if you are looking for a population planning job in either Thailand or Indonesia, you may want to broaden your geographic preference to "Asia" since the population revolution successfully passed through Thailand and Indonesia more than 15 years ago! There simply isn't much demand for expatriates with population planning skills in these countries because the local medical profession and other support groups are already well organized, funded, and competent in this area. Population planning jobs are more likely to be found in other Asian countries, such as the Philippines, Bangladesh, India, and Pakistan. Africa and Latin American are even more promising geographic choices.

As you develop your objective statement, keep in mind that employers want to know how you will achieve **their** goals. Always remember to develop a work-related objective responsive to the needs of your audience. Above all, tell employers what you have to offer—strengths, skills, competencies—and what you will do for them and where. Emphasize that you are a **doer** who produces concrete results.

While you have certain self-centered goals you wish to achieve for yourself, employers are less interested in what they can do for you. They have organizational, program, and project goals that must be met with the best mix of personnel they can create. As many employees quickly learn, they are expendable commodities. Regardless of how important you may think you are to an organization, operation, or project, you can always be replaced. While you may leave memories behind, others will forget your importance after a short period of time as they adjust to your replacement. Indeed, you are never as important as you think you are. Although they may develop parent-children management styles with their employees, few employers feel a need to love you, take care of you, or become sensitive to your personal and professional needs. Employment is a business transaction—their money for your talent. *"You're fired!"* expresses the fact that employers did not get **value** for their money. Communicate your value loud and clear from the very beginning of your job search.

Tell employers what you have to offer—
strengths, skills, competencies—and
what you will do for them and where.

CONDUCT JOB RESEARCH

You should continuously conduct research on the international job market. Research will provide you with a strong knowledge base from which to plan and implement your job search. It will give you critical information for writing your resume and letters, networking, interviewing, and negotiating salaries.

Research, the process of uncovering information, is central to every step in your job search. It should be a continuous process aimed at two general areas:

1. Information for understanding the structure and operation of employment—both the advertised and hidden international job markets.

2. Information for targeting key elements in the international job markets—individuals and organizations.

You gather this information by conducting research in libraries, writing and telephoning people, and communicating with potential job leads and employers in face-to-face meetings. This research begins the first day of your job search and continues until the final day and beyond.

Advertised Versus Hidden Job Markets

Your research should be directed initially toward understanding the structure of the international job market. The so-called job market actually consists of two structurally different arenas for locating job opportunities. Both are characterized by a high degree of decentralization. Neither should be underestimated nor over-estimated.

The **advertised job market** consists of job vacancy announcements and listings found in newspapers, professional and trade journals, newsletters, employment agencies, and personnel offices. Most people focus on this market because it is relatively easy to locate, and because they believe it accurately reflects available job vacancies at any given moment. In reality, however, the advertised job market may include no more than 25 percent of actual job openings. Furthermore, this market tends to represent positions at the extreme ends of the job spectrum—low paid unskilled or high paid highly skilled jobs. The majority of positions lying between these two extremes are not well represented in the listings. And many of the advertised jobs are either nonexistent or are filled prior to being advertised. Government agencies and international organizations normally advertise all of their positions through personnel offices and some published sources, although many of these positions are "wired" for specific individuals.

On the other hand, don't neglect the advertised job market. Many high level and exotic international jobs are advertised because organizations have difficulty recruiting individuals by other means. Many of these jobs will require specific technical skills or some exotic combination of skills and experience. Some may also involve working in a remote, dangerous, or boring location where personal hardships incurred with such jobs outweigh their ostensible financial and travel benefits. Indeed, many contractors working in developing countries have difficulty filling top level project management positions precisely because of these problems.

At the same time, many international job seekers have no interest whatsoever in working in Third or Fourth World countries or even in the most developed parts of the Middle East, Latin America, Africa, or Asia—regardless of how well the jobs may pay. Many of these jobs may involve hardships that are beyond the call of duty or require lifestyles that are simply difficult to manage. These jobs are best advertised in the hope that some unusual individual will be attracted to them because of the international "challenge." In fact, many international job seekers we encounter only want to "go international" in the best parts of Europe.

Even working next door in Central and Eastern Europe would be out of the question for them.

You should spend a minimum amount of time looking for employment on the advertised international job market. Monitor this market well by regularly reviewing the listings found in the best job listing services, but don't assume it represents the entire spectrum of job opportunities. Your job search time and money may be better spent elsewhere—on the hidden job market.

The **hidden job market** should be the most important arena for your job search. Lacking a formal structure, this job market may encompass as many as 75 percent of all international job openings at any given moment. Many employers turn to the advertised job market only **after** they fail to recruit candidates through word-of-mouth or networking efforts. The lag time between when a position becomes vacant, is listed, and then filled is a critical period for your attention and **intervention**. Your goal should be to locate high quality job vacancies on the hidden international job market **before** they become listed on the advertised job market.

Your goal should be to locate high quality job vacancies before they become listed.

Your research efforts will be the key to penetrating the hidden job market. Consider, for example, the hiring problems of employers by putting yourself in their place. Start this scenario by supposing one of your employees suddenly gives you two weeks notice, or you terminate someone. Now you have a problem —you must hire a new employee. It's time consuming, it's troublesome, and it's a risky business—especially if the employee is to be relocated abroad—you would prefer to avoid. Your field operation or project may experience serious problems if you do not recruit a highly qualified individual quickly. Except for some unemployed individuals, not many people are prepared to pick up stakes and move abroad on a moment's notice. After hours of reading resumes and interviewing, you still will be hiring an unknown who might create new problems for you rather than solve the ones you are hiring someone to resolve. Like many other employers, you want to **minimize your time and risks**. You can do this by calling your friends and acquaintances and letting them know you are looking for someone; you would appreciate it if they could refer some good candidates to you. Based on these contacts, you should receive referrals. At the same time, you want to hedge your bets by listing the job vacancy in the newspaper or professional newsletter. While 100 people respond by mail to your classified ad, you also get referrals from the trusted individuals in your network. In the end, you conduct 10 telephone interviews and three face-to-face interviews. You hire the **best** candidate—the one your former classmate recommended to you on the first day you informed her of your need to fill the vacancy. You are satisfied with your excellent choice; you are relatively certain this new employee will be a good addition to your organization.

This scenario is played out regularly in many organizations—both public and private. It demonstrates the importance of getting into the hidden job market and devoting most of your time and energy there. If you let people know you are looking for employment, chances are they will keep you in mind and refer you to others who may have an unexpected vacancy. Your research will help you enter and maneuver within this job market of interpersonal networks and highly personalized information exchanges. Chapter Six outlines how to do this with maximum impact.

Work the Library

Libraries are filled with useful job and career information. Reference and documents rooms of libraries have some of the best career resources. Career planning offices at colleges and universities have a wealth of job and career information in their specialized libraries—a wider selection than most general libraries.

Your goal should be to acquire as much written information as possible on individuals and organizations relating to your international job objective. Normally this means examining directories, books, magazines, and reports. These publications will provide general surveys of occupational fields, information on particular individuals and organizations, as well as names, addresses, and telephone numbers of key individuals within organizations. At this stage you need to understand the organizations and collect many names, addresses, and telephone numbers for initiating your writing and telephoning activities.

You should start your research by examining several of the following resources normally found in the reference sections of libraries:

Directories of Reference Materials

- *Ayer Directory of Publications*
- *Applied Science and Technology*
- *Business Periodicals Index*
- *Guide To American Directories*
- *Readers' Guide To Periodical Literature*
- *Standard Periodical Directory*
- *Ulrich's International Periodicals Directory*
- *Working Press of the Nation*

Career and Job Alternatives

- *Ad Search*
- *Advance Job Listings*
- *Affirmative Action Register*
- *The College Placement Annual*
- *Dictionary of Occupational Titles*
- *Encyclopedia of Careers and Vocational Guidance*
- *Enhanced Guide To Occupational Exploration*
- *Guide To Occupational Exploration*
- *Occupational Outlook Handbook*
- *Occupational Outlook Quarterly*
- *Work Related Abstracts*

Business

- *American Encyclopedia of International Information*
- *American Export Register*
- *American Register of Exporters and Importers*
- *Career Guide To Professional Associations*
- *China's Foreign Trade Corporations and Organizations*
- *Directory of American Firms Operating In Foreign Countries*
- *The Directory of Corporate Affiliations: Who Owns Whom*
- *Directory of Foreign Automotive Companies In the U.S.*
- *Directory of Foreign Firms Operating In the U.S.*
- *Directory of Foreign Forwarders and Custom House Brokers*
- *Directory of Japanese Firms and Offices In the U.S.*
- *Directory of Leading U.S. Export Management Companies*
- *Directory of Management Consultants*
- *Directory of State Industrial and Economic Departments, Commerce Departments, and Purchasing Agents*
- *Directory of U.S. Firms Operating In Latin America*
- *Dun & Bradstreet's Exporter's Encyclopedia*
- *Dun & Bradstreet's Middle Market Directory*
- *Dun & Bradstreet's Million Dollar Directory*
- *Dun & Bradstreet's Reference Book of Corporate Managements*
- *East-West Business Directory*
- *Encyclopedia of Business Information Services*
- *Europages: The European Business Directory*
- *Fitch's Corporate Reports*
- *Fortune 500: Top 50 Exporters*
- *Geographical Index*
- *Hoover's Handbook of American Business*
- *Hoover's Handbook of World Business*

- *How to Find Information About Companies*
- *Industrial Reps of Overseas Countries and Overseas Buying Reps*
- *International Bankers Directory*
- *The International Corporate 1,000*
- *Job Prospector*
- *Jane's Major Companies of Europe*
- *Major Companies of Europe*
- *Marconi's International Register*
- *MacRae's Blue Book—Corporate Index*
- *Moody's Industrial Manual*
- *The Multinational Marketing and Employment Directory*
- *Principal International Business*
- *Product Export Riches Opportunities*
- *Standard Directory of Advertisers*
- *The Standard Handbook of Industrial Distributors*
- *The Standard Periodical Directory*
- *Standard & Poor's Industrial Index*
- *Standard & Poor's Register of Corporations, Directors, and Executives*
- *Taiwan Register*
- *Thomas' Register of American Manufacturers*
- *Trade Directories of the World*
- *Who's Who In Banking*
- *Worldwide Riches Opportunities*

Government

- *American Almanac of Politics*
- *Commerce Business Daily*
- *Congressional Directory*
- *Congressional Record*
- *Congressional Staff Directory*
- *Congressional Yellow Book*
- *Directory of Federal Executives*
- *Federal Register*
- *Federal Yellow Book*
- *Taylor's Encyclopedia of Government Officials*
- *United States Government Manual*
- *Washington Information Directory*

Peripheral Public Institutions

- *The Consultants and Consulting Organizations Directory*
- *Encyclopedia of Associations* (4 vols.)

- *The Foundation Directory*
- *National Trade and Professional Associations*
- *Research Center Directory*
- *Washington* (yearly)
- *Washington Representatives*
- *Who's Who in Consulting*

International

- *Encyclopedia of Associations* (Vol. 4: *"International Organizations"*)
- *Europa Year Book*
- *Yearbook of International Organizations*
- *Yearbook of the United Nations*

Other Resources

- Trade journals (the *Directory of Libraries and Subject Collections: A Guide to Special Book Collections in Libraries* compiles information on specialized business, government, and association libraries).
- Publications of internationally relevant nonprofit organizations; contractors; trade and professional associations; foundations; research organizations; Federal government agencies.
- Telephone books—especially the Yellow Pages (if not in library, contact your local telephone company which may have a telephone book collection).
- Trade books on how to get an international job

If you are currently living abroad, you may find many of the business and government directories at the libraries of the United States Information Agency or U.S. Department of Commerce. In some countries these two libraries have excellent collections of international directories that are more extensive than many libraries back home. Contact the U.S. embassy or the local consulate for information on where these libraries can be found. They are often housed in buildings outside the embassy compound. Many regional offices of the United Nations also have excellent libraries with numerous international directories and publications worth reviewing for information on opportunities abroad.

As you accumulate names and addresses from your library research, write or call individuals and organizations for further information. Many organizations will give you copies of their annual reports and related literature. Government agencies publish reports and newsletters which are worth examining. Your library may have additional job-related international resources.

Talk to People

Beware of becoming **too** preoccupied with library research. This research may give you a false sense of making progress with your job search. Stop when you feel you have enough information to begin other types of research or start other job search activities. Two weeks or 40 hours in the library should get you off to a good start. If you are examining a highly specialized field where there are few names and addresses, you may achieve a high degree of redundancy within 10 hours.

Informal, word-of-mouth communication is still the most effective channel for job search information.

Your most productive research activity will be talking to people. Informal, word-of-mouth communication is still the most effective channel for job search information. In contrast to reading books, people have more current, and probably more accurate, information. In addition, most people are flattered to be asked for advice. Many people freely give it and will be happy to assist you with referrals to others. Don't hide the fact you are looking for an international job, but don't ask for a job. Ask people about:

- Occupational fields
- Job requirements and training
- Interpersonal environments
- Performance expectations
- Their problems
- Salaries
- Advancement opportunities
- Future growth potential of the organization
- How best to acquire more information and contacts in a particular field
- How you can improve your resume

Techniques for conducting this type of research—referred to as networking and informational interviewing—are outlined in Chapter Seven.

You may be surprised how willing friends, acquaintances, and strangers give useful job information. But before you talk to people, do your library research so you are better able to ask thoughtful questions.

Knowledge is power. Research will help increase your power in the international job market. You should always collect new information, revise previous conceptions, and adjust your job search efforts to new realities uncovered through your research. As you do this, your research will help refine your original objective, provide appropriate language and substance for your resume, and guide your networking and informational interviewing activities into productive directions. Your power to give some structure and coherence to the hidden job market in your area of interest should increase accordingly.

Chapter Six

PROJECT A POSITIVE IMAGE WITH QUALITY RESUMES, LETTERS, AND PERSONAL APPEARANCE

Communicating a positive image to potential employers is central to every action you take during your international job search. The initial impression you make on an employer through applications, resumes, letters, telephone calls, faxes, or informational interviews will determine whether the employer is interested in interviewing you and offering you a position.

Developing and managing effective job search communication should play a central role in everything you do related to finding employment. This communication takes many verbal and nonverbal forms. Your first communication with employers will most likely be by letter or in a face-to-face meeting. Job search letters often include your calling card—the resume. These documents are important forms of communication.

Face-to-face meetings involve both verbal and nonverbal communication. However, the nonverbal aspect is especially important for the informational and job interviews (Chapter Seven). Employers place a great deal of emphasis on how you look. Whether you like it or not, your dress and appearance play a key role in determining the outcomes of your job search.

In this chapter we examine important nonverbal aspects of three communication activities during the job search: resumes, letters, and dress. How you develop, target, and manage this communication will largely determine how far you progress through the interpersonal job search processes in Chapter Seven.

MAKING JUDGMENTS
AT HOME AND ABROAD

People do make important judgments about others based upon initial impressions relating to the quality of their stationery, length of their resume, what they wear, how they look, and how they shake hands and eat their food. Managing your image and observing proper social and cultural etiquette will play important roles in every stage of your international job search. As a stranger to most employers, you are more likely to be "sized up" initially on the basis of these seemingly non-quantitative, somewhat superficial, and nonverbal factors than on your educational background, skills, abilities, and qualifications for the job. In the eyes of many employers **how you do something** is often more important than what you do in terms of your work-content and transferable skills.

> *How you do something is often more important than what you do.*

Form or image considerations are especially important when applying for an international job. Indeed, it is critical in many countries where status and class play key roles in personnel decisions and where status and class are primarily communicated nonverbally. If you are applying for an international job where the status of the position and its occupant are important, you must observe the local rules for proper social behavior. The nonverbal choices you make in the presence of the potential employer—where you stay, how and when you arrive, what you wear, how you greet others, how you direct your eyes, whom you sit next to, and how you eat and pass food—convey important messages about you as well as your future with the employer. Therefore, you must pay particular attention to how well you communicate a positive image cross-culturally. This image management activity may become the decisive factor in determining whether you or someone else gets the job.

INTERNATIONAL IMAGES

International job seekers are often more concerned with where they want to work, what they can do, and what they say than with maintaining a positive nonverbal image. Not surprising, they often produce unattractive resumes and letters, dress inappropriately, stay in the wrong places, and communicate the wrong messages about their capabilities to function well abroad. Their resume is either too long or too short, distributed inappropriately, or sent to the wrong people. If they have lived abroad for an extended period of time, they may be unfamiliar with current dress and appearance practices, especially types of apparel, choice of fabrics, and selection of colors. In fact, international job seekers are some of the least well dressed people we have encountered. They violate many rules of good dress and appearance. Applying past dress and appearance practices and observations to the job search, they often make poor impressions on employers. Indeed, many international workers are used to informal wardrobes or are only familiar with dress codes on their last job.

If there are two areas which international job seekers can quickly improve upon, it is their resume and personal appearance. What you write and how you appear in person communicates as much about who you as your stated education, skills, and accomplishments and what you say in interviews. First impressions count a great deal. Most of all, you want to communicate a positive image to international employers.

Within American culture we can say with some degree of certainty what qualifies as an excellent resume and how one should best dress for job search success. In America we prefer brevity, efficiency, closure, and individualism in what we write and wear. We prefer setting goals, getting to the point, and being different rather than orchestrating a somewhat pointless performance that conforms to group norms. Many countries in the international arena do not share the same values when recruiting employees. They may evaluate a candidate on the basis of breadth, status, conformity to group norms, power, and the ability to control the situation. Instead of looking for one or two specialty skills to be used in what may well be an ill-defined job, they may want someone who has lots of different skills and many different experiences—the Renaissance individual rather than the specialist—who will be hired to define the job and acquire the necessary power to take the job and organization into new directions.

The one to two-page resume that works well in the U.S. is not necessarily well received in other cultures which place higher value on the length and weight of resumes. A ten page resume, for example, may be preferred over a one page resume. In some countries written communication is not important to decision-making. Greater reliance is placed on personal contacts, referrals, and face-to-face meetings for exchanging information and sizing up the "qualifications" and "status" of candidates.

The same is true for dress and appearance. Clothing has different meanings in different cultures. In many countries formal dress implies a great deal about one's position and status—moreso that in the U.S. and other less formal countries such as Australia and New Zealand. In many hot and humid countries, where a suit seems to be impractical attire given the climatic conditions, nonetheless, a suit or sport coat worn with a long-sleeved shirt would be appropriate attire for a job interview. Wearing a short-sleeve shirt—even under the sport coat or a suit—might be inappropriate because it communicates low status. Indeed, in many status conscious societies, a long-sleeved shirt is considered "polite" while a short-sleeved shirt is "impolite" in important or formal situations. A similar principle applies to women who should wear a tailored suit or long-sleeved tailored dress rather than a short-sleeved blouse and skirt or dress.

The one to two-page resume that works well in the U.S. is not necessarily well received in other cultures.

Dining customs also differ. In some cultures, for example, it's impolite and even rude to pass things with your left hand, reach for items on the table, eat everything on your plate, or drink the last half inch of beverage in your glass. And where you stay and how you arrive at an interview say something about your status.

Your choice of hotel and transportation says something about you and your status. If you stay at the best hotel in town and rent a car with driver, you may impress upon the employer that your behavior may be equal to the status of the position. Staying at a cheap, low status hotel and taking an inexpensive crowded bus to the interview say negative things about how you view your status and the employer's position.

If you violate these norms of good behavior, you may be politely thanked for your interest in the job but rejected in the end. Thus, you should be aware of these and other important cross-cultural differences before you interview for a job.

Whatever you do, be sure you know the local customs concerning written communications and proper attire and interpersonal behavior. There is no quicker way to disqualify yourself from consideration for an international job than to demonstrate an "insensitivity" to the local cultural norms. Regardless of how qualified you are on paper, you may be telling potential employers loud and clear through your nonverbal behaviors that you will have difficulty adjusting to the job and thus "fitting in" with the local organization.

WRITING RESUMES

Resumes are important tools for communicating your purpose and capabilities to employers. While many jobs only require a completed application form, you should always prepare a resume for influencing the hiring process. Application forms do not substitute for resumes.

Many myths surround resumes and letters. Some people still believe a resume should summarize one's history. Others believe it will get them a job. And still others believe they should be mailed in response to classified ads. The reality is this: A resume advertises your qualifications to prospective employers. It is your calling card for getting interviews. For many international jobs, it also may become your plane ticket to an interview abroad.

A resume advertises your qualifications to prospective employers. It is your calling card for getting interviews.

Ineffective Resumes

Most people write ineffective resumes. Misunderstanding the purpose of resumes, they make numerous mistakes commonly associated with weak resumes and poor advertising copy. Their resumes often lack an objective, include unrelated categories of information, are too long, and appear unattractive. Other common pitfalls identified by employers include:

- Poor layout
- Misspellings and punctuation errors
- Poor grammar
- Unclear purpose
- Too much jargon
- Include irrelevant data
- Too long or too short
- Poorly typed and reproduced
- Unexplained time gaps
- Too boastful
- Deceptive or dishonest
- Difficult to understand or interpret

Your resume, instead, should incorporate the characteristics of strong and effective resumes:

- Clearly communicate your purpose and competencies in relation to employers' needs.
- Be concise and easy to read but still respond to the need for breadth and depth of information.
- Motivate the reader to read it in-depth.
- Tell employers that you are a responsible and purposeful individual— a doer who can solve their problems.

Keep in mind that most employers are busy people who normally glance at a resume for only 20 to 30 seconds. Your resume, therefore, must sufficiently catch their attention to pass the 20 to 30 second evaluation test. When writing your resume, ask yourself the same question asked by employers: *"Why should I read this or contact this person for an interview?"* Your answer should result in an attractive, interesting, unique, and skills-based resume.

Employers are busy people who normally only glance at a resume for 20 or 30 seconds.

Types of Resumes

You have four types of resumes to choose from: chronological, functional, combination, or resume letter. Each format has various advantages and disadvantages, depending on your background and purpose. For example, someone first entering the job market or making a major career change should use a functional resume. On the other hand, a person who wants to target a particular job may choose to use a resume letter. Examples of these different types of resumes as well as in-depth assistance in developing each section of a resume is found in Krannich's and Banis' comprehensive resume development book, *High Impact Resumes and Letters* and our *Dynamite Resumes*.

The **chronological resume** is the standard resume used by most applicants. It comes in two forms: traditional and improved. The **traditional chronological resume** is also known as the "obituary resume," because it both "kills" your chances of getting a job and is a good source for writing your obituary. Summarizing your work history, this resume lists dates and names first and duties and responsibilities second; it includes extraneous information such as height, weight, age, marital status, sex, and hobbies. While relatively easy to write, this is the most ineffective resume you can produce. Its purpose at best is to inform people of what you have done in the past as well as where, when, and with whom. It tells employers little or nothing about what you want to do, can do, and will do for them. This is the ultimate self-centered resume.

The **improved chronological resume** communicates directly to employers your purpose, past achievements, and probable future performance. You should use this type of resume when you have extensive experience directly related to a position you seek. This resume should include a work objective which reflects both your work experience and professional goals. The work experience section should include the names and addresses of former employers followed by a brief description of your accomplishments, skills, and responsibilities; inclusive employment dates should appear at the end. Do not begin with dates; they are the least significant element in the descriptions. Be sure to stress your **accomplishments** and **skills** rather than your formal duties and responsibilities. You want to inform your audience that you are a productive and responsible person who gets things done—a doer.

If you are changing careers or have an unstable employment history, avoid using a chronological resume. It communicates the wrong messages—you lack direct work experience, you are an unstable worker, or you have not advanced in your career. If you have such a career pattern, consider writing a functional or combination resume.

Functional resumes should be used by individuals making a significant career change, first entering the workforce, or re-entering the job market after a lengthy absence. This resume should stress your accomplishments and transferable skills regardless of previous work settings and job titles. This could include accomplishments as a housewife or house husband, volunteer worker, or Sunday school teacher. Names of employers and dates of employment should not appear on this resume.

Functional resumes have certain weaknesses. While they are important bridges for the inexperienced and for those making a career change, some employers dislike these seemingly vague resumes. Since many employers— especially those abroad—still look for names, dates, direct job experience, positions, titles, duties, and responsibilities, this resume does not meet their expectations. You should use a functional resume only if your past work experience does not strengthen your objective when making a major career change.

Combination resumes are a compromise between chronological and functional resumes. Having more advantages than disadvantages, this resume may be exactly what you need if you are making a career change with related experience from one career to another.

Combination resumes have the potential to both **meet** and **raise** the expectations of employers. You should stress your accomplishments and skills as well as include your work history. Your work history should appear as a separate section immediately following your presentation of accomplishments and skills in the "Areas of Effectiveness" or "Experience" section. It is not necessary to include dates unless they enhance your resume. This is the perfect resume for someone wishing to change to a job in a related career field.

Resume letters are substitutes for resumes. Appearing as a job inquiry or application letter, resume letters highlight various sections of your resume, such as work history, experience, areas of effectiveness, objective, or education, in relation to employers' needs. These letters are used when you prefer not sending your more general resume. Resume letters have one major weakness: they give employers insufficient information and thus may prematurely eliminate you from consideration.

International Resume Choices

The brief one to two-page American resume communicates the wrong messages to many international employers who either feel you have little in-depth experience or you are not interested enough in the position to take the time to detail your qualifications and experience. Many international employers expect to receive a five to eight-page resume—commonly referred to as a curriculum vita (CV)—from serious candidates. After all, shouldn't a big job be the object of a big resume from those who have big experience and skills? Don't argue with this logic—just use it to your advantage.

We prefer the improved chronological or combination resume for internation-al jobs. These resumes have the best potential to meet the expectations of international employers as well as clearly communicate your international experience and qualifications to them. The functional resume is too vague for most serious international jobs. It often says little or nothing about work-content skills and qualifications other than provide some highly generalized and somewhat "canned" resume statements about experiences that anyone can include on a resume regardless of their particular work experience.

Since many international employers prefer lengthy resumes or curriculum vitas which list numerous positions, duties, responsibilities, names, dates, locations, professional memberships, and references, you can provide such information in the improved chronological and combination resume. However, we recommend that you write these resumes in a nontraditional manner. Rather than just provide an eight-page resume with long listings of experience, job titles, and skills, write a one to two-page improved chronological or combination resume that essentially synthesizes the information or documentation found on the remaining pages of the resume. Consequently, your resume may be seven pages long but the first-page actually functions like an "executive summary" for a report; it synthesizes for the reader all of the back-up information provided in the remaining five or six pages. These other pages should be well organized by functional information categories that summarize and list important accomplish-ments relevant to your education and experience. These might include the actual titles and dates of speeches and presentations you gave or articles you published; the formal duties and responsibilities of your past jobs along with a listing of actual accomplishments and any special recognition received for your perfor-mance; a listing of honors and awards, complete with dates and a summary of their significance; information on your professional memberships; and contact information on three or four references. In the process of doing such a resume, you are permitted to include many of the prohibitions normally associated with the brief one or two-page American resume. Yes, in many cases it's okay to list publications, speeches, memberships, references, hobbies, interests, family data, age, sex, religion, and health. Remember, international employers want to know a lot more about you than just your skills. They are interested in looking at you as an individual with many characteristics which may or may not qualify you for both the job and the international living situation.

Structuring Your Resume

After choosing an appropriate resume format, you should generate the necessary information for structuring each category of your resume. You developed much of this information when you identified your strengths and specified your objective in Chapter Five. To complete your data base for the resume, include the following information on separate sheets of paper:

CONTACT INFORMATION:	name, address, telephone number, fax number if applicable.
WORK OBJECTIVE:	refer to your data in Chapter Seven on writing an objective.
EDUCATION:	degrees, schools, dates, highlights, special training.
WORK EXPERIENCE:	paid, unpaid, civilian, military, and part-time employment. Include job titles, employers, locations, dates, skills, accomplishments, duties, and responsibilities. Use the functional language developed in Chapter Five.
OTHER EXPERIENCE:	volunteer, civic, and professional memberships. Include your travel, contributions, demonstrated skills, offices held, names, and dates.
SPECIAL SKILLS OR LICENSES/ CERTIFICATES:	foreign languages, teaching, paramedical, etc. relevant to your objective.
PERSONAL:	citizenship, age, religion, marital status, family data, interests, hobbies.
MISCELLANEOUS INFORMATION:	references, expected salary, willingness to relocate and travel, availability dates.

Producing Drafts

Once you generate the basic data for constructing your resume, your next task is to reduce this data into draft resumes. If, for example, you write a combination resume, the internal organization of the resume should be as follows:

- Contact information
- Work objective
- Education
- Qualifications or functional experience
- Work history or employment
- Professional memberships/activities (optional, depending on job)
- Publications/speeches (optional, depending on job)
- References (optional, depending on job)
- Personal information (optional, depending on job)

Be careful about including any other type of information on your resume. Other information most often is extraneous or negative information. You should only include information designed to strengthen your objective.

While your first draft may run more than 10 pages, try to get everything into five to eight pages, with a one to two-page "executive summary" for the final draft. Most employers lose interest after reading the second page, even international employers who may prefer lengthy resumes. If you include a one to two-page summary resume attached to the remaining five pages of what is essentially a curriculum vita with back-up documentation for the first two pages, you should have a powerful resume that both meets the needs of employers as well as clearly and accurately represents your qualifications.

Your final draft should conform to the following rules for creating an excellent resume:

RESUME "DON'TS"

- **Don't** use abbreviations except for your middle name.
- **Don't** make the resume cramped and crowded; it should be pleasing to the eyes.
- **Don't** make statements you can't document.
- **Don't** use the passive voice.
- **Don't** change tense of verbs.
- **Don't** use lengthy sentences and descriptions.
- **Don't** refer to yourself as "I".
- **Don't** include negative information.
- **Don't** include extraneous information unless is appears appropriate for particular employers who want to know more about you than just your skills and work qualifications.

RESUME "DOS"

- **Do** use action verbs and the active voice.
- **Do** be direct, succinct, and expressive with your language.
- **Do** appear neat, well organized, and professional.
- **Do** use ample spacing and highlights (all caps, underlining, bulleting) for different emphases.
- **Do** maintain an eye pleasing balance. Try centering your contact information at the top, keeping information categories on the left in all caps, and describing the categories in the center and on the right.
- **Do** check carefully your spelling, grammar, and punctuation.
- **Do** clearly communicate your purpose and value to employers.
- **Do** communicate your strongest points first.

Evaluating

You should subject your resume drafts to two types of evaluations. An **internal evaluation** consists of reviewing our lists of "dos" and "don'ts" to make sure your resume conforms to these rules. An **external evaluation** should be conducted by circulating your resume to three or more individuals whom you believe will give you frank, objective, and useful feedback. Avoid people who tend to flatter you. The best evaluator would be someone in a hiring position similar to one you will encounter in the actual interview. Ask these people to critique your draft resume and suggest improvements in both form and content. This will be your most important evaluation. After all, the only evaluation that counts is the one that helps get you an interview. Asking someone to critique your resume is one way to spread the word that you are job hunting. As we will see in Chapter Seven, this is one method for getting invited to an interview!

Checklist criteria and forms for conducting an internal resume evaluation are included in Krannich's and Banis' *High Impact Resumes and Letters* and our *Dynamite Resumes*.

Final Production

How you produce your resume will say a great deal about you and your image. Your final resume can be typed, typeset, or word processed. If you type it, be sure it looks professional. Use an electric typewriter with a carbon ribbon. Varying the typing elements and styles can produce an attractive copy. Do not use a portable typewriter with a nylon ribbon since it does not produce professional copy. Many typists will do your resume on the proper machine for about $5 to $10 per page.

If you have it word processed, be sure the final copy is printed on a letter quality printer using a carbon ribbon or on a laser printer. Dot matrix and near letter quality printers make your resume look mass produced. In addition, many international employers want resumes to look "original"—as if they were produced only for them and their job vacancy.

Alternatively, you can have a printer typeset your resume. This may cost anywhere from $20 to $50 per page. The final product should look first-class. However, it may look **too** professional or **too** slick; some employers may think you had someone else write the resume for you and it will not appear custom designed for particular international employers and jobs—something you want to achieve in your resume writing.

Whichever method you use, be sure to proofread the final copy for spelling, grammatical, and typing errors. Many people spend good money on production only to later find such errors.

When reproducing the resume, you must consider the quality and color of paper as well as the number of copies you need. By all means use good quality paper that communicates your professionalism and class. You should use watermarked 20-pound or heavier bond paper. Costing 3¢ to 7¢ per sheet, this paper can be purchased through stationery stores and printers. It is important not to cut corners at this point by purchasing cheap paper or using copy machine paper. You may save $25 on 100 copies, but you also will communicate an unprofessional and low class image to employers—something you must especially avoid in the international job arena.

Use one of the following paper colors: white, off-white, light tan, light gray, or light blue. Avoid blue, yellow, green, pink, orange, red, or any other bright colors. Conservative, light-muted colors are the best. Any of these colors can be complemented with black ink. In the case of light gray—our first choice—a navy blue ink looks best. Dark brown ink is especially attractive on light tan paper.

Your choices of paper quality and color say something about your personality and professional style. They communicate nonverbally your attention to detail as well as that you do things "first class." Employers will use these as indicators for screening you in or out of an interview. At the same time, these choices may make your resume stand out from the crowd of standard black-on-white resumes.

It's best to send an original copy of your resume since many international employers prefer receiving a resume produced specifically for them. This is easy to do if you have a word processor and letter quality or laser printer. Better still, you can custom-design the resume specifically around the particular employer and job. If not, go ahead and reproduce your more general resume from an original copy.

If you choose to reproduce your resume from an original, you have two choices: a copy machine or an offset process. Many of the newer copy machines give good reproductions on the quality paper you need—nearly the same quality as the offset process. You should be able to make such copies for 10-20¢ per page. The offset process produces the best quality because it uses a printing plate. It also is relatively inexpensive—5¢ to 10¢ per page with a minimum run of 100 copies. The cost per page decreases with large runs of 300, 500, or 1000. In the end, you should be able to have your resume typed and 100 copies reproduced on high quality colored bond paper for less than $60. If you have it typeset, the same number of copies may cost you $100. Obviously, it's much cheaper and your resume will be more effective if you have the in-house word processing and printing capabilities to produce original custom-designed resumes for individual employers.

Whatever your choices, do not try to cut costs when it comes to producing your resume. It simply is not worth it. Remember, your resume is your calling card—it should represent your best professional image. Put your best foot forward at this stage. Go in style; spend a few dollars on producing a first-class resume.

Remember, your resume is your calling card—it should represent your best professional image.

JOB SEARCH LETTERS

Resumes sent through the mail are normally accompanied by a cover letter. After interviewing for information or a position, you should send a thank-you letter. Other occasions will arise when it is both proper and necessary for you to write different types of job search letters.

Your letter writing should follow the principles of good resume and business writing. Job hunting letters are like resumes—they advertise you for interviews. Like good advertisements, these letters should follow four basic principles for effectiveness:

1. Catch the reader's attention.
2. Persuade the reader of your benefits or value.
3. Convince the reader with evidence.
4. Move the reader to acquire the product.

Basic Preparation Rules

Before you begin writing a job search letter, ask yourself several questions to clarify the content of your letter:

- What is the **purpose** of the letter?
- What are the **needs** of my audience?
- What **benefits** will my audience gain from me?

- What is a good opening sentence or paragraph for grabbing the **attention** of my audience?
- How can I maintain the **interests** of my audience?
- How can I best end the letter so that the audience will be **persuaded** to contact me?
- If a resume is enclosed, how can my letter best **advertise the resume**?
- Have I spent enough **time** revising and proofreading the letter?
- Does the letter represent my **best professional effort**?

Since your letters are a form of business communication, they should conform to the rules of good business correspondence:

- Plan and organize what you will say by outlining the content of your letter.

- Know your purpose and plan the elements of your letter accordingly.

- Communicate your message in a logical and sequential manner.

- State your purpose immediately in the first sentence and paragraph; main ideas always go first.

- End your letter by stating what your reader can expect next from you.

- Use short paragraphs and sentences; avoid overly complex sentences.

- Punctuate properly and use correct grammar and spelling.

- Use simple and straight forward language; avoid jargon.

- Communicate your message as directly and briefly as possible.

The rules stress how to both **organize and communicate** your message with impact. At the same time, you should always have a specific purpose in mind as well as know the needs of your audience.

Types of Letters

Cover letters provide cover for your resume. You should avoid overwhelming your resume with a two-page letter or repeating the contents of the resume in the letter. A short and succinct one-page letter which highlights one or two points in your resume is sufficient. Three paragraphs will suffice. The first paragraph should state your interests and purposes for writing. The second paragraph should highlight your possible value to the employer. The third paragraph should state that you will call the individual at a particular time to schedule an interview.

Approach letters should get employers to engage in the 5R's of informational interviewing.

Approach letters are written for the purpose of developing job contacts, leads, or information as well as for organizing networks and getting interviews—the subjects of Chapter Seven. Your primary purposes should be to get employers to engage in the 5R's of informational interviewing:

- **Reveal** useful information and advice.
- **Refer** you to others.
- **Read** and **revise** your resume.
- **Remember** you for future reference.

These letters help you gain access to the hidden job market.

Approach letters can be sent out en masse to uncover job leads, or they can target particular individuals or organizations. It is best to target these letters since they have maximum impact when personalized in reference to particular positions.

The structure of approach letters is similar to other letters. The first paragraph states your purpose. In so doing, you may want to use a personal statement for openers, such as *"Mary Tillis recommended that I write to you..."* or *"I am familiar with your..."* State your purpose, but do not suggest that you are asking for a job—only career advice or information. In your final paragraph, request a meeting and indicate you will call to schedule such a meeting at a mutually convenient time.

Thank-you letters may well become your most effective job search letters. They especially communicate your thoughtfulness. These letters come in different forms and are written for various occasions. The most common thank-you letter is written after receiving assistance, such as job search information or a critique of your resume. Other occasions include:

- **Immediately following an interview:** Thank the interviewer for the opportunity to interview for the position. Repeat your interest in the position.

- **Receive a job offer:** Thank the employer for his or her faith in you and express your appreciation.

- **Rejected for a job:** Thank the employer for giving you the "opportunity" to interview for the job. Ask to be remembered for future reference.

- **Terminate employment:** Thank the employer for the experience and ask to be remembered for future reference.

- **Begin a new job:** Thank the employer for giving you this new opportunity and express your confidence in producing the value he or she is expecting from you.

Examples of each type of letter are presented in Krannich's and Banis' *High Impact Resumes and Letters* and our other two books, *Dynamite Cover Letters* and *Job Search Letters That Get Results*.

Being remembered by employers is the closest thing to being invited to an interview and offered a job.

Several of these thank-you letters are unusual, but they all have the same goal in mind—to be remembered by potential employers in a positive light. In a job search, being remembered by employers is the closest thing to being invited to an interview and offered a job.

DISTRIBUTION AND MANAGEMENT

The only good resumes are the ones that get read, remembered, referred, and result in a job interview. Therefore, after completing a first-rate resume and job search letters, you must decide what to do with them. Are you planning to only respond to classified ads? What other creative distribution methods might you use, such as sending it to friends, relatives, and former employers? What is the best way to proceed?

Responding To Classified Ads

Except for government agencies, most of your writing activities should focus on the hidden job market. At the same time, you should respond to job listings in newspapers, magazines, and personnel offices. While this is largely a numbers game, you can increase your odds by the way you respond to the listings.

You should be selective in your responses. Since you know what you want to do, you will be looking for only certain types of positions. Once you identify them, your response entails little expenditure of time and effort—an envelope, letter, stamp, resume, and maybe 20 minutes of your time. You have little to lose. While you have the potential to gain by sending a letter and resume in response to an ad, remember the odds are usually against you.

The only good resumes are the ones that get read, remembered, referred, and result in a job interview.

It is difficult to interpret job listings. Some employers place blind ads with P.O. Box numbers in order to collect resumes for future reference. Others wish to avoid aggressive applicants who telephone or "drop-in" for interviews. Many employers work through professional recruiters who place these ads. While you may try to second guess the rationale behind such ads, respond to them as you would to ads with an employer's name, address, or telephone number. Assume there is a real job behind the ad.

Most ads request a copy of your resume. You should respond with a cover letter and resume as soon as you see the ad. Depending on how much information about the position is revealed in the ad, your letter should be tailored to emphasize your qualifications vis-a-vis the ad. Examine the ad carefully. Underline any words or phrases which relate to your qualifications. In your cover letter you should use similar terminology in emphasizing your qualifications. Keep the letter brief and to the point.

If the ad asks you to state your salary history or salary requirements, you may wish to state "negotiable" or "open." Alternatively, you can include a figure by stating a salary range 20 percent above your present salary base. For example, if you are making $40,000 a year, you can state this as "in the $40,000 to $46,000 range." Use your own judgment in addressing the salary question. There is no hard and fast rule on stating a figure or range. A figure helps the employer screen-out individuals with too high a salary expectation as well as those whose low figures suggest they must not have the experience and qualifications appropriate for the position. You are usually safer to keep salary considerations to the end of the interview—after you know more about the position and have demonstrated your value.

Keep your letter brief and concise and highlight your qualifications as stated in the employer's ad.

You may be able to increase your odds by sending a second copy of your letter and resume two or three weeks after your initial response. Most applicants normally reply to an ad during the seven day period immediately after it appears in print. Since employers often are swamped with responses, your letter and resume may get lost in the crowd. If you send a second copy of your application two or three weeks later, the employer will have more time to give you special attention. By then, he or she also will have a better basis on which to compare you to the others.

Keep in mind that your cover letter and resume may be screened among 400 other resumes and letters. Thus, you want your cover letter to be eye catching and easy to read. Keep it brief and concise and highlight your qualifications as stated in the employer's ad. Don't spend a great deal of time responding to an ad or waiting anxiously at your mailbox or telephone for a reply. Keep moving on to other job search activities.

Self-Initiated Methods

Your letters and resumes can be distributed and managed in various ways. Many people shotgun hundreds of cover letters and resumes to prospective employers. This is a form of gambling where the odds are against you. For every 100 people you contact in this manner, expect one or two might be interested in you. After all, successful direct-mail experts at best expect only a 2 percent return on their mass mailings!

On the other hand, many international companies welcome such mailings because they maintain an in-house resume bank to which they constantly refer to identify candidates for future job openings. International contracting and consulting firms in particular need to quickly identify qualified international experts who are available for overseas assignments. If you are interested in working with such companies, you should get a list of names and addresses and send them a copy of your resume for their resume data bank. Many of these firms will keep your resume on file for two to five years. They also welcome receiving an annual updated version of your resume. The more exotic your skills, the more welcome will be your resume. If they receive a contract for a project related to skills identified on your resume, they may call you for a telephone screening interview which may lead to a formal job interview and a job offer. Our experience is that many firms take their in-house resume data banks seriously, regularly referring to them for identifying qualified candidates. Don't neglect these firms when you get around to distributing your resume and letters.

If you choose to use the shotgun methods, you can increase your odds by using the **telephone**. Call the prospective employer within a week after he or she receives your letter. This technique will probably increase your effectiveness rate from 1 to 5 percent. For a good book on this subject, see John Truitt's *Telesearch: Direct Dial the Best Job of Your Life* (New York: Macmillan or Facts on File).

However, many people are shotgunning their resumes today. As more resumes and letters descend on employers with the increased use of word processing equipment, the effectiveness rates may be even lower. This also can be an expensive marketing method.

Your best distribution strategy will be your own modification of the following procedure:

- Selectively identify whom you would be interested in working for.
- Send an approach letter.
- Follow up with a telephone call seeking an appointment for an interview.

If you use this approach, you will get an interview in more than 50 percent of the cases. It is best not to include a copy of your resume with the approach letter. Keep your resume for the end of the interview. Chapter Seven outlines the procedures for conducting this informational interview.

Recordkeeping

Once you begin distributing letters and resumes, you also will need to keep good records for managing your job search writing campaign. Purchase file folders for your correspondence and notes. Be sure to make copies of all letters you write since you may need to refer to them over the telephone or before interviews. Record your activities with each employer—letters, resumes, telephone calls, interviews—on a 4x6" card and file it according to the name of the organization or individual. These files will help you quickly access information and enable you to evaluate your job search progress.

Always remember the purpose of resumes and letters—**advertise you for interviews**. They do not get jobs. Since most employers know nothing about you, **you must effectively communicate your value in writing prior to the** critical interview. While you should not overestimate the importance of this written communication, neither should you underestimate it.

PROJECT A PROFESSIONAL IMAGE

Let's assume you present a positive image in your written and telephone communication. Based on these impressions, someone agrees to meet with you for an informational interview or invites you to a job interview. At this stage, you must convey a positive image in the way you look as well as the way you behave both verbally and nonverbally. Your appearance becomes a powerful indicator of your value to individuals who do not know you.

Appearance is the first thing you communicate to others.

Appearance is the first thing you communicate to others. Before you have a chance to speak, others notice how you dress and accordingly draw certain conclusions about your personality and competence. Indeed, research shows that appearance makes the greatest difference when an evaluator has little information about the other person. This is precisely the situation you find yourself in at the start of the interview.

Many people object to having their capabilities evaluated on the basis of their appearance and manner of dress. *"But that is not fair,"* they argue. *"People should be hired on the basis of their ability to do the job—not on how they look."* But debating the lack of merit or complaining about the unfairness of such behavior does not alter reality. Like it or not, people do make initial judgments about others based on their appearance. Since you cannot alter this fact and bemoaning it will get you nowhere, it is best to learn to use it to your advantage. If you learn to effectively manage your image, you can convey marvelous messages regarding your authority, credibility, and competence.

Some estimates indicate that as much as 65 percent of the hiring decision may be based on the nonverbal aspects of the interview! Employers sometimes refer to this phenomenon with such terms as "chemistry," "body warmth," or that "gut feeling" the individual is right for the job. This correlates with findings of communication studies that approximately 65 percent of a message is communicated nonverbally. The remaining 35 percent is communicated verbally.

Rules of the Game

Knowing how to dress appropriately for the interview requires knowing important rules of the game. Like it or not, employers play by these rules. Once you know the rules, you at least can make a conscious choice whether or not you want to play. If you decide to play, you will stand a better chance of winning by using the often unwritten rules to your advantage.

Much has been written on how to dress professionally, especially since John Molloy first wrote his books on dress for success in the 1970s. While this approach has been criticized for promoting a "cookie cutter" or "carbon copy" image, it is still valid for most interview situations. The degree to which employers adhere to these rules, however, will depend on particular individuals and situations. Although Molloy's research was conducted in the U.S. setting, its application is just as valid—perhaps moreso—in many international settings. In many cultures the manner of dress is even more important than it is here. Status, class, and competence are often more interconnected abroad than in our society where egalitarian goals have been pursued and where high value is placed on being different, unique, and individualistic. One's manner of dress is equated with his or her status. Your job is to know when, where, and to what extent these rules apply to you. When in doubt, follow our general advice on looking professional.

Knowing and playing by the rules does not imply incompetent people get jobs simply by dressing the part. Rather, it implies that qualified and competent job applicants can gain an extra edge over a field of other qualified, competent individuals by dressing to convey positive professional images.

Winning the Game

Much advice has been written about how to dress for success—some of it excellent. However, there is a major flaw in most of the advice you encounter. Researchers on the subject have looked at how people in positions of power view certain colors for professional attire. Few have gone beyond this to note that colors do different things on different people. Various shades or clarities of a color or combinations of contrast between light and dark colors when worn together may be unenhancing to some individuals and actually diminish that person's "power look."

For example, the combination of a white shirt or blouse paired with a navy suit—one of the success and power looks promoted by many—will be enhancing both to the appearance and the image of power on some individuals, but will be unenhancing and actually over-power the appearance of others. Or suppose you take the advice that a medium to charcoal gray suit is a good color in the professional world. It is, but the advice to wear medium to charcoal gray only recognizes differences of light to dark. In that medium to charcoal range we could pick scores of shades of gray from very blue grays to taupe grays. The wrong gray shade on individuals can make them look unattractive, unhealthy, and even older than their age. Who wants to hire someone who appears to be in poor health?

If we combine the results of research done by John Molloy on how colors relate to one's power look and that done by JoAnne Nicholson and Judy Lewis-Crum as explained in their book *Color Wonderful* (New York: Bantam) on how colors relate to us as unique individuals, we can achieve a win-win situation. You can retain your individuality and look your most enhanced while, at the same time, achieving a look of success, power, and competence.

Your Winning Appearance

The key to effective dressing is to know how to relate the clothing you put on your body to your own natural coloring. Let's pose a few questions to start you thinking about color in what may be some new ways. Ask yourself these questions:

- Can you wear black and white together and look good, or does that much contrast wear you?

- Can you wear navy and white together and retain your "power look" or does that much contrast actually diminish your look of power and authority?

- Can you wear a pure white or is a slightly cream toned white more flattering?

- Do you look better in clear or toned down shades of colors?

The answers to these questions varies with each individual and their own natural coloring. So it is important to know what the appropriate answer is for you.

Into which category does your coloring fit? Let's find out where you belong in terms of color type:

- **Contrast coloring:** If you are a contrast color type, you have a definite dark-light appearance. You have very dark brown or black hair and light to medium ivory or olive toned skin. Black men and women in this category will have clear light to dark skin tones and dark hair.

- **Light-bright coloring:** If you are of this color type, you have golden tones in your skin and golden tones in your blond or light to medium brown hair. Most of you had blond or light brown hair as children. Black men and women in this category will have clear golden skin in their face and dark hair.

- **Muted coloring:** If you are a muted color type, you have a definite brown-on-brown or red-on-brown appearance. Your skin tone is an ivory-beige, brown-beige, or golden-beige tone—that is, you have a beige skin with a golden-brown cast. Your hair could be red or light to dark brown with camel, bronze, or red highlights. Black men and women in this category will have golden or brown skin tones and dark hair.

- **Gentle coloring:** If you are of this color type, you have a soft, gentle looking appearance. Your skin tone is a light ivory or pink-beige tone and your hair is ash blond or ash brown. You probably had blond or ash brown hair as a child. Black men and women in this category will have pink tones in their skin and dark hair.

There are also some individuals who may be a combination of two color types. If your skin tone falls in one category and your hair color in another, you are a combination color type.

These color types will be referred to in the next two sections when guidelines are given for effectively combining shirts, suits, and ties for men, and skirted suits, blouses, and accessories for women to both enhance and maximize each individual's professional look.

However, if you are not certain which hair or skin tone is yours and are hence undecided as to which color type category you belong to, you may wish to contact Color 1 Associates at 1/800-523-8496 (2211 Washington Circle, NW, Washington, DC 20037).

Color 1 can provide you with an individualized color chart that allows you to wear every color in the spectrum, but in your best **shade** and **clarity** as well as written material telling you how you can combine your colors for the best amounts of contrast for your natural coloring (color type).

The color chart is an excellent one-time investment considering the costs of buying the wrong colored suit, shirt, or blouse. It will more than pay for itself if it contributes to an effective interview as you wear your suit in your best shade and put your clothing together to work with, rather than against, your natural coloring. It can help you convey positive images during those crucial initial minutes of the interview—as well as over a lifetime.

Male Images of Success

John Molloy has conducted extensive research on how individuals can dress effectively. Aimed at those already working in professional positions who want to communicate a success image, his advice is relevant for someone interviewing for a public or private sector job at home or abroad.

Although you should find out as much as you can about the appropriate apparel for the area where you will be interviewing, in general, conservative business attire as suggested here should be your choice. Western business attire for men is being adopted throughout most of the world. Even in areas where it may not be the normal dress for the nationals, it would usually be the expected mode of dress for a foreigner arriving for an interview or business meeting.

Except for some blue collar jobs, basic attire for men interviewing for a position is a suit. Let's look at appropriate suits in terms of color, fabric, and style. The suit color can make a difference in creating an image of authority and competence. In general, blue, gray, camel, or beige are proper colors for men's suits. Usually the darker the shade, the greater amount of authority it conveys to the wearer. Given your situation (the interview) and your audience (the interviewer), you should aim at conveying enough authority to command attention and a positive regard, but not so much as to threaten the interviewer. Hence, the medium to charcoal gray or navy blue would be good suit colors. Black, a basic funeral or formal attire in most societies, can threaten the interviewer by conveying too much authority.

When selecting your gray, navy, camel, or beige suit, choose a shade that is enhancing to you. Should you wear a blue-gray, a taupe-gray, or a shade in-between? Do you look better in a somewhat bright navy or a more toned-down navy; a blue navy or a black navy; a navy with a purple or a yellow base to it?

In general, most people will look better in somewhat blue grays than in grays that are closer to the taupe side of the spectrum. Most people will be enhanced by a navy that is not too bright or contain so much black that it is difficult to distinguish whether the color is navy or black. When selecting a beige or a camel, select a tone that complements your skin color. If your skin has pink tones, avoid beiges and camels that contain gold hues and select pink based beiges/camels that enhance your skin color. Similarly, those of you who have gold/olive tones to your skin should avoid the pink based camel and beiges. If you are going to spend a lot of money on a suit—and if you buy a good, well-made suit you are going to spend a lot of money—buy a suit that will work for you.

Your suit(s) should be made of a natural fiber. A good blend of a natural fiber with some synthetic is acceptable as long as it has the "look" of the natural fiber. The very best suit fabrics are wool, wool blends, or fabrics that look like them. Even for the warmer summer months, men can find summer weight wool suits that are comfortable and look marvelous. They are your best buy. For really hot climates, linen, or a fabric that looks like linen tests well. Normally a linen will have to be blended with another fiber, often a synthetic, in order to retain a pressed, neat look. The major disadvantage of pure linen is that it wrinkles. For hot climates a good silk (nubby weave) sport jacket is acceptable if you make a deliberate choice not to wear a suit. Avoid 100 percent polyester materials, or anything that looks like it—especially double-knits—like the plague! Because polyester doesn't breathe, it will be unbearably hot in a hot climate, and it is a definite negative for your look of competence, power, and success.

The style of your suit should be classic. It should be well-tailored and well-styled. A conservative suit that has a timeless classic styling and also looks up-to-date will serve you best not only for the interview, but it will give you several years wear once you land the job.

Select a long-sleeved shirt that is lighter than the color of your suit—probably white. John Molloy's book on appearance and dress for men, *Molloy's New Dress For Success*, goes into great detail on shirts, ties, and practically everything you might wear or carry with you. We recommend Molloy's book over others because it is based on research rather than personal opinion and promotional fads.

A conservative suit that has a timeless classic styling and also looks up-to-date will serve you best.

However, you must take Molloy's advice one step beyond where he takes you: keep in mind your color type. If you have contrast or light-bright coloring, you will look great wearing your shade of white in a shirt with your navy blue shade in a suit. But if you have muted or gentle coloring, **this is too much contrast for you.** For muted or gentle coloring, the combination of navy and white will visually overpower you and you will not look your most enhanced.

If you are a muted or gentle color type, the look that gives you the greatest power look and yet does not overpower you will be a suit in your most flattering shade of gray worn with a shirt in your shade of white. You can expect your white to be less of a "pure" white (more creamy) than the white a contrast or a light-bright would wear. When you wear a navy suit, pair it with a blue shirt rather than a white one. This combines your colors in a level of contrast effective for your coloring.

If you are traveling to a hot climate for your interview(s), be sure to take several dress shirts. You are likely to find you need to change them more frequently than you do at home, especially when you discover your single job interview may involve two or three days of interviewing with several people involved with an organization or project.

Female Images of Success

Few men would consider wearing anything other than a suit to a job interview—especially an interview for a managerial or professional position. Women are often less certain what is appropriate. As a result of research conducted by John Molloy and others, we are told a skirted suit is generally the choice for the interview. This attire allows a woman to best convey images of professionalism, authority, and competence.

A skirted suit allows a woman to best convey images of professionalism, authority, and competence.

As you travel abroad, you may feel that business attire for women is not as well defined as for men. In many countries there may be few women holding professional positions, and women who dress other than casually may tend to "dress up"—wearing somewhat frilly or even low-cut clothing we view as evening attire. If your best reading of the situation leads you to believe a suit is too austere, consider a tailored business dress and perhaps at least carry a jacket you could put with it if you change your mind. Remember, long sleeves are considered "polite" in many cultures.

Although you should be aware of and sensitive to local customs when interviewing abroad, keep in mind that there are expectations held for foreigners that will be somewhat different than those for the nationals. If you adhere to conservative business dress, you will probably be well accepted.

Let's survey appropriate suits in terms of color, fabric, and style. As in the case of men's suits, the color of your suit can help create an image of authority and competence. The suit colors that make the strongest positive statements for you are **your shade** of gray in a medium to charcoal depth or **your shade** of blue in a medium to navy depth of color. Other dark shades, such as maroon, test well as does camel. Avoid black, which can convey so much authority many interviewers find it threatening. For a hot climate or to lessen the authority of a dark color, your beige shade can be a good choice for a suit.

When selecting your gray, navy, camel, beige, or any other colored suit, follow the same rules we outlined for men: choose a shade that is enhancing to you. If you are uncertain which shades are best for you, contact a Color 1 Associate for advice.

Similar to men's suits, your suit should be made of a natural fiber or have the "look" of a natural fiber. The very best winter-weight suit fabrics are wool or wool blends. For the warmer climates or the summer months, women will find few, if any, summer weight wool suits made for them. Hence linen, blended with a synthetic so it will not look as if it needs constant pressing, or a textured silk are good choices. Other fabrics, such as polyester blended with rayon, in clothing of good quality often has the definite look of linen but without the hassles of caring for real linen. But the key word here is **quality**. A cheap polyester/rayon fabric will look just that. Avoid 100 percent polyester material, or anything that looks like it—especially double-knits—like the plague it is. In addition to conveying the wrong look, polyester doesn't breathe and will be unbearably hot in a very hot climate.

Your suit style should be classic. Following similar rules as for men, women's suits should be well-tailored, well-styled, and avoid a "trendy" look unless appropriate for certain occupations. A conservative, classic suit will last for years and is an excellent investment. Indeed, you can afford to buy good quality clothing if you know you will get a lot of use from the item. When deciding on your professional wardrobe, always buy clothes to last and buy quality.

When deciding on your professional wardrobe, always buy clothes to last and buy quality.

Quality also means buying silk blouses if you can afford them. Keep in mind not only the price of the blouse itself, but the cleaning bill. There are many polyester blouse fabrics that have the look and feel of silk—this is an exception to the "no polyester" rule. Silk or a polyester that has the look and feel of silk are the fabrics for blouses to go with your business suits. Polyester will be hot though, so keep your climate in mind. Choose your blouses in your most flattering shades and clarity of color. John Molloy's book on appearance and dress for women, *The Woman's Dress For Success Book*, goes into great detail on the blouse styles that test best as well as expands on suit colors. It includes information on almost anything you might wear or carry with you to the interview or on the job.

But remember, as in the case of men, you must take Molloy's advice one step further: keep in mind your color type. Contrast or light-bright coloring types look great wearing their shade of white in a blouse with their navy blue shade in a suit. Muted and gentle color types will find this to be too much contrast and thus overpower their natural coloring. Such a color combination actually diminishes their power look.

If you are a muted or gentle color type, why not try your coral red shade blouse with your navy suit or wear your shade of white with your gray shade suit. Most of your best colors will go well with your beige. Once you are aware of your color type and how to best enhance it while retaining visual authority, you will find many new and flattering combinations.

Give your outfit a more "finished and polished" look by accessorizing it effectively. Collect silk scarves and necklaces of semiprecious stones in your suit colors. Wear scarves and necklaces with your suits and blouses in such a way that they repeat the color of the suit. For example, a woman wearing a navy suit and a red silk blouse could accent the look by wearing a necklace of navy sodalite beads or a silk scarf that has navy as a predominate color. The *Color Wonderful* book includes a great deal of information to help you accessorize your look geared to your color type.

The most appropriate shoe to wear with a business suit is a classic pump with a closed heel and toe and little or no decoration. Not only does this shoe stand by itself as creating the most professional look, it also teams best with a business suit and is flattering at the same time. A sling-back shoe (heel open with a strap across the heel) can be worn with a suit, but will slightly diminish the wearer's professional look. Avoid shoes with both the heel and toe open as well as any sandal look. They can be beautiful shoes, but save them for evening wear. We have observed many women arriving for job interviews wearing suits, but ruining their professional image by wearing strappy sandal looks. In general, wear shoes as dark or darker than your skirt. If not, you may draw the other person's eyes to your feet when, instead, you want them to focus on your face and on what you are saying.

You may choose to carry a purse **or** an attache case, but not both at the same time. It is difficult not to look clumsy trying to handle both a purse and an attache case, and it is likely to diminish your power look as well. One way to carry both is to keep a slim purse with essentials such as lipstick, mirror, and money inside the attache case. If you need to go out to lunch, or any place where you choose not to carry the attache case, just pull out your purse and you're off.

Buy Quality Apparel

Aside from information on what articles of apparel to wear, a word on the quality of what you purchase is in order. Buy the best you can afford. If you are not gainfully employed, this may seem like impractical advice. But it still remains the most practical advice. Two really good suits with a variety of shirts or blouses will look better from the first day you own them than four suits of inferior quality—and will outlast them as well. To buy quality rather than quantity is a good habit to form.

Stretch your money by shopping sales or good discount outlets if you wish. But remember, it isn't a bargain if it isn't right for you. A suit that never quite fits or isn't exactly your best shade is not a bargain no matter how many times it has been marked down. John Molloy's books have useful hints on how to overcome a middle-class background and learn to buy good quality clothing at reasonable prices.

In addition to buying natural fibers in clothing whenever possible, invest in real leather for shoes, attache case, and handbag—if you carry one. Leather conveys a professional look and will outlast the cheap looking imitations you might buy. However, when traveling abroad, consider whether there are any local customs which might limit your obvious use of leather.

Buy the best you can afford.

One word of caution for those who enjoy purchasing tailored clothes and handmade items abroad, especially in Third World countries. While much of the clothing and accessory pieces may initially appear attractive, unique, and inexpensive, tailoring in many countries is neither stylish nor presents a finished look. Many of the clothes and fabrics are inappropriate. Often handmade items, such as shoes and purses, have a decided homemade look to them. Such items often do not look good compared to the ready-made clothes and accessories found back home.

Unless you are purchasing clothes and accessories from top quality tailors, shops, or department stores in places like Hong Kong, Italy, France, Germany, or England, we generally recommend shopping for clothes and accessories in places that offer good quality ready-made items. You can get good buys and quality items elsewhere, but be careful. Examine fabrics carefully, check tailoring on finished items waiting to be picked up, and communicate everything in detail—pinstripes that go around your body rather than lengthwise on a business suit will not enhance your professional look. Make certain you have time for several fittings before your departure.

Remember, quality fabrics and workmanship will not be cheap anywhere in the world. They may cost less than at home, but you can't get something for nothing. The old adage—it sounds too good to be true, it probably is—is generally validated in experience.

Chapter Seven

NETWORK FOR INFORMATION, ADVICE, AND REFERRALS

You won't get an international job unless you first go through an interview process. And you probably won't get many job interviews unless you network for job leads. The networking and interviewing processes are closely linked to one another. They will take place either at home or abroad, or possibly in both locations.

How do you get the interview and then interview well enough to be offered a job? What role will your job objective, research, and resume play in getting the interview and job offer? What is this thing called "networking" that everyone talks about as if it were some type of magical ingredient for getting a job? More importantly, how does one network for international jobs which may be located 12,000 miles from your present location?

The job search skills discussed thus far prepare you for the most critical stages of the job search: networking, interviewing, and negotiating various terms of employment. These are the face-to-face marketing and implementation stages of the job search that take place **after** you have identified your strengths, stated an objective, conducted research, and produced a powerful resume or curriculum vita.

Specific skills and strategies are also associated with successful networking, interviewing, and salary negotiations. Assuming you have completed the previous stages of your job search, you should now be well prepared to implement these critical final stages that hopefully will lead quickly to job offers and career success. This chapter, as well as Chapter Eight, outlines practical methods for developing the necessary interpersonal skills and for implementing the face-to-face strategies for finding an international job.

PROSPECTING, NETWORKING, AND INFORMATIONAL INTERVIEWS

What do you do after you complete your resume? Most people send cover letters and resumes in response to job listings. They then wait to be called for a job interview. Viewing the job search as basically a direct-mail operation, many are disappointed in discovering the realities of direct-mail—a 5 percent response rate is considered outstanding! A 1-2 percent response rate is typical of most direct-mail efforts.

Successful international job seekers break out of this relatively passive job search role by orienting themselves toward face-to-face action. Being proactive, they develop interpersonal strategies in which the resume plays a **supportive** rather than a central role in the job search. They first present themselves to employers; the resume appears only at the end of a face-to-face conversation.

Throughout the job search you will acquire useful names and addresses as well as meet people who will assist you in contacting potential international employers. Such information and contacts become key building blocks for generating job interviews and offers.

The informal, interpersonal system of communication is the central nervous system of the international job market.

Since the best and most numerous international jobs are found on the hidden job market, you must use methods appropriate for this job market. Indeed, research and experience clearly show the most effective means of communication are face-to-face and word-of-mouth. The informal, interpersonal system of communication is the central nervous system of the international job market. Your goal should be to penetrate this job market with proven methods for success. Appropriate methods for making important job contacts are **prospecting and networking**. Appropriate methods for getting these contacts to provide you with useful job information are **informational and referral interviews**.

COMMUNICATING YOUR QUALIFICATIONS

Taken together, these interpersonal methods help you **communicate your qualifications to employers**. Although many job seekers may be reluctant to use this informal communication system, they greatly limit their potential for success if they do not. Swamped with 400 to 500 resumes for a single position, many employers prefer this informal system. In addition, many employers are uncertain what type of individual they should hire. By using this informal system, you help employers identify their needs, limit their alternatives, save them time and money, and thus make decisions in your favor. In other words, they need not look any further since they now have you.

Employers generally seek individuals they like both personally and professionally.

Most employers also want more information on candidates to supplement the "paper qualifications" represented in application forms, resumes, and letters. Studies show that employers in general seek candidates who have these skills: communication, problem solving, analytical, assessment, and planning. Surprising to many job seekers, technical expertise ranks third or fourth in employers' lists of most desired skills. These findings support a frequent observation made by employers: the major problems with employees relate to communication, problem solving, and analysis. Indeed, most individuals get fired because of political and interpersonal conflicts rather than technical incompetence.

Employers generally seek individuals they **like** both personally and professionally. While it is essential that you communicate your technical competence to employers—especially for international jobs that require specific technical skills—you must also communicate that you have the requisite personal **and** professional skills for performing the job both with the employer and within the specific social and cultural settings that will be critical for successful job performance. Informal prospecting, networking, and informational interviewing activities are the best methods for communicating such "qualifications" to employers. If you use these methods properly, you should communicate loud and clear that you have both the technical and interpersonal skills to perform well in the international arena.

DEVELOPING YOUR NETWORKS

Networking is the process of developing relations with others for a variety of purposes. When applied to the international job search, networking involves connecting and interacting with other individuals who can assist you by providing useful international job information, advice, and referrals. The process of networking is the quickest and easiest way to cross national boundaries for the purpose of developing important international job contacts. The more you develop, maintain, and expand your networks, the more successful should be your international job search.

Your network is your interpersonal environment. While you know and interact with hundreds of people, on a day-to-day basis you probably encounter no more than 20 people. You frequently contact these people in face-to-face situations. Some people are more **important** to you than others. You **like** some more than others. And some will be more **helpful** to you in your job search than others. Your basic network may encompass the following individuals and groups: friends, acquaintances, immediate family, distant relatives, professional colleagues, spouse, supervisor, fellow workers, close friends, and local business people and professionals, such as your banker, lawyer, doctor, minister, and insurance agent. You should contact many of these individuals for advice relating to your international job search even though you may not think they will have useful information and advice on international jobs. You may be surprised at what you learn!

You need to **identify everyone in your network** who might help you with your international job search. You first need to expand your basic network to include individuals you know and have interacted with over the past 10 or more years. Make a list of 200 people you know. Include friends and relatives from your Christmas card list, past and present neighbors, former classmates, politicians, business persons, foreign visitors, previous employers, professional associates, travel acquaintances, ministers, insurance agents, lawyers, bankers, doctors, dentists, former professors, accountants, and social acquaintances. Your preference should be for individuals who have some international work experience or who know others working in the international arena.

However, don't prematurely eliminate anyone from your contact list. You may be surprised at what you learn from those you already know. Many people you might never think of as having international contacts do indeed know others who work in the international arena. If, for example, you casually mention to your neighbor your interest in gathering information on international jobs, your neighbor just might surprise you with important secondary contact information:

"It's funny you should mention that. Your job interest really sounds fascinating, especially being able to live and work in Europe. You know, I have a friend at work who often talks about her daughter who either lives in Germany at present or did so during the past five

*years. In fact, I think she's visiting her mother next week. I'll ask
her for her daughter's address and telephone number. Maybe I can
get more information on what she does and check to see if she will
be in town next week. Perhaps you might have a chance to meet and
talk with her about your interests. If not, give her a call or write her
a letter. Her mother is always worried she's not getting enough mail
from home! She should know several people in Germany whom you
could contact for job information and advice. I think she was
working with one of the banks, or maybe she was with some large
manufacturing firm. It could be the State Department. I really didn't
pay that close attention to what she did. But I do know she worked
there for a few years and really loved it. I'm sure she'll be happy
to talk to you about your interests in Germany."*

Such an unexpected contact from a neighbor whom you never thought might be
helpful could lead to valuable international job information that could materialize
into a job in Germany.

Again, don't neglect anyone in your network just because you believe they
don't have international experience or interests. People know other people who
may very well lead to a valuable set of contacts for international job information
and advice that eventually leads to a satisfying international job.

After identifying your extended network, you should try to **link your
network to others' networks**. Individuals in these other networks also have job
information and contacts. Ask people in your basic network for referrals to
individuals in their networks. This approach should greatly enlarge your basic job
search network. More important, it will help extend your local network both
nationally and internationally. You should be able to quickly expand your
network—as noted in our example of the neighbor with a secondary contact to
someone in Germany—to include many strangers who will be happy to share
with you their information on international jobs.

GOING "COLD TURKEY"

On the other hand, what do you do if individuals in your immediate and
extended network do not provide you with useful international job information
and contacts? While it is much easier and more effective to meet new people
through personal contacts, on occasion you may need to **approach strangers
without prior contacts**. In this situation it's necessary to try the "cold turkey"
approach. One useful approach is to write a letter to someone you feel may be
useful to your job search. Research this individual so you are acquainted with
their background and accomplishments. In the letter, refer to their accomplishments, mention your need for job information, and specify a date and time you
will call to discuss your interests or schedule a meeting.

It's not necessary to always physically meet with such networking contacts. Indeed, since much of your international job search will be conducted long-distance, it's simply impractical to schedule meetings with everyone you contact. You can quickly develop your networks and gain valuable job information and advice over the telephone. Many people are happy to give you a few minutes of telephone time, but really busy people simply don't have time to meet with individuals other than those who are central to their day-to-day business dealings.

> *You can quickly develop your networks and gain valuable job information and advice over the telephone.*

Another approach is to introduce yourself to someone by telephone and request a meeting and/or job information prior to writing a letter of introduction.

While you may experience many rejections in using these approaches, you also will experience numerous successes if you persist in repeating the approaches. And those successes should lead to further expansion of your job search network.

PROSPECT FOR JOB LEADS

The key to successful networking is an active and routine **prospecting campaign**. Salespersons in insurance, real estate, Amway, Shaklee, and other direct-sales businesses understand the importance and principles of prospecting. For them, people are a renewable resource. The more people they can include in their always expanding network, the higher the probability of job success.

Seasoned salespeople use two prospecting methods: third party referrals and cold calls. The third party referral is usually the most preferred and productive method. Using this method, the salesperson asks for referrals from present contacts: *"Do you know anyone else who might be interested in benefiting from this type of program?"* In addition, good salespeople must continually replenish their pool of prospective customers by making cold calls for sales leads. Like junk mail, most cold calls are "junk telephone calls." You may receive them in early evening or on weekends. The caller offers potential prizes by asking you dumb questions anyone can answer; asking you to answer survey questions; or throwing you the standard "positive response" question as an opener to their sales pitch—*"If I could show you how to save more money, would you . . . ?"* The basic problem is that these salespeople are all offering the same junk product—nothing special or unique that would appeal to most potential buyers.

Many salespeople have turned the art of prospecting into a science. In a traditional sales situation, the basic operating principle underlining a productive prospecting campaign is **probability**: The number of "sales" you make is a direct function of the amount of effort you put into developing new contacts and following-through. Expect no more than a 10 percent acceptance rate: for every 10 people you meet, 9 will reject you—but 1 will accept you. Not surprising, the more people you contact, the more acceptances you will receive. If you want to be successful, you must collect many more *"nos"* than *"yeses."* In a 10 percent probability situation, you need to contact 100 people for 10 successes.

The basic requirements for a good prospecting campaign are persistence, tenacity, a willingness to approach strangers, acceptance of numerous rejections, and a good quality and unique product. If you are too shy to approach strangers, can't stick with the method, can't take many rejections, and don't have much to offer, then don't expect to be successful in networking for job information, advice, and leads. You simply must be willing to approach strangers, handle rejections, repeat your approach over and over again with numerous individuals, and communicate that you are an excellent product that someone should quickly acquire.

The job search is a highly ego-involved activity characterized by numerous rejections accompanied by a few acceptances.

These prospecting principles are extremely useful for your job search if adapted properly and refocused around different goals. Like sales situations, the job search is a highly ego-involved activity characterized by numerous rejections accompanied by a few acceptances. While no one wants to be rejected, few people are willing and able to handle more than a few rejections. They take a *"no"* as a sign of personal failure—and quit prematurely. If they persisted longer, they would achieve success after a few more *"nos."* Furthermore, if their prospecting activities were focused on gathering information rather than making sales, they would considerably minimize the number of rejections. Therefore, these should be your prospecting goals and strategies:

- Prospect for job leads.
- Accept rejections as part of the game.

- Link prospecting to informational interviewing.
- Keep prospecting for more information and *"yeses"* which will eventually translate into job interviews and offers.

A good international job search prospecting pace to start with is to make two new contacts each day. Start by contacting people in your immediate network. Let them know you are conducting an international job search—but emphasize that you are only doing research at this point. Ask for a few moments to discuss your information needs. You are only seeking **information and advice** at this time—not a job.

It should take you about 20 minutes to make a contact by letter or telephone. If you make two contacts each day, by the end of the first week you will have 10 new contacts for a total investment of less than seven hours. By the second week you may want to increase your prospecting pace to four new contacts each day or 20 each week. The more contacts you make, the more useful information, advice, and job leads you will receive. If your job search bogs down, you probably need to increase your prospecting activities.

Expect each contact to refer you to two or three others who will also refer you to others. Consequently, your contacts should multiply considerably within only a few weeks.

The key to networking success is to focus on gathering information while also learning to handle rejections.

HANDLING AND MINIMIZING REJECTIONS

These prospecting and networking methods have proved effective for millions of people. While they are responsible for building, maintaining, and expanding multi-million dollar businesses, they work extremely well for job hunters. But they only work if you are patient and persist. The key to networking success is to focus on gathering information while also learning to handle rejections. Learn from rejections, forget them, and go on to more productive networking activities. The major reason direct-sales people fail is because they don't persist. The reason they don't persist is because they either can't take, or get tired of taking, rejections.

Rejections are no fun, especially in such an ego-involved activity as a job search. But you will encounter rejections as you travel on the road toward job search success. This road is strewn with individuals who quit prematurely because they were rejected three, four, or five times. Don't be one of them!

Our prospecting and networking techniques differ from sales approaches in one major respect: we have special techniques for minimizing the number of rejections. If handled properly, at least 50 percent—maybe as many as 90 percent —of your prospects will turn into *"yeses"* rather than *"nos."* The reason for this unusually high acceptance rate is how you introduce and handle yourself before your prospects. Many insurance agents and direct distributors expect a 90 percent rejection rate, because they are trying to sell specific products potential clients may or may not need. Most people don't like to be put on the spot—especially when it is in their own home or office—to make a decision to buy a product which is of questionable quality and utility.

BE HONEST, SINCERE, AND APPEALING

The principles of selling yourself in the job market are similar. People don't want to be put on the spot. They feel uncomfortable if they think you expect them to give you a job. Thus, you should never introduce yourself to a prospect by asking them for a job or a job lead. You should do just the opposite: relieve their anxiety by mentioning that you are not looking for a job from them—only job information and advice. You must be honest and sincere in communicating these intentions to your contact. The biggest turn-off for individuals targeted for informational interviews is the insincere job seeker who tries to use this as a mechanism to get a job.

Your approach to prospects must be subtle, honest, and professional. You are seeking **information, advice, and referrals** relating to several subjects:

- International job and career opportunities
- Regional and country settings
- International lifestyles and worklifes
- Your job search approach and your resume
- Others who may have similar information, advice, and referrals

Most people gladly volunteer such information. They generally like to talk about themselves, their careers, and others. They like to give advice. This approach flatters individuals by placing them in the role of the expert-advisor. Who doesn't want to be recognized as an expert-advisor, especially on such a critical topic as one's employment?

This approach should yield a great deal of information, advice, and referrals from your prospects. One other important outcome should result from using this approach: people will **remember** you as the person who made them feel at ease and who received their valuable advice. If they hear of international job opportunities for someone with your qualifications, chances are they will contact you with the information. After contacting 100 prospects, you will have created 100 sets of eyes and ears to help you in your job search!

The guiding principle behind prospecting, networking, and informational interviews is this: the best way to get a job is to ask for information, advice, and referrals; never ask for a job. Remember, you want prospects to engage in the 5-R's of informational interviewing:

- **Reveal** useful information and advice.
- **Refer** you to others.
- **Read** and **revise** your resume.
- **Remember** you for future reference.

If you follow this principle, you should join the ranks of thousands of successful job seekers who paid a great deal of money learning it from highly-paid professionals.

> ## *The best way to get a job is to ask for job information, advice, and referrals; never ask for a job.*

APPROACHING KEY PEOPLE

Whom should you contact within an organization for an informational interview? Ideally, you should contact people who are busy, who have the power to hire, and who are knowledgeable about the organization. The least likely candidate will be someone in the personnel department. Most often the heads of operating units are the most busy, powerful, and knowledgeable individuals in the organization. However, getting access to such individuals may be difficult. Some people at the top may appear to be informed and powerful, but they may lack information on the day-to-day personnel changes or their influence is limited in the hiring process. It is difficult to give one best answer to this question.

Therefore, we recommend contacting a variety of people. Aim for the busy, powerful, and informed, but be prepared to settle for less. Secretaries, receptionists, and the person you want to meet may refer you to others. From a practical standpoint, you may have to take whomever you can schedule an appointment with. Sometimes people who are not busy can be helpful. Talk to a secretary or receptionist sometime about their boss or working in the organization. You may be surprised with what you learn!

The best way to initiate a contact with a prospective employer is to **send an approach letter**. Begin this letter with a personal statement, such as: *"James Chance suggested that I contact you..."* Briefly state your purpose—seek information and advice—and mention you will call at a specific time to discuss your interests or schedule a meeting. Do not enclose a resume with this letter. Remember, your purposes are to get information, advice, referrals, and remembered. While this is not a formal interview, it may well lead to one.

Most people will talk or meet with you, assuming you are sincere in your approach. If the person tries to put you off when you telephone for an appointment, clearly state your purpose and emphasize that you are not looking for a job through this person—only information and advice. If the person insists on putting you off, make the best of the situation: try to interview the person over the phone. If you are unsuccessful with this approach, write a nice thank-you letter in which you again state your intended purpose; mention your disappointment in not being able to learn from the person's experience; and ask to be remembered for future reference. Enclose your resume with this letter. Don't linger nor lament the fact that you didn't get more access to this individual. Just move on to potentially more productive contacts and referrals.

While you are ostensibly seeking information and advice, treat this meeting as an important preliminary interview. You need to communicate your qualifications—that you are competent, intelligent, honest, and likable. These are the same qualities you should communicate in a formal job interview as well.

STRUCTURING THE INFORMATIONAL INTERVIEW

An informational interview will be relatively unstructured compared to a formal interview. Since you want the interviewer to advise you, you reverse roles by asking questions which should give you useful information. You, in effect, become the interviewer. You should structure this interview with a particular sequence of questions. Most questions should be open-ended, requiring the individual to give specific answers based upon his or her experience.

The structure and dialogue for the informational interview might go something like this. You plan to take no more than 45 minutes for this interview. The first three to five minutes will be devoted to small talk—the weather, traffic, the office, mutual acquaintances, or an interesting or humorous observation. Since these are the most critical moments in the interview, be especially careful how you communicate nonverbally. Begin your interview by stating your appreciation for the individual's time:

> *"I want to thank you again for scheduling this meeting with me. I know you're busy. I appreciate the special arrangements you made to see me on a subject which is very important to my future."*

Your next comment should be a statement reiterating your purpose as stated in your letter:

> *"As you know, I am exploring international job and career alternatives. I know what I do well and what I want to do. Before I commit myself to a new job, I need to know more about various career options. I thought you would be able to provide me with some insights into international career opportunities, job requirements, and possible problems or promising directions in the field of _____."*

This statement normally will get a positive reaction from the individual who may want to know more about what it is you want to do. Be sure to clearly communicate your job objective. If you can't, please don't waste this person's time by communicating that you are lost, indecisive, or uncertain about yourself. The person is prepared to give you valuable job information—not therapy or advice on what you should do with the rest of your life. You supposedly took care of such "preliminaries" when you identified your strengths and stated your objective.

Be a good listener, but make sure you move along with the questions.

Your next line of questioning should focus on "how" and "what" questions centering on (1) specific jobs and (2) the job search process. Begin by asking about various aspects of specific jobs:

- Duties and responsibilities.
- Knowledge, skills, and abilities required.
- Work environment relating to fellow employees, work flows, deadlines, stress, initiative.
- Advantages and disadvantages.
- Advancement opportunities and outlook.
- Salary ranges, benefits, especially if they relate to specific international jobs and country locations.
- Relocation and travel requirements.
- Living conditions and lifestyles.
- Employment opportunities for spouses.

Your informer will probably take a great deal of time talking about his or her experience in each area. Be a good listener, but make sure you move along with the questions.

Your next line of questioning should focus on your job search activities. You need as much information as possible on how to:

- Acquire the necessary skills.
- Best find a job in this field.
- Overcome any objections employers may have to you. Uncover job vacancies which may be advertised.
- Develop job leads.
- Approach prospective employers.

Your final line of questioning should focus on your resume. Do not show your resume until you focus on this last set of questions. The purpose of these questions is to: (1) get the individual to read your resume in-depth, (2) acquire useful advice on how to strengthen it, (3) be referred to prospective employers, and (4) be remembered. With the resume in front of you and your interviewee, ask the following questions:

- Is this an appropriate type of resume for the international jobs I have outlined?
- If an employer received this resume in the mail, how do you think he or she would react to it?
- What do you see as possible weaknesses or areas that need to be improved?
- What should I do with this resume? Shotgun it to hundreds of international employers with a cover letter? Use resume letters instead?
- What about the length, paper quality and color, layout, and typing? Are they appropriate?
- How might I best improve the form and content of the resume?

You should receive useful advice on how to strengthen both the content and use of your resume. Most important, these questions force the individual to **read** your resume which, in turn, may be **remembered** for future reference.

Your last question is especially important in this interview. You want to be both **remembered** and **referred**. Some variation of the following question should help:

> *"I really appreciate all this advice. It is very helpful and it should improve my job search considerably. Could I ask you one more favor? Do you know two or three other people who could help me with my job search? I want to conduct as much research as possible, and their advice might be helpful also."*

Before you leave, mention one more important item:

> *"During the next few months, should you hear of any job opportunities for someone with my interests and qualifications, I would appreciate being kept in mind. And please feel free to pass my name on to others."*

Send a nice thank-you letter within 48 hours of completing this informational interview. Express your genuine gratitude for the individual's time and advice. Reiterate your interests, and ask to be remembered and referred to others.

Follow-up on any useful advice you receive, particularly referrals. Approach referrals in the same manner you approached the person who gave you the referral. Write a letter requesting a meeting. Begin the letter by mentioning:

> *"Mr./Ms. _____ suggested that I contact you concerning my research on careers in _____."*

If you continue prospecting, networking, and conducting informational interviews, soon you will be busy conducting interviews and receiving job offers. While 100 informational interviews over a two-month period should lead to several formal job interviews and offers, the pay-offs are uncertain because job vacancies are unpredictable. We know cases where the first referral turned into a formal interview and job offer. More typical cases require constant prospecting, networking, and informational interviewing activities. The telephone call or letter inviting you to a job interview can come at any time. While the timing may be unpredictable, your persistent job search activities will be largely responsible for the final outcome.

TELEPHONING AND
FAXING FOR JOB LEADS

Telephone communication should play an important role in prospecting, networking, and informational interviews. However, controversy centers around how and when to use the telephone for generating job leads and scheduling interviews. Some people recommend writing a letter and waiting for a written or telephone reply. Others suggest writing a letter and following it with a telephone call. Still others argue you should use the telephone exclusively rather than write letters.

How you use the telephone will indicate what type of job search you are conducting. Exclusive reliance on the telephone is a technique used by highly formalized job clubs which operate phone banks for generating job leads. Using the Yellow Pages as the guide to employers, a job club member may call as many as 50 employers a day to schedule job interviews. A rather aggressive yet typical telephone dialogue goes something like this:

"Hello, my name is Jim Morgan. I would like to speak to the head of the training department. By the way, what is the name of the training director?"

"You want to talk to Ms. Stevens. Her number is 723-8191 or I can connect you directly."

"Hello, Ms. Stevens. My name is Jim Morgan. I have several years of international training experience as both a trainer and developer of training materials. I'd like to meet with you to discuss possible openings in your department for someone with my qualifications. Would it be possible to see you on Friday at 2pm?"

Not surprising, this telephone approach generates many "nos." If you have a hard time handling rejections, this telephone approach will help you confront your anxieties. The principle behind this approach is **probability**: for every 25 telephone *"nos"* you receive, you will probably get one or two *"yeses."* Success is just 25 telephone calls away! If you start calling prospective employers at 9am and finish your 25 calls by 12 noon, you should generate at least one or two interviews. That's not bad for three hours of job search work. It beats a direct-mail approach.

The telephone is more efficient than writing letters. However, its effectiveness is questionable.

The telephone is more efficient than writing letters. However, its effectiveness is questionable. When you use the telephone in this manner, you are basically asking for a job. You are asking the employer: *"Do you have a job for me?"* There is nothing subtle or particularly professional about this approach. It is effective in uncovering particular types of job leads for particular types of individuals. If you need a job—any job—in a hurry, this is one of the most efficient ways of finding employment. However, if you are more concerned with finding a job that is right for you—a job you do well and enjoy doing, one that is fit for you—this telephone approach is inappropriate.

You must use your own judgment in determining when and how to use the telephone in your job search. There are appropriate times and methods for using the telephone, and these should relate to your job search goals and needs. We prefer the more conventional approach of writing a letter requesting an informational interview and following it up with a telephone call. While you take the initiative in scheduling an appointment, you do not put the individual on the spot by asking for a job. You are only seeking information and advice. This low-keyed approach results in numerous acceptances and has a higher probability of paying off with interviews than the aggressive telephone request. You should be trying to uncover jobs that are right for you rather than any job that happens to pop up from a telephoning blitz.

The telephone can be an effective networking tool if used appropriately. If, for example, someone gives you a referral and suggests that you call the person, go ahead and initiate this new contact by telephone. In some cases you may want to call an organization to get information on their hiring procedures, names of people to contact, and whether or not they maintain an international resume bank. Sometimes these calls result in talking to a helpful person who provides you with very useful international job information, advice, and more referrals.

We also recommend using the telephone for some long-distance networking abroad. Long-distance calls are not expensive when considering the amount of valuable job information you are likely to receive for a few minutes and dollars of investment. The cost of international phone calls can be kept down if you know the least expensive time to call abroad. If you rely solely on writing letters, you will waste a great deal of time, and you will seldom receive much quality information for further targeting your job search. While many countries rely more heavily on fax machines than the U.S. for communicating information, do not fax information unless you are requested to do so. Sending unsolicited faxes in the form of letters and resumes can be a negative for any job search—at home or abroad. However, be prepared to fax information about yourself to contacts you make by phone or letter if the person requests this information. Alternatively, you might ask: *"Could I fax you information on my background?"* The sooner you get this information in the hands of the individual you are talking to, the better. Follow-up this fax with both a phone call (*"Did you get my fax? Do you have any questions?"*) and mail a copy of the original paper work that generated the fax.

USING JOB CLUBS
AND SUPPORT GROUPS

The techniques we outlined thus far are designed for individuals conducting a self-directed job search. Job clubs and support groups complement a self-directed job search.

Job clubs are designed to provide a group structure and support system to individuals seeking employment. These groups consist of about 12 individuals who are led by a trained counselor and supported with telephones, copying machines, and a resource center.

Highly formalized job clubs, such as the 40-Plus Club, organize job search activities for both the advertised and hidden job markets. As outlined by Azrin and Besalel in their book *Job Club Counselor's Manual*, job club activities include:

- Signing commitment agreements to achieve specific job search goals and targets.
- Contacting friends, relatives, and acquaintances for job leads.
- Completing activity forms.
- Using telephones, typewriters, photocopy machines, postage, and other equipment and supplies.
- Meeting with fellow participants to discuss job search progress.
- Telephoning to uncover job leads.
- Researching newspapers, telephone books, and directories.
- Developing research, telephone, interview, and social skills.
- Writing letters and resumes.
- Responding to want ads.
- Completing employment applications.

In other words, the job club formalizes many of the prospecting, networking, and informational interviewing activities within a group context and interjects the role of the telephone as the key communication device for developing and expanding networks.

Job clubs place excessive reliance on using the telephone for uncovering job leads. Members call prospective employers and ask about job openings. The Yellow Pages become the job hunting bible. During a two-week period, a job club member might spend most of his or her mornings telephoning for job leads and scheduling interviews. Afternoons are normally devoted to job interviewing.

We do not recommend joining such job clubs for obvious reasons. Most job club methods are designed for the hardcore unemployed or for individuals who need a job—any job—quickly. Individuals try to fit into available vacancies; their objectives and skills are of secondary concern. We recommend conducting your own job search or forming a support group which adapts some job club methods to our central concept of finding a job fit for you—one appropriate to your objective and in line with your particular mix of skills, abilities, and interests.

Support groups are a useful alternative to job clubs. They have one major advantage: they may cut your job search time in half. Forming or joining one of these groups can help direct as well as enhance your individual job search activities.

Your support group should consist of three or more individuals who are job hunting. Try to schedule regular meetings with specific purposes in mind. While the group may be highly social, especially if it involves close friends, it also should be **task-oriented**. Meet at least once a week and include your spouse. At each meeting set **performance goals** for the week. For example, your goal can be to make 20 new contacts and conduct five informational interviews. The contacts can be made by telephone, letter, or in person. Share your experiences and job information with each other. **Critique** each other's progress, make suggestions for improving the job search, and develop new strategies together. By doing this, you will be gaining valuable information and feedback which is normally difficult to gain on one's own. This group should provide important psychological supports to help you through your job search. After all, job hunting can be a lonely, frustrating, and exasperating experience. By sharing your experiences with others, you will find you are not alone. You will quickly learn that rejections are part of the game. The group will encourage you, and you will feel good about helping others achieve their goals. Try building small incentives into the group, such as the individual who receives the most job interviews for the month will be treated to dinner by other members of the group.

Chapter Eight

CONDUCT EFFECTIVE JOB INTERVIEWS AND SALARY NEGOTIATIONS

Your resume, letters, and networking activities should eventually result in invitations to job interviews. An important element of probability operates here: the more resumes and letters you circulate and the more networking you do, the more job interviews you will receive. If you circulate few resumes and letters and neglect to network for job information, advice, and referrals, expect to receive few invitations to job interviews.

THE INTERVIEW DIFFERENCE

Formal job interviews are required by nearly 95 percent of all organizations. The normal pattern is for an organization to announce a position, request the submission of applications, including a resume and letter, and call for interviews based upon an evaluation of the paper qualifications. On the other hand, some organizations—especially firms attending job fairs—reverse this normal pattern by skipping the application phase and going directly to a job interview. The job interview itself becomes the application. They may ask you to complete an application form a few minutes prior to the interview as well as give them a copy of your resume at the beginning of the interview. Others may ask you to complete an application form and perhaps submit a copy of your resume **after** you have completed the job interview.

Whatever the pattern, the job interview is the single most important step to getting a job offer. Everything you have done thus far in organizing your job search should come together in the job interview. In fact, job interviews take on special importance in the case of international jobs. Many employers want to interview candidates because they are particularly sensitive to how an individual looks and behaves in face-to-face cross-cultural situations. In addition, the international interview incorporates many questions and considerations normally not associated with interviews for jobs in the U.S. How well you handle this interview is more important than your previous work experience, recommendations, and educational record. As such, it is much more than just the final step in the job search process. It represents all elements in your job search and puts you on stage for communicating all your paper and personal qualifications to employers.

The job interview also is the most stressful job search experience. Your application, resume, and letters may get you to the interview, but you must perform well in person in order to get a job offer. Knowing the stakes are high, most people face interviews with dry throats and sweaty palms; it is a time of great stress. You will be on stage, and you are expected to put on a good performance.

How do you prepare for the interview? First, you need to understand the nature and purpose of the interview. Second, you must prepare to respond to the interview situation and the interviewer. Make sure whomever assists you in preparing for the interview evaluates your performance. Practice the whole interviewing scenario, beginning with entering the door to leaving at the end. You should sharpen your nonverbal communication skills and be prepared to give positive answers to questions as well as ask intelligent questions. The more you practice, the better prepared you will be for the real job interview.

COMMUNICATIONS

An interview is a two-way communication exchange between an interviewer and interviewee. It involves both verbal and nonverbal communication. While we tend to concentrate on the content of what we say, research shows that approximately 65 percent of all communication is nonverbal. This percentage may be even higher in some cultures. Furthermore, we tend to give more credibility to nonverbal than to verbal messages. Regardless of what you say, how you dress, sit, stand, use your hands, move your head and eyes, and listen communicate both positive and negative messages.

Job interviews can occur in many different settings and under various circumstances. You will write job interview letters, schedule interviews by telephone, be interviewed over the phone, and encounter one-on-one as well as panel, group, and series interviews at home and abroad. Each situation requires a different set of communication behaviors. For example, while telephone communication is efficient, it may be ineffective for interview purposes. Only certain types of information can be effectively communicated over the telephone because this medium limits nonverbal behavior. For example, honesty, intelligence, and likability—three of the most important values you want to communicate to employers—are primarily communicated nonverbally. Therefore, you should be very careful of telephone interviews—whether giving or receiving them.

Honesty, intelligence, and likability are primarily communicated nonverbally.

Job interviews have different purposes and can be negative in many ways. From your perspective, the purpose of an initial job interview is to get a second interview, and the purpose of the second interview is to get a job offer. However, for many employers, the purpose of the interview is to eliminate you from a second interview or job offer. The interviewer wants to know why he or she should **not** hire you. The interviewer tries to do this by identifying your weaknesses. These differing purposes create an adversarial relationship and contribute to the overall interviewing stress experienced by both the applicant and the interviewer.

Since the interviewer wants to identify your weaknesses, you must counter by **communicating your strengths** to lessen the interviewer's fears of hiring you. Recognizing that you are an unknown quantity to the employer, you must raise the interviewer's expectations of you.

ANSWERING QUESTIONS

Hopefully your prospecting, networking, informational interviewing, and resume and letter writing activities result in several invitations to interview for jobs appropriate to your objective. Once you receive an invitation to interview, you should do a great deal of work in preparation for your meeting. You should prepare for the interview as if it were a $500,000 prize. After all, that may be what you earn with the employer over the next several years.

The invitation to interview will most likely come by telephone. In some cases, a preliminary interview will be conducted by telephone. The employer may want to shorten the list of eligible candidates from 10 to 3. By calling each individual, the employer can quickly eliminate marginal candidates as well as up-date the job status of each individual. When you get such a telephone call, you have no time to prepare. You may be dripping wet as you step from the shower or you may have a splitting headache as you pick up the phone. Telephone interviews always seem to occur at bad times. Whatever your situation, put your best foot forward based upon your thorough preparation for an interview. You may want to keep a list of questions near the telephone just in case you receive such a telephone call.

Telephone interviews often result in a face-to-face interview at the employer's office. Once you confirm an interview time and place, you should do as much research on the organization and employer as possible as well as learn to lessen your anxiety and stress levels by practicing the interview situation. **Preparation and practice** are the keys to doing your best.

During the interview, you want to impress upon the interviewer your knowledge of the organization by asking intelligent questions and giving intelligent answers. Your library and networking research should yield useful information on the organization and employer. Be sure you know something about the organization. Interviewers are normally impressed by interviewees who demonstrate knowledge and interest in their organization.

Interviewers are normally impressed by interviewees who demonstrate knowledge and interest in their organization.

You should practice the actual interview by mentally addressing several questions most interviewers ask. Do not develop answers and then memorize them. While promoted in many interview books, such "canned" or "role playing" approaches to the job interview can lead to disaster if you either forget your answers in the interview situation or sound "rehearsed" for the interview. Rather, develop an **orientation** to the interview situation and potential interview questions that always emphasizes responding to questions in a positive, professional, mature, and intelligent manner. Eliminate any negative responses.

Most interview questions will relate to your educational background, work experience, career goals, personality, international job setting, and related concerns. The most frequently asked questions include:

Education

- Describe your educational background.
- Why did you attend _____ University (College or School)?
- Why did you major in _____?
- What was your grade point average?
- What foreign languages have you studied?
- What subjects did you enjoy the most? The least? Why?
- What leadership positions did you hold?
- How did you finance your education?
- If you started all over, what would you change about your education?

- Why were your grades so low? So high?
- Did you do the best you could in school? If not, why not?
- Do you think your educational background prepared you well for international employment and living?

Work Experience

- What were your major achievements in each of your past jobs?
- Why did you change jobs before?
- What other international work experience do you have?
- What is your typical workday like?
- What functions do you enjoy doing the most?
- What did you like about your boss? Dislike?
- Which job did you enjoy the most? Why? Which job did you enjoy the least? Why?
- Have you ever been fired? Why?

Career Goals

- Why do you want to join our organization?
- Why do you think you are qualified for this position?
- Why are you looking for another job?
- Why do you want to make a career change?
- What ideally would you like to do?
- Why should we hire you?
- How would you improve our operations?
- What do you want to be doing five years from now?
- How much do you want to be making five years from now?
- What are your short-range and long-range career goals?
- If you could choose your job and organization, where would you go?
- What other types of jobs are you considering? Other companies?
- When will you be ready to begin work?
- How do you feel about relocating, traveling, working over-time, and spending weekends in the office?
- What attracted you to our organization?

Personality and Other Concerns

- Tell me about yourself.
- How did you get involved in international work?
- If you had to choose any place in the world to work, where would it be? Why there?
- What other countries have you worked in? How did you end up there?

- What kind of work were you doing there? What did you enjoy the most about that job?
- What are your major weaknesses? What are your major strengths?
- What causes you to lose your temper?
- What do you do in your spare time? Any hobbies?
- What types of books do you read?
- What role does your family play in your career?
- Will your family accompany you abroad or will you come alone? What about your spouse's career? What will your spouse do if he/she can't find a job in the new location? Do your foresee any problems arising from such a situation?
- Are you prepared to relocate within the next six weeks?
- What will be your relocation requirements in terms of shipping household goods, local housing, and schools?
- How well do you work under pressure? In meeting deadlines?
- Tell me about your management philosophy.
- Have you worked with a cross-cultural staff before?
- How well did you get along with the local staff?
- Have you supervised local staff before?
- What do you see as potential problems in such a relationship?
- How is your language proficiency?
- How much initiative do you take?
- What types of people do you prefer working with?
- How _____(creative, analytical, tactful, etc.) are you?
- If you could change your life, what would you do differently?

Your answers to each question should be positive and emphasize your **strengths**. Remember, the interviewer wants to know about your **weaknesses**. For example, if you are asked *"What are your weaknesses?"*, one could turn this potential negative question into a positive by answering something like this:

> *"I sometimes get so involved with my work that I neglect my family as well as forget to complete work around the house. My problem is that I'm somewhat of a workaholic."*

What employer could consider this a negative? You have taken a potential negative and raised the expectations of the employer by basically saying you are a hard and persistent worker; the organization will get more for its money than expected.

However, there is one line of questioning that you may be unprepared to deal with since it is no longer prevalent among many employers in the United States. It's a personal line of questioning that may appear unrelated to the specific job. Interviewers may be poorly prepared or incompetent in what they do and thus fall into areas of questioning that may seem inappropriate for the situation. In fact, you may encounter few polished and professional interviewers in the international job arena. Many are amateurs who don't know what they want as well as have difficulty focusing on what they should be doing—gathering the best information for determining the best candidates.

Much of the problem is also cultural. American culture tends to make sharp distinctions between professional and personal concerns. It further gives legitimacy to such concepts as fairness, equity, and discrimination in the workplace. As a result, we expect an interviewer to only raise questions that directly pertain to the skill content and professional qualifications of the job. Many personal questions are even designated as "illegal questions"—employers are prohibited by law to ask questions about your age, race, sexual behavior, height, weight, marital status, and family situation.

> *While some employment questions may be illegal to ask in the U.S., they are not illegal in many other countries.*

While some employment questions may be illegal to ask in the U.S., they are not illegal in many other countries that do not make such distinctions between what is private and personal versus what is professional and job-related. Indeed, in many cultures these lines are blurred. The personal element is central in performing the job and is given as much—if not more—weight than the professional element defining one's qualifications. Hence, many international employers want answers to questions concerning your private life, family situation, and lifestyle. Like it or not, your sex, race, marital status, spouse, and willingness to socialize will be important to many international jobs and thus you should be prepared to handle such questions. Since you purposefully left these off of your resume, the employer may especially want to ask you these personal questions during the interview.

Many international employers routinely ask personal questions as part of their screening process. Given your cultural sensitivity to many of these questions, they may make you feel uncomfortable and at times angry. Consider how you would respond to these questions:

- Are you married, divorced, separated, or single?
- How old are you?
- How much to you make at present?
- Do you go to church regularly?
- Do you have many debts?

- Do you own or rent your home?
- Do you drink much?
- Do you socialize a lot?
- Do you like our food? What about our women?
- What social and political organizations do you belong to?
- What does your spouse think about your career?
- Are you living with anyone?
- Are you gay?
- Have you been tested for AIDS?
- Are you practicing birth control?
- Were you ever arrested?
- How does your spouse feel about living in _____?
- Is your spouse prepared to give up her/his career while you are living in _____?
- How many children do you have?
- How old are they?
- Who will care for the children when you travel?
- How much do you weigh?

Don't get upset and say *"That's a very personal question and it's an illegal one back home. . . I refuse to answer it!"* While you may be perfectly right in saying so, this response lacks cultural tact and sensitivity as well as familiarity with the other culture—which may be exactly what the employer is looking for. For example, if an interviewer asks if you are divorced, and if indeed you are and you know a divorce is a negative in the interviewer's culture, you might respond by putting your divorce into a positive light related to the job:

> *"Yes, I am. Unlike me, my former spouse was not interested in living abroad and pursuing an international career. Since the divorce I have been able to focus more attention on my international career and am better prepared to meet the travel demands of my work."*

Some employers may ask very sensitive questions just to see how you answer or react under stress. Others may do so out of ignorance and lack of sensitivity to other cultures. Whatever the case, you must be prepared to offer thoughtful answers to these questions since many are central concerns of the international employment process.

On the other hand, many international employers, especially U.S.-based firms, will ask the type of questions you would normally expect from a U.S. company or a government agency. Our best advice is that you prepare for the interview by first **analyzing your audience**. What is it they are most likely to ask about you both professionally and personally? If the job requires relocating abroad, you can expect most employers to be concerned about your family situation and spouse. After all, they don't want to go to the expense of moving you abroad and then discover you have an unhappy family as well as an unemployed and unhappy spouse who wants to return home as soon as possible! Be prepared for these types of questions, whether or not they are raised by the interviewer. In fact, you may want to ask these questions yourself since they will be important to your international adjustment.

ASKING QUESTIONS

Interviewers expect candidates to ask intelligent questions concerning the organization and the nature of the work. Moreover, you need information and should indicate your interest in the employer by asking questions. Since international jobs involve many important lifestyle concerns and travel considerations, you should be prepared to ask many professional **and** personal questions. Consider asking some of these questions if they haven't been answered early in the interview:

- Tell me about the duties and responsibilities of this job.
- How does this position relate to other positions within this organization?
- How long has this position been in the organization?
- How long do you expect this position to continue?
- Is this a permanent position or is it funded through a contract? What is the contract source—local or international funding?
- What would be the ideal type of person for this position? Skills? Personality? Working style? Background?
- Can you tell me about the people who have been in this position before? Backgrounds? Promotions? Terminations?
- Whom would I be working with in this position?
- Tell me something about these people? Strengths? Weaknesses?
- Performance expectations?
- Are there any special language, travel, or social requirements for this position?
- What am I expected to accomplish during the first year?
- How will I be evaluated?
- Are promotions and raises tied to performance criteria?
- Can you tell me how this system works?
- What is the normal salary range for such a position?
- Based on your experience, what type of problems would someone new in this position likely encounter?
- I'm interested in your career with this organization. When did you start? What are your plans for the future?
- I would like to know how people get promoted and advance in this organization?
- What is particularly unique about working in this organization?

- Can you explain the various benefits employees receive?
- What does the future look like for this organization?

You should also be prepared to ask many **personal questions** that are not normally associated with interviews for jobs in the United States. Like the interviewer who asks personal questions, you too should ask your own set of such questions. If the job involves relocating abroad, for example, feel free to ask several questions relating to your lifestyle and family situation. If you don't, you may be in for some surprises! You may want to ask several of these personal questions:

- Do you take care of all immigration matters, including work permits and visas for me and my family?
- Will my salary be subject to local taxes?
- How do you handle the packing and shipping of household goods? What are the allowances both coming here and returning home?
- How about bringing in personal goods, such as my computer system and photo equipment, that are subject to local import duties? What is your policy in this area?
- What kind of housing is normally provided for someone in this position?
- What about a car, driver, and servants? Are these provided with this job?
- Tell me about the local schools since we have two children, one in the fifth grade and the other in the ninth grade?
- What is the company's contribution toward tuition at the international school or for the expenses of a private boarding school our children may need to attend?
- Tell me about the quality of the local medical facilities.
- What's the local political climate like these days?
- Have previous employees had any trouble in the local community with thefts or violence? How safe is it here? What special precautions should one take?
- What's it really like living here?
- Is there anything we should especially know about this community?
- Is there a large and active expatriate community?
- What about the cost of living? For example, how much does one normally spend on housing?
- How difficult is it to get certain imported items, especially foods? How much do these imported goods cost?
- What about local job opportunities for my spouse? Will the company assist my spouse in finding employment? Could you tell me more about the local job market for spouses?

- What type of home leave policy do you have? Does this include round-trip transportation for all members of the family?
- Are salaries paid in local currency or deposited in a U.S. dollar account? How do you draw on the account?

You may want to write these questions on a 3x5" card and take them with you to the interview. Although it's best if you can remember most of your questions, you may want to refer to your list to make certain you have forgotten nothing that is important. You might do this by saying: *"Yes, I jotted down a few questions which I want to make sure I ask you before leaving."* Then pull out your card and refer to the questions.

Interviewers normally make a positive or negative decision based upon the impression you make during the first four or five minutes of the interview.

NONVERBAL COMMUNICATION

The interview is an image management activity. Interviewers normally make a positive or negative hiring decision based upon the impression you make during the first four or five minutes of the interview. The major factors influencing this decision are your nonverbal cues communicated at the very beginning of the interview. Therefore, what you wear, how you look, the way you greet others, how you smell, whether you are interested and enthusiastic, where and how you sit, and how you initiate the small talk are extremely important to the interviewer's decision. These factors may be more important than your answers to specific interview questions. Indeed, in some cultures as much as 80 percent of communications will be nonverbal in nature. Your verbal answers to questions will tend to either reinforce or alter initial nonverbal impressions.

Certain nonverbal behaviors have different meanings in different cultures. For example, while Americans tend to use frequent eye contact as indications of attentiveness and active listening, in some cultures frequent eye contact may make people feel uneasy. The same is true for body language. Crossing one's legs, folding one's arms, and passing items with the left hand may communicate impoliteness and rudeness is some cultures but not in other cultures.

Our basic rule for nonverbal behavior is to know your audience. Most of the following nonverbal rules pertain to an American audience, which is the most likely audience you will be interviewing with. However, many interviews held abroad will place you in a different cultural context that involves interviewing with several people from the local culture who may adhere to different nonverbal rules of behavior. If this is the situation you find yourself in, the best thing to do is to know your audience. Gather information on cross-cultural behavior in the particular country and make sure you do not engage in any faux pas that would be embarrassing to you and thus be a real negative for the job interview. You can find several good books on the subject of cross-cultural business behavior, dining customs, and nonverbal communication that should be helpful. Know what is proper and improper behavior in your particular country, from dressing right to observing social etiquette and table manners. In the meantime, the following rules of nonverbal behavior should be valid in most international job interview situations.

While it may seem unfair for employers to make snap decisions based on only a few minutes of nonverbal impressions, it happens nonetheless. Accept it as an important reality of the job search, and learn to adjust your behavior to your best advantage. Remember, those first five minutes may be the most critical moments in your job search and for your future job or career. Put your best foot forward with the most positive image you can generate.

Be sure you dress appropriately for the interview. Whether an interview takes place in the U.S. or abroad, there are certain basic dress codes you need to observe for the job interview. Other nonverbal behaviors to sensitize yourself to are how you sit, stand, and listen. You may want to think through or practice each step of the interview, from arriving to leaving. Be sure you arrive at the interview on time if interviewing in a culture where this is appropriate—10 minutes early is recommended in the U.S. When you enter the office area, remove your coat. On meeting the interviewer, extend your hand; women should do the same, particularly when interviewing with a male. Next, sit when and where the interviewer indicates; don't rush to a seat as if you are in a hurry to get started and finished.

Be particularly sensitive to **your listening behavior**. While most interviewers expect more than single *"yes"* and *"no"* answers to questions, an interviewer also needs nonverbal feedback in order to take you seriously. Indicate your attention and interest by maintaining frequent eye contact, nodding, smiling, and interjecting verbal responses. Listening is an active process, and effective listeners make others feel good about their communication.

CLOSING THE INTERVIEW

Be prepared to end the interview. Many people don't know when or how to close interviews. They go on and on until someone breaks an uneasy moment of silence with an indication that it is time to go.

Interviewers normally will initiate the close by standing, shaking hands, and thanking you for coming to the interview. Don't end by saying *"Goodbye and thank you."* As this stage, you should summarize the interview in terms of your interests, strengths, and goals. Briefly restate your qualifications and continuing interest in working with the employer. At this point it is proper to ask the interviewer about selection plans: *"When do you anticipate making your final decision?"* Follow this question with your final one: *"May I call you next week to inquire about my status?"* By taking the initiative in this manner, the employer will be prompted to clarify your status soon, and you will have an opportunity to talk to her further.

Many interviewers will ask you for a list of references. Be sure to prepare such a list prior to the interview. Include the names, addresses, and phone numbers of four individuals who will give you positive professional and personal recommendations.

TELEPHONE INTERVIEWS

Few people are effective telephone communicators. Several channels of nonverbal communication, such as eye contact, facial expression, and gestures, are absent in telephone conversations. People who may be dynamic in face-to-face situations may be dull and boring over the telephone. Since critical communication relating to the interview will take place over the telephone, pay particular attention to how you handle your telephone communication.

Two potential telephone interview situations may arise at any time. First, you may request an interview by calling an employer. Second, the employer may call you and conduct a screening interview over the phone. While the rules for both types of telephone conversations vary, certain principles should be followed.

When you telephone to request an interview, always know the name of the person you wish to contact. If you don't know the person's name, you can easily get the name by making two phone calls: one to the receptionist or secretary and another to the person you want to speak to. When calling the receptionist or secretary, just ask for the name of the person you wish to contact: *"Who is the head of the _____ office?"* Your second call should be directly to the person you wish to contact.

Most often your telephone calls will go through a secretary. The easiest way to avoid being screened out is to sound like you know the person or he or she is expecting your call. Do not ask: *"May I speak with Mr. Casey?"* This question often results in being screened out; a secretary next asks who you are and the nature of your business. Instead, try a more direct and authoritative statement for openers: *"This is Mary Allen calling for David Casey."* A surprising number of secretaries will put you directly through to the individual without asking you a series of screening questions.

Should the secretary want more information about the nature of your call, say you wish to make an appointment to see the person about some business. If the secretary persists in trying to identify what exactly you want, say it's "personal business." If this line of questioning fails to get you through, try to call at odd times, such as one half hour before the office opens and a half hour after it closes. Many managers arrive early and leave late—times when no one else is around to answer the telephone.

Telephone introductions are easier if you are following-up on a letter you sent earlier. You might begin by saying,

> *"Hello, this is Mary Allen. I'm calling in regards to the letter I sent you last week. I mentioned I would call you today to see if we could meet briefly. You may recall my interests and experience in international training and development. I would like to meet with you briefly to discuss..."*

However, if this is a "cold turkey" request-for-interview call, you may have difficulty scheduling an interview. Many employers will not invite you to a job interview based on this aggressive approach. Be straightforward, assertive, and hope for the best. Try to avoid the "give-me-a-job" mentality often associated with such calls. Use an appropriate variation of one of these opening statements to ease the aggressiveness of this call:

> *"I heard about the innovative work you are doing in technical training..."*

> *"I've always wanted to learn more about opportunities with your organization. Would it be possible for us to get together briefly to discuss your training needs?"*

> *"I was told you might know someone who would be interested in my background: 10 years of increasingly responsible international training and development experience in Africa and Asia..."*

It is best to write down these opening statements and refer to them in your conversation. Avoid a lengthy phone conversation. You do not want to turn this into a job interview. Your goal is to schedule a face-to-face interview. If the individual asks you interview-type questions, stress your strengths and specify an interview time.

Keep in mind that your telephone voice will be a slightly higher pitch than your normal voice. Therefore, lower your pitch and speak in a moderate volume and rate. If you vary your volume, rate, and pitch for emphasis, you will sound relatively enthusiastic and interesting over the phone.

The second type of telephone encounter, as we noted earlier, is the unexpected call from the employer who is attempting to eliminate several finalists by conducting a telephone screening interview. If you receive such a call, be prepared for questions probing both your strengths and weakness-

es. Although this may be a stressful situation for you, try to sound as enthusiastic, interested, and positive as possible. Stress your strengths and try to arrange
an interview. Keep your list of questions near the telephone so you also can
interview the employer. Close the conversation by arranging an interview:

> *"I would appreciate an opportunity to meet with you to further
> discuss how my skills might best meet your needs. Would it possible
> for us to meet briefly sometime in the next few days?"*

Many interviewers will probe salary questions with you over the phone. They
want to know if you are within a realistic range for further consideration. While
it is always best to keep this question to the end of the final interview, be
prepared to answer it over the telephone. Based on your research, you should already know the salary range for the position. You should either respond with
"I'm open to discussions on this question," or state your range which also
includes part of the employer's range as common ground for negotiations. Use
this question as the basis for requesting an interview. Mention that you need
more information on the position. Out of fairness to the employer, he or she
needs to know more about you and your value. A job interview would be most
appropriate at this time.

You can prepare for these telephone conversations. Role play them with a
friend. Tape-record various conversation scenarios, but do not look at each other
during these conversations. Have someone else critique the tape and discuss how
you might improve your telephone answers and questions.

FAX COMMUNICATIONS AND INTERVIEWS

International firms increasingly use the fax machine for most of their
important communication, including the selection of personnel. Consequently, be
prepared to both receive faxes related to international jobs and transmit faxes to
potential employers. You may want to find a friend who already has a fax
machine and arrange to receive and transmit faxes through that number.
Alternatively, you may want to purchase your own fax machine or arrange to
receive and transmit faxes through a local business. Whatever you do, it's a good
idea to include a fax number with all of your written correspondence, including
placing the fax number next to your telephone number on your resume.

The fax machine has much wider use abroad than in the United States.
Consequently, many employers will use the fax as part of the selection process.
If you can't receive nor transmit faxes, you simply are not part of this
international communication culture and thus you will make an important
nonverbal statement about your international orientation.

Many international employers will conduct part of the job interview via fax
by asking you to respond to particular questions normally asked during an
interview, provide additional information on your background, or send a list of

questions you need answered. In these situations you have more time to provide thoughtful answers to questions. These same employers may tentatively hire you based on the content of the fax traffic. Their final decision may involve a telephone interview and an invitation to visit the job site abroad where you will finally get into the details of the job, meet all of the individuals involved in the final decision-making process, and negotiate the job offer. The job interview actually becomes the final step of the normal interview sequence. In the end, you may discover you were hired in a rather non-conventional manner: 10 fax transmissions, one telephone interview, and one job interview. On the other hand, some people get hired these days based solely on fax communications.

If you can't receive nor transmit faxes, you simply are not part of this international communication culture.

Whatever your do, make sure you are in the international mainstream with quick access to a fax machine. It is becoming increasingly difficult to function in the international arena without such access. Purchasing your own machine may well be a very wise investment when looking for an international job. Fax machines are much cheaper and probably more effective than taking a trip abroad to look for a job. Fax your qualifications to employers before you make any unnecessary trips to contact potential employers. You may quickly discover that your fax machine plays a critical role in your international job search. Not only will it speed written communication, but it also functions as a long-distance interview tool. After you land the job, you may wonder how you ever survived without your fax machine!

DEALING WITH OBJECTIONS

Interviewers must have a healthy skepticism of job candidates. They expect people to exaggerate their competencies and overstate what they will do for the employer. They sometimes encounter dishonest applicants, and many people they hire fail to meet their expectations. Being realists who have made poor hiring decisions before, they want to know why they should **not** hire you. Although they do not always ask you these questions, they think about them nonetheless:

- Why should I hire you?
- What do you really want?
- What can you really do for me?

- What are your weaknesses?
- What problems will I have with you?

Underlying these questions are specific employers' objections to hiring you:

- You're not as good as you say you are; you probably hyped your resume or lied about yourself.
- All you want is a job and security.
- You have weaknesses like the rest of us.
- Is it alcohol, sex, drugs, finances, shiftlessness, petty politics?
- You'll probably want my job in another 5 months.
- You won't stay long with us.

Employers raise such suspicions and objections because it is difficult to trust strangers in the employment game, and they may have been "burned" before. Indeed, there is an alarming rise in the number of individuals lying on their resumes or falsifying their credentials.

How can you best handle employers' objections? You must first recognize their biases and stereotypes and then **raise** their expectations. You do this by stressing your strengths and avoiding your weaknesses. You must be impeccably honest in doing so. Take, for example, the question *"Why are you leaving your present job?"* If you have been fired and you are depressed, you might blurt out all your problems:

> *"I had a great job, but my crazy boss began cutting back on personnel because of budgetary problems. I got the axe along with three others."*

You might be admired for your frankness, but this answer is too negative; it reveals the wrong motivations for seeking a job. Essentially you are saying you are unemployed and bitter because you were fired. Furthermore, that's probably how you will talk about your new employer should things turn sour. A better answer would be:

> *"My position was abolished because of budget reductions. However, I see this as a new opportunity for me to use the skills I acquired during the past 10 years to improve profits. Having worked regularly with people in your field, I'm now anxious to use my experience to contribute to a growing organization."*

Let's try another question reflecting objections to hiring you. The interviewer asks:

> *"Your background bothers me somewhat. You've been with this organization for 10 years. You know, its different working in our organization. Why should I hire you?"*

One positive way to respond to this probing question is to clearly communicate your understanding of the objection and then give evidence that you have resolved this issue in a positive manner:

> *"I understand your hesitation in hiring someone with my background. I would too, if I were you. Yes, many people don't do well in different occupational settings. But I don't believe I have that problem. I'm used to working with people. I work until the job gets done, which often means long hours and on weekends. I'm very concerned with achieving results. But most important, I've done a great deal of thinking about my goals. I've researched your organization as well as many others. From what I have learned, this is exactly what I want to do, and your organization is the one I'm most interested in joining. I know I will do a good job as I have always done in the past."*

Always try to avoid confessing weaknesses, negatives, or lack of experience. You want to communicate your strengths and positives loud and clear to the interviewer. Be honest, but not stupid!

FOLLOW-UP

Once you have been interviewed, be sure to follow through to get nearer to the job offer. One of the best follow-up methods is the thank-you letter. After talking to the employer over the telephone or in a face-to-face interview, send a thank-you letter. This letter should be typed on good quality bond paper. In this letter express your gratitude for the opportunity to interview. Re-state your interest in the position and highlight any particularly noteworthy points made in your conversation or anything you wish to further clarify. Close the letter by mentioning that you will call in a few days to inquire about the employer's decision. When you do this, the employer should remember you as a thoughtful person.

If you call and the employer has not yet made a decision, follow through with another phone call in a few days. Send any additional information to the employer which may enhance your application. You might also want to ask one of your references to call the employer to further recommend you for the position. However, don't engage in overkill by making a pest of yourself. You want to tactfully communicate two things to the employer at this point: (1) you are interested in the job, and (2) you will do a good job.

SALARIES AND BENEFITS

Salary is one of the most important yet least understood considerations in the job search. Many individuals do well in handling all interview questions except the salary question. They are either too shy to talk about money—nice people don't talk about salaries—or they believe you must take what you are offered because salary is predetermined by employers. In some cases—especially government—salaries are specified for each position and thus are non-negotiable. But even in government, what is specified is often a salary **range**.

Lacking experience in negotiating salaries, many people generally do not know the first step to dealing with money questions. As a result, you may be paid much less than you are worth. Over the years, you will lose thousands of dollars by having failed to properly negotiate your salaries.

---

*Many applicants are paid much
less than they are worth.*

Except for many government salaries and salaries for entry-level positions, most salaries are negotiable. Even within government negotiation is often possible within a limited range.

The salary question may arise at any time. Employers like to raise the question as soon as possible in order to screen candidates in or out. You, on the other hand, want to deal with the salary question toward the end—after you learn more about the job and demonstrate your value to the employer. Your goal should be to get a job interview and job offer as well as negotiate as high a salary as possible.

Strategies

A standard salary negotiation scenario is for the employer to raise this question:

"What are your salary requirements?"

When faced with this question, you should turn it around by asking the employer:

*"What is the normal range in your organization for a position such
as this as well as for someone with my qualifications?"*

The employer will either try again to get you to state a figure by restating the original question or reveal the actual range. Expect a frank answer most of the time. If the employer indicates a range, the rest of the salary negotiation is relatively simple.

Having done your homework on international salaries and cost of living differentials abroad as well as knowing what you are worth and what the employer is willing to pay, you are now ready to do some friendly but earnest haggling. If, for example, the employer says his range for the position is $50,000 to $54,000, you might respond by saying *"$54,000 is within my range."* If his range is much more or less than you anticipated, avoid being emotional or overly positive or negative. Disregard the bottom figure and concentrate on working from the top by putting his highest figure into the bottom of your range. For example, if he says *"$50,000 to $54,000,"* you should move the top figure into your $54,000 to $60,000 range. By doing this, you create common ground from which to negotiate or you neutralize the salary issue until later negotiations.

However, if the employer does not state a range or states only a single figure, such as $50,000, rely on your salary research or multiply this figure by 25 percent to arrive at a figure for negotiation. Thus, the $50,000 figure now becomes your $57,500 expectation. Respond by saying, *"I'm thinking more in terms of $57,500."* A $7,500 difference should give you room for negotiation. If you state $65,000, you may appear unreasonable, unless you can support this figure based upon your salary research on comparable positions. But your previous salary research should result in stating a reasonable salary range which can be documented for similar positions in this or other organizations.

Employers may praise their "benefits" package prior to talking about a cash figure. Be wary of such benefits. Most are standard and thus come with the job regardless of the salary figure you negotiate. Unless you can create some special benefits, such as an extra two weeks of paid vacation each year, you should focus your attention primarily on the base salary figure.

Raising the Base

The salary figure you negotiate will influence subsequent salaries with this and other organizations. In fact, many employers figure your present worth based on your salary history; they simply add 10 to 15 percent to what you made in your last job to arrive at your new salary. If you were a $25,000 a year teacher, such a procedure will discriminate against you and your talents. In this case, you need to change the rules of game. Disregard your salary history and, instead, focus on both your worth and the value of the position to the employer—not on what the employer can get you for. On the other hand, if you are coming from a $65,000 a year job to a $55,000 one, you must convince the employer that you will be happy with a salary decrease—if, indeed, you can live with it. Many employers will not expect you to remain long if you take such a salary cut; thus, they may be reluctant to offer you a position.

Renegotiations

You should make sure your future salary reflects your value. One approach to doing this is to reach an agreement to renegotiate your salary at a later date, perhaps in another six to eight months. Use this technique especially when you feel the final salary offer is less than what you are worth, but you want to accept the job. Employers often will agree to this provision since they have nothing to lose and much to gain if you are as productive as you tell them.

However, be prepared to renegotiate in both directions—up and down. If the employer does not want to give you the salary figure you want, you can create good will by proposing to negotiate the higher salary figure down after six months, if your performance does not meet the employer's expectations. On the other hand, you may accept his lower figure with the provision that the two of you will negotiate your salary up after six months, if you exceed the employer's expectations. It is preferable to start out high and negotiate down, if necessary, rather than start low and negotiate up.

Renegotiation provisions stress one very important point: you want to be paid on the basis of your performance. You demonstrate your professionalism, self-confidence, and competence by negotiating in this manner. More important, you ensure that the question of your monetary value will not be closed in the future. As you negotiate the present, you also negotiate your future with this as well as other employers.

International Costs and Benefits

Salaries and benefits for international jobs will involve many more considerations than those normally associated with jobs in the United States. If living abroad, an international job involves moving expenses, currency issues, housing considerations, and a host of other questions that could have a very negative impact on your salary base. If, for example, you have two school-age children who will move abroad with you and you fail to ask about educational provisions and allowances, you may be shocked to discover that it costs $12,000 a year for tuition per child to send them to the private international school. Even a $65,000 a year salary will not go far if you have to pay such tuition costs. Hopefully, the employer will take care of such educational expenses—but only if you address this question as part of the salary and benefit negotiations.

Some of the most important salary and benefit-related questions you need to raise prior to accepting a position are these. While they may not be important for some international jobs, they are very important for other jobs. If you fail to raise many of these questions prior to accepting a job, you may be in for some unpleasant surprises that could very well sour your international experience:

- **Immigration, visas, work permits, and customs:** Who will take care of all the legal matters involved in working in this country? This includes getting the proper visas and work permits for you and your family. And who deals with customs, especially if you want to bring your computer and camera with you and the local regulation prohibit duty-free entry of such goods? The employer should have a policy regarding these matters as well as staff members who handle the details of immigration and customs. While the employer may handle the work permit for your particular job, what about a work permit for your spouse who may want to work in this country? How difficult will it be to get one? What are the restrictions in terms of entering and exiting the country? In some countries your visa may prohibit multiple entry into the country. In other countries the government requires tax clearances every time expatriates leave the country, which can be a very time consuming and expensive process. You don't want to discover that this attractive international job which ostensibly permits you to travel abroad actually prohibits you from traveling outside the country once you begin working there!

- **Moving expenses:** Who pays what for moving you, your family, and household goods abroad? Most employers will provide round-trip air transportation for you and your family. They also provide allowances for household goods—both to and from the job destination. These allowances are either a dollar or a sea freight weight amount. Be sure you also ask about packing along with freight. Freight normally does not include packing, which can be very expensive. You want the whole package—packing, pick-up, delivery to the docks, sea freight shipping, dock fees, trans-shipping, delivery, unpacking, and any special fees involved in moving your goods from your original destination to the final destination. Most employers will pay all of these costs, but only within certain ranges. Try to get the maximum range possible. You might want to "back-load" the shipping allowances—a smaller figure for shipping your goods to your destination but a larger figure for shipping your goods home. Our assumption is that you will purchase many things abroad and thus return home with more items than you left with. In fact, you might consider taking as few household goods as possible with you in expectation of making many purchases abroad. Your shipping allowance will enable you to "import" a great deal. Keep in mind that sea freight takes anywhere from six weeks to three months before you will receive your shipment. Consequently, you should also negotiate both an excess baggage amount and air freight allowance for moving those things you will need immediately upon settling in abroad. If you don't, you will either arrive abroad with two suitcases per person or incur a very expensive excess baggage and air freight bill that may be several thousands of dollars.

- **Air transportation:** Most employers will provide round-trip air transportation for you and your family. However, make sure this provision is in writing. Also, many employers will provide business-class rather than economy-class transportation. Don't expect first-class transportation. Some employers may only provide one-way transportation. Many may expect you to reimburse them for both the air transportation and moving expenses should you voluntarily quit your job within the first 12 months. This is common practice since moving an employee abroad is very expensive. International employers expect some type of minimum commitment on your part.

- **Home leave and vacations:** Most international employers have home leave provisions in their employment contracts. The home leave provision usually provides round-trip air transportation for the employee and family after a one year, 18-month, or two year period and involves three or four weeks of paid vacation. Make sure there is enough money built into this provision so you can make several stops along the way home. Many employees use this home leave time to do some much needed international pleasure travel.

- **Housing:** One of your major expenses will be local housing. Depending on where you live, you may well be paying US$2,500 to $5,000 per month for housing. Make sure the employer covers most of this cost or the cost is significantly reflected in your salary base. In many cases employers will provide a housing allowance which allows you to choose your own level of housing. In other cases the employer provides the housing directly. This may involve a company apartment or housing compound. Also figure in your housing the cost of utilities —which can be very expensive in some countries, especially electricity —and maids, servants, guards, and gardeners. In many countries it is essential that you hire maids and servants because they are not do-it-yourself societies. Simple living matters, such as shopping for groceries, cooking meals, and washing laundry, are still major chores in many countries. You may need full-time staff to get these things done. In many countries you will also need to hire a full-time private guard to look after your home. Hopefully, this person will also have some gardening skills. You may also want to discuss a home furnishing allowance. In some countries housing is very basic—devoid of such items as closets, window treatments, air-conditioning, and telephones. If you have to purchase your own cupboards, wardrobe cabinets, bookshelves, window blinds and curtains, air-conditioners, and a telephone connection, you may discover you just added another US$5,000 to your housing expenses.

- **Local transportation:** Will the employer provide you with a car, a car and driver, or arrange to have your automobile shipped abroad. You will be better off with a car and driver in those countries where driving is a hassle, the cost of purchasing a car is prohibitive, and importing is not a viable option given high local import duties. In many countries the local transportation issue may not be important because of the excellent public transportation system. Perhaps you can negotiate a local transportation allowance should you frequently need to take a taxi to work or hire your own car and driver.

- **Education allowances:** If you have school-age children accompanying you abroad, make sure you address the educational expense questions. In countries with good international schools tuition costs can be very high—from US$10,000 to $15,000 per child. In other countries which lack good schools, you may have to send your children to a boarding school in another country. Expect to pay another US$5,000 to $8,000 for such schools.

- **Currency and salary payments:** How will you be paid? Will the employer pay you in local currency or in U.S. dollars? If in U.S. dollars, will your paycheck be deposited in a local U.S. dollar account or in a bank back home? While these questions may not seem important, they become very important if you work in a country with high inflation rates. A seemingly high salary paid in local currency may be quickly eroded in an high inflationary economy. If you work in Latin American, it's best to be paid in U.S. dollars. If you work in Germany or Japan, it may be best to be paid in local currency which is stronger that the U.S. dollar. In many other countries which tie their local currency to the U.S. dollar, it's best to get paid in U.S. dollars as well as have your paycheck deposited in a bank back home since many of these countries have restrictions on how much money you can take out of their countries. You don't want to accumulate savings in the country and then discover you can't take the money with you!

- **Insurance:** Most international employers have some type of insurance coverage. However, some may not or their policies provide limited coverage. Be sure to look over your insurance provisions in detail. Keep in mind that if you should have to be evacuated for medical reasons, the cost of special medical air transportation back home can run from US$8,000 to $20,000. If your insurance policy does not provide such coverage, consider taking out special coverage for such medical evacuation. Many a tourist—as well as international employees —have been shocked to discover such medical bills were not covered in their insurance policies.

- **Special privileges:** In some cases, especially for government workers and consultants and contractors working on U.S. government contacts, employees receive special privileges not normally provided to other international workers. These might include access to shopping in the commissary, international mail at U.S. domestic rates, and importing and exporting personal goods duty-free, including an automobile.

- **Spousal employment:** One of the most difficult problems today's international workers encounter is the spouse who is unhappy with his or her employment situation abroad. This has increasingly become a major problem in two-career families where the one spouse is hired for the job but the other is left languishing in the local community with nothing to do other than attend the house and look after the children. It is a cause for many divorces among international workers. Increasingly more and more families are either choosing not to move abroad or are terminating early because the spouse is unable to find fulfilling work. We recommend that you address this potential problem head-on with both your spouse and potential employer. You and your spouse must be prepared for an unemployed spouse situation abroad. On the other hand, many international employers are increasingly sensitive to this problem and will provide job assistance for the spouse. In some cases—depending on the job requirements and skills of your spouse— a job-sharing arrangement can be worked out where you and your spouse work on the same job together. In other situations the employer can offer another rewarding job within the organization or knows of other local organizations that might be interested in hiring your spouse. The employer then provides you with the necessary contacts for approaching these other employers. Whatever the situation, we highly recommend that you raise the question of your spouse's employment at this stage. While it is a personal question that some candidate may feel is inappropriate to raise with a potential employer, it is one of the very important personal questions you must raise if it is likely to become a problem. More and more international employers understand this concern and are willing to assist employees in making sure their family situations remain stable and supportive throughout while living and working abroad. In the meantime, a good book on this subject is Fran Bastress' *The Relocating Spouse's Guide To Employment: Options and Strategies In the U.S. and Abroad.* Couples and families should not move abroad before reading this book and considering this critical employment question.

- **Starting on the payroll and advances:** This can be an important negotiation point that makes a significant difference in your initial income and cash flow. When will be employer start you on the payroll? The day you arrive in the office? The day you depart for the job? One, two, three, or four weeks before your departure? Remember, the process of arranging your private affairs and moving abroad takes time. In addition, you may have to do some special preparation work or meet with the employers representatives prior to arriving in country. Many employers will start you on the payroll prior to departing for the job or arriving at the job site. Try to get on the payroll as soon as possible, especially if you are leaving one job and then having to spend several days or a few weeks arranging your personal and professional affairs. Someone should pay for this time since you have to take it in direct preparation for the job. In some cases the employer will give you a per diem—a per day rate—for this transition period rather than put you directly on the payroll. At this point, anything is better than receiving compensation only when you arrive at the job site. In many cases the employer will also advance you the money to cover your moving expenses, transportation, and per diem and perhaps some of your first month's salary. It's best to raise these questions with the employer **before** you find yourself cash poor for financing your transition and move abroad.

Acceptance

You should accept an offer only after reaching a salary agreement which should address many of the issues we have outlined thus far. If you jump at an offer, you may appear needy. Take time to consider your options. Remember, you are committing your time and effort in exchange for money and status. Is this the job you really want? Take some time to think about the offer before giving the employer a definite answer. But don't play hard-to-get and thereby create ill-will with your new employer. How you interview and negotiate your salary will influence how well you get along with your employer on the job.

While considering the offer, ask yourself several of the same questions you asked at the beginning of your job search:

- What do I want to be doing five years from now?
- How will this job affect my personal life?
- Do I know enough about the employer and the future of this organization?
- Are there other jobs I'm considering which would better meet my goals?

Accepting a job is serious business. If you make a mistake, you could be locked into a very unhappy situation for a long time.

If you receive one job offer while considering another, you will be able to compare relative advantages and disadvantages. You also will have some external leverage for negotiating salary and benefits. While you should not play games, let the employer know you have alternative job offers. This communicates that you are in demand, others also know your value, and the employer's price is not the only one in town. Use this leverage to negotiate your salary, benefits, and job responsibilities.

If you get a job offer but you are considering other employers, let the others know you have a job offer. Telephone them to inquire about your status as well as inform them of the job offer. Sometimes this will prompt employers to make a hiring decision sooner than anticipated. In addition, you will be informing them that you are in demand; they should seriously consider you before you get away!

Some job seekers play a bluffing game by telling employers they have alternative job offers even though they don't. Some candidates do this and get away with it. We don't recommend this approach. Not only is it dishonest, it will work to your disadvantage if the employer learns that you were lying. But more important, you should be selling yourself on the basis of your strengths rather than your cleverness and greed. If you can't sell yourself by being honest, don't expect to get along well on the job. When you compromise your integrity, you demean your value to others and yourself.

Your job search is not over with the job offer and acceptance. One final word of advice. Be thoughtful by sending your new employer a nice thank-you letter. This is one of the most effective letters to write for getting your new job off on the right foot. The employer will remember you as a thoughtful individual whom he or she looks forward to working with.

The whole point of our job search methods is to clearly communicate to employers that you are competent and worthy of being paid top dollar. If you follow our advice, you should do very well with employers in interviews and in negotiating salary and benefits as well as working on the job.

PART III

FINDING YOUR
BEST WORK SETTING

FINDING YOUR
BEST WORK SETTING

So far we've explored some of the most critical steps involved in finding an international job related to your motivations, interests, skills, and goals. If you carefully follow these steps, luck should come your way in finding an international job that is right for you. However, understanding myths, predicting future trends, and acquiring effective job search skills are not enough to get you where you eventually need to go—into an international arena of real jobs.

This final section brings closure to the international job search by linking "how-to" strategies to the real nuts-and-bolts of finding an international job— where the jobs can be found. In addition, we focus on some of the best international job and career opportunities available given the changing nature of today's international job market. As such, this section links the previous sections on future trends, myths, and job search skills to information on the real world of international jobs.

Regardless of how good you think you are in finding a job, you must be able to locate the right organizations functioning in the countries and regions of your choice. Thus, specific organizations and geography play important roles in the international job search.

While we provide greater in-depth treatment of these subjects in our *Almanac of International Jobs and Careers*, this section outlines the basic elements for locating places and organizations that yield some of the best international job and career opportunities. It also goes further in addressing one of the most exciting international employment arenas for the decade ahead—the travel industry. Furthermore, it examines one other major employment arena for the decade ahead—the self-employment option for those interested in working for themselves by starting their own international-related business.

We conclude this section, as well as this volume, with a discussion of the best resources for conducting additional research on international jobs and careers. We do this from a user's decision-making perspective—what practical and quality resources you most need to make critical international job and career decisions. Once you complete this section, along with the previous sections, you should be in a very strong position to find the international job you want. Better still, you will clearly communicate your international qualifications to the people who count—those in organizations needing your skills to solve their problems.

Chapter Nine

THE BEST PLACES
AND ORGANIZATIONS

Your major choices in finding an international job are both geographic and organizational in nature. You first need to decide where it is you want to work in the international arena—your **geographic preference**. Are you willing to go anywhere, or do you have particular geographic interests by region, country, or city? Are you interested in working in developing, Third and Fourth World countries of Africa, Asia, Latin America, Eastern Europe, and the Middle East or only in the developed countries of Western Europe, North America, Japan, Australia, and New Zealand? Maybe you have a favorite city, such as London, Paris, Rome, Geneva, Berlin, Madrid, Athens, Istanbul, Rio, Sydney, Tokyo, Hong Kong, Singapore, or Bangkok?

Or perhaps you're interested in working in the newly emerging industrial nations of the Pacific Rim, such as South Korea, Taiwan, Hong Kong, Singapore, Thailand, and Malaysia? Maybe you're into the "real" developing world of the Philippines, Indonesia, Bangladesh, China, India, Pakistan, Nepal, Poland, Romania, Egypt, Morocco, Tunisia, Rwanda, Ghana, Kenya, Haiti, Mexico, or Peru?

If you work for certain types of organizations, such as the United Nations, the Agency for International Development, International Monetary Fund, CARE, or the Chase Manhattan Bank, you can expect to work in only certain types of countries and cities. Whatever your preference, each region as well as type of country will yield a different international work and lifestyle experience.

WHERE TO WORK

You also need to decide for whom you will work. You will want to learn about the different **types of organizations** that operate in these countries. Therefore, you will need to link your motivations, skills, and job search techniques to the specific organizations that operate in different countries and offer specific job opportunities. Knowing **what** are the organizations and **where** they operate will be central to conducting a successful international job search.

Your organizational choices are numerous, including government agencies, international organizations, businesses, educational institutions, nonprofit organizations, trade and professional organizations, contractors and consulting firms, and a variety of organizations that make up the travel industry. If you are primarily interested in working in poor Third and Fourth World countries on development-related issues or have a missionary zeal to save souls, you'll want to consider organizations that have primary interests in these countries— government agencies, international lending institutions, nonprofit organizations, contracting firms, and religious groups.

Job opportunities are disproportionately dispersed according to the economic development levels and political climates of each country. Developed countries, as well as Newly Industrialized Countries (NICs), have a disproportionate number of job opportunities available in business. While some of these jobs require technical skills, many of the jobs are managerial and marketing in nature —two of the major skills Americans are especially noted for abroad. Many underdeveloped countries with histories of colonial rule may still express xenophobic attitudes through restrictive legislation that prevents foreigners from engaging in many types of employment.

Both education and the travel industry tend to be made up of generic forms of organizations that function in all countries regardless of their level of economic development.

At the same time, you will find more and more international businesses operating in Third and Fourth World countries. Indeed, previous direct government development assistance to these countries has been modified and redirected to place increased emphasis on promoting greater foreign investment and business activity. During the next decade more and more businesses that traditionally operated in developed countries will move into Third and Fourth World countries where they will play a key role in the overall development. The traditional development roles of nonprofit organizations, contracting firms, and government agencies will shift to further promote and strengthen private sector initiatives and institutions that have been overshadowed and dominated by decades of inefficient and ineffective public bureaucracies. The name of the game throughout the 1990s will be to further privatize the public sector, encourage greater foreign investment, and develop local entrepreneurial skills that can be transformed into long-term sustainable growth of an innovative, dynamic, and strong private sector.

SELECTING YOUR BEST PLACE

Where do you want to work and live? Do you want to be based in New York City, Washington, DC, or San Francisco from where you make occasional forays into the international arena? Maybe you would like to be based in London from where you would conduct business in New York, Berlin, Rome, Bombay, Hong Kong, or Tokyo? Perhaps Hong Kong would be an excellent choice from where you can work in China, Japan, Thailand, Indonesia, India, Germany, England, or the United States?

Most people who are interested in international employment have a specific region or country in mind. Perhaps they once visited the country or region and fell in love with it. Perhaps they took a foreign language course and found the language and culture intriguing enough to want to visit the region as well as live and work abroad. Or perhaps ethnic roots or intellectual curiosity drew them to particular countries or regions. We know few people who are truly global in their interests. Most want to live and work in certain countries within Latin America, Europe, Africa, **or** Asia, but not in just any country that offers opportunities. They have their own ranking of "favorite" places to live and work; other places have little or no appeal. Indeed, some people get hooked on England, Germany, Italy, Turkey, Morocco, Kenya, Thailand, Indonesia, Hong Kong, or South Korea and would rather return home to live and work than expand the scope of their employment to include other countries.

You'll have to decide for yourself where would be the best place in the world to work. Our point is that your motivations will largely determine where you should look for employment. We love Southeast Asia, especially Thailand, Malaysia, Singapore, Indonesia, the Philippines, and Hong Kong. Our interests and motivations are more oriented toward the people, their products, the exotic cultures, and public policy issues than to making money or pursuing particular social causes.

Nonetheless, if you are mainly motivated by **making money**, you should consider working in the major capitals of Europe and Asia in the fields of finance and sales. There's lots of money to be made in London, Geneva, Tokyo, and Hong Kong for those who have the proper financial skills. If you are primarily looking for **adventure**, you should consider looking for employment in countries with a high degree of unpredictability—developing countries of Asia, Africa, and Latin America. If you are **pursuing important causes**, or want to make a difference in the lives of less fortunate people, look toward the Third and Fourth World countries of South Asia and Africa—the poorer, the more challenging and potentially the most personally rewarding. If you are looking for **unique and exotic experiences**, consider such countries as India, Thailand, Indonesia, Turkey, Morocco, and Ecuador.

NETWORKS OF OPPORTUNITIES

The best place in the world to work is where your interests and motivations fit the mission of particular organizations involved with your interests. Therefore, other-directed people who want to assist the less fortunate should seriously consider working for nonprofit organizations and private contracting firms with government development contracts as well as government agencies and international organizations involved in promoting Third and Fourth World development efforts in Asia, Africa, and Latin America. These organizations include everything from the Peace Corps, Agency for International Development, the United Nations, the African Development Bank, and the World Bank to such nonprofit organizations as CARE, the Red Cross, and the Catholic Relief Services as well as such contracting firms as Robert Nathan Associates and Coopers and Lybrand. All work in the same regions and countries. Many pursue their own development agendas.

The best place in the world to work is where your interests and motivations fit the mission of organizations involved with your interests.

Most of these organizations also work with one another in a competitive yet mutually dependent fashion. They develop important networks of relationships amongst themselves whereby each organization depends on the other for survival and prosperity. They accomplish their missions with the help of each other. Individuals working in one organization may leave to work in another organization within this network. For example, nonprofit organizations and contracting firms depend on contracts, grants, and cooperative agreements from government agencies, international organizations, and foundations for their survival and prosperity. Government agencies and international organizations, in turn, depend on the same nonprofit organizations and contracting firms to develop and implement projects they fund in the field. Each has an interest in seeing the other succeed to a certain degree. As a result, while there is some competition between the players operating in the same territory, they generally cooperate amongst themselves in the process of pursuing similar goals and interlocking agendas. Individuals working for a nonprofit organization may resign to join a counterpart foundation, contracting firm, government agency, or international organization operating in the same area and dealing with similar issues.

The network of relationships amongst organizations pursuing similar agendas becomes an important "opportunity structure" for those interested in moving from one type of international organization to another, both within and between countries and regions. This network and relationships are best illustrated as follows:

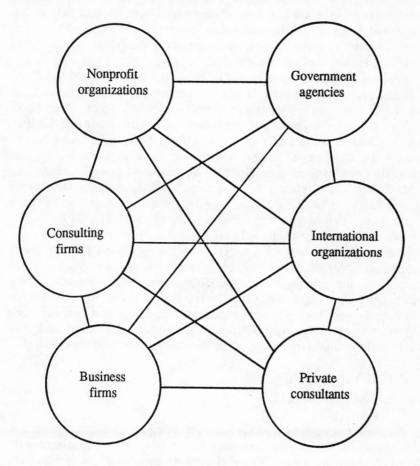

Wherever you work in whatever job, you will encounter some version of this basic network of organizations offering numerous international job opportunities. Be it Tokyo, Hong Kong, Manila, Bangkok, Bombay, Cairo, Rome, or London, similar organizations operate in pursuing their own international agendas. They more or less compete with one another, but they all have an interest in seeing each other succeed as long as the other's success is not at their expense. Best of all, these organizations may provide important job opportunities for those with the proper mix of work skills and networking relationships. You will want to cultivate professional as well as personal relationships with individuals working in these other organizations.

As you begin identifying the best place in the world to work, start looking at regions and countries as being made up of specific communities consisting of similar networks of international organizations. For the most part, the key communities are the capital cities where most government, international banking, educational, nonprofit, and business institutions are centered and from where they operate within the region as well as the country's hinterland. These are the centers for international job opportunities.

Your initial job search task should be to identify the institutions that define this local opportunity network. If you are interested in working in Southeast Asia, for example, you might begin by identifying which complex of international organizations is most heavily concentrated in Singapore, Kuala Lumpur, Bangkok, Jakarta, or Manila. You will, for example, find a major United Nations presence in Bangkok. Government agencies, nonprofit organizations, and consulting firms involved in development are disproportionately headquartered in Manila and Jakarta. Manufacturing firms and banking institutions are heavily concentrated in Bangkok and Singapore. All of these organizations will be more or less found in all major cities, but only a few of the cities offer a complete network of interlocking international organizations.

If you understand how these networks operate and target your job search around specific organizations within this network, you should be able to position yourself well for later making strategic job and career moves amongst the key organizations operating within a specific country or region. For example, you may initially work for a nonprofit organization in Manila and then two years later move to an educational institution or perhaps an international lending or development institution operating within the country or within the larger region.

IDENTIFYING THE BEST ORGANIZATION

Wherever you work, you are likely to be working for a specific organization. It may be a large bureaucratic organization, such as the State Department or the United Nations, a small nonprofit organization or contracting firm, or a medium-sized multinational firm or business.

Your organizational choices are numerous. The remainder of this chapter examines some of the major institutional and organizational complexes that offer international job opportunities. These consist of government agencies, international organizations, businesses, trade and professional organizations, nonprofit organizations, contracting and consulting firms, and a complex of organizations we generically call "the travel industry". An enormous subject in and of itself, we examine these organizations in terms of the types of jobs they offer, the outlook for opportunities in the decade ahead, and information on further researching each organizational complex.

Before looking at each of these organizations, it's necessary to again stress the importance of treating each organization as a component within a larger and more important **network of international organizations**. These organizations offer numerous opportunities for enterprising job seekers who understand how the network operates. Therefore, you should never think of these organizations in isolation of one another nor as competitors to one another. If you are interested in working for nonprofit organizations in Third World countries, keep in mind that the nonprofits operate alongside, and in cooperation with, government agencies, international lending institutions, international development organizations, private contracting firms, educational institutions, foundations, businesses, and a host of other types of organizations. Working for one of these organizations also requires working with many other organizations that function as key players within this larger international network of organizations. Once you begin working for one organization you will quickly discover numerous other job opportunities related to your own work, but not necessarily within your present organization or even in another counterpart nonprofit organization. Indeed, your next job may be with the international lending institution that provided the bulk of the funds for financing the operations of your nonprofit organization!

Not surprising, you will discover an important "revolving door" operates in the international arena. It operates similarly to the revolving door found amongst the network of interdependent domestic U.S. public and private institutions that define the public procurement process involving contractual arrangements among government agencies and private contracting firms and businesses. This network and its revolving door dispenses opportunities to those who are members of the network and who understand how it can operate to their advantage. The ubiquitous "personal contact" becomes the key to moving within this network. The only problem is that you need to initially break into the network before you can position yourself for moving within the network. That problem should be partly resolved as you complete the remainder of this book.

For a more extended discussion of these and other organizations operating in the international arena, please refer to the resources recommended in each of the following chapters. You will find many useful publications that provide overviews of specific organizations operating within the international arena. Many of these resources also include important contact information on the "who," "where," and "how" of contacting each organization for job vacancy information.

PUBLIC AND PRIVATE ORGANIZATIONS

The line between many public and private organizations in the international arena is not a sharp one. Indeed, many different types of ostensibly private sector organizations are closely interwoven into a network of relationships with themselves and government agencies for the purpose of promoting public goals. Each of these organizations provide numerous job opportunities for enterprising job seekers who know about these organizations and how to contact them for job vacancies. In addition, this network of organizations provides easy access to numerous job opportunities with other organizations within the network.

While public organizations are normally associated with government agencies, many other types of organizations lie at the periphery of government performing public functions similarly to those of government agencies. Nonprofit organizations, consulting and contracting firms, foundations, and research organizations all have their own public agendas as well as depend upon government for much of their funding. The major players in what is best termed the "international public sector" include:

1. **Federal, state, and local government agencies:** Most Federal executive agencies have international interests and functions. They engage in everything from foreign policy, trade, and military to public safety and crime prevention activities. The U.S. Congress and legislative agencies are also deeply involved in international issues. Furthermore, many state governments are very active in promoting international trade and tourism. Some cities even hire international experts to promote trade, tourism, and foreign investment for the purposes of local economic development.

2. **Contracting and consulting firms:** In addition to many military contractors involved in providing military hardware for the Department of Defense, several specialized consulting firms compete for Federal government contracts to perform a variety of international tasks, such as designing projects, providing support services, and implementing development projects abroad. The major funding sources for these firms are the U.S. Agency for International Development (USAID) and the World Bank.

3. **International organizations:** Numerous international and regional organizations, such as the United Nations and the Organization of American States, are structured to promote world peace, international cooperation, economic development, and social welfare.

4. **Nonprofit organizations:** A variety of organizations are designed to promote particular international causes. These include nonprofit charitable and social welfare organizations such as CARE and Project Hope. Other organizations are primarily private development organizations engaged in promoting particular types of development projects in the areas of population planning, health, education, energy, and rural development. Religious organizations are active in promoting health, education, and welfare services in developing countries. Several

foundations specialize in funding nonprofit organizations throughout the world.

5. **Educational and training organizations:** Schools, colleges, universities, training institutions, and educational support groups with international interests and orientations are found in abundance both at home and abroad.

6. **Trade and professional associations:** Thousands of trade and professional associations have international interests, including members and affiliated offices. Most of these associations are head-quartered in Washington, DC, New York City, and Chicago.

7. **Foundations:** Numerous private foundations, such as the Rockefeller Foundation and Ford Foundation, are major players in international development efforts. They are major funding sources for many nonprofit organizations, academic researchers, and educational institutions involved in promoting economic and social development in Third and Fourth World countries.

8. **Public policy and research organizations:** These organizations are involved in providing information to both government and nongovernmental organizations as well as influencing the direction of public policy. Numerous research organizations, such as the Brookings Institution and the American Enterprise Institute, and think tanks such as the World Resources Institute and the International Institute of Economics, have major international interests.

Organizations that primarily function within the private sector include the news media, commercial banks, and businesses offering a wide range of products and services, from automobiles and computer software to petroleum, sports goods, and accounting services. The private sector also includes a complex of organizations commonly associated with the travel industry. While many of these organizations maintain close relationships with government agencies and other public sector organizations, they are primarily driven to make a profit from their international ventures. Many do provide funding to international nonprofit and research organizations as well as sponsor foundations which, in turn, fund nongovernmental organizations.

Chapter Ten

UNITED STATES GOVERNMENTS

The largest number of international job opportunities in the United States are found with various agencies of the Federal government. Approximately 140,000 Federal civilian employees work abroad. Another 500,000 U.S. military work in overseas U.S. installations.

But these numbers represent less than half of all government employees working in international affairs. The majority of international-related government jobs are based in the United States. These jobs either provide support for agency field operations or they direct international operations from U.S.-based offices. Each agency has some international interest and staff themselves accordingly. At the same time, since many state and local governments are involved in international affairs, they too need international staff expertise.

In this chapter we outline the basics for locating international opportunities with various government agencies at all levels. While many of the jobs are based in the United States and require occasional travel abroad, many other international-al jobs require residence in foreign countries and rotation from one field site to another as well as between field and headquarter offices. For example, the U.S. Information Agency (USIA) has nearly 8,200 employees of whom 3,600 work in the U.S. They provide support for field operations consisting of 4,200 foreign nationals hired by USIA.

For an detailed examination of overseas opportunities with Federal agencies, we highly recommend Cantrell's and Modderno's newly released 430-page guide, *How To Find an Overseas Job With the U.S. Government*. It can be ordered directly from the publisher: send $28.95 (includes postage) to Worldwise Books, P.O. Box 3030, Oakton, VA 22124, or call 703/620-1972 for information.

FEDERAL EXECUTIVE AGENCIES

The Federal government hires all types of individuals for international positions, ranging from highly skilled intelligence specialists to clerk-typists. Most positions deal with international politics, economics, administrative, commercial, and information affairs as well as all support services required to perform the international activities.

The distinction between what is an international or a non-international job is not always clear. For example, one may be employed as a Department of State librarian in charge of maintaining an excellent international resource collection. While this position involves a great deal of knowledge and skill concerning international affairs, it does not involve overseas travel nor the use of foreign languages. Yet, the position could lead to other international positions requiring overseas travel and the use of foreign languages.

For our purposes, we consider any position which to some degree involves international affairs to be an international position. This broad definition includes Foreign Service Officers, Peace Corps volunteers and staff, U.S. Agency for International Development employees, as well as thousands of individuals in other agencies promoting U.S. foreign, military, economic, and social goals in both policy and support staff positions at the Federal, state, and local levels. Some agencies and positions are primarily oriented toward foreign policy whereas others are mainly concerned with promoting domestic policies through the use of international resources.

Executive Office of the President

The Executive Office of the President, while employing only 1,500 individuals, has a few international positions. The major offices with such positions include:

- Council of Economic Advisors
- National Security Council
- Office of Management and Budget
- Office of Science and Technology Policy
- Office of the United States Trade Representative
- White House Office

Executive Departments

Most international jobs in the Federal government are found among the following executive departments:

- **Department of Agriculture**
  - Foreign Agricultural Service
  - Office of International Cooperation and Development
  - Economics and Statistics Service (International Economic Division)
  - Agricultural Market Service
  - Animal and Plant Health Inspection Service
  - Forest Service (International Forestry Staff)
  - Office of Transportation
  - Science and Education Administration
  - World Food and Agricultural Outlook and Situation Board
- **Department of Commerce**
  - International Trade Administration
  - Foreign Commercial Service
  - Bureau of the Census
  - National Oceanic and Atmospheric Administration
  - Bureau of Economic Analysis
  - United States Travel Service
  - Maritime Administration
  - National Bureau of Standards
  - National Telecommunications and Information Administration
  - Office of Products Standards Policy
  - Patent and Trademark Office
- **Department of Defense and Related Agencies**
  - Office of the Assistant Secretary for International Security Affairs
  - Office of the Undersecretary of Defense for Research and Engineering
  - Army Materiel Development and Readiness Command
  - Planning and Policy Directorate of the Organization of the Joint Chiefs of Staff
  - Office of the Secretary of Defense
    NOTE: Department of Defense maintains a special service to assist individuals with overseas employment: Department of Defense Automated Overseas Employment Referral Program (DOD AOEFP)
  - Defense Advanced Research Projects Agency
  - Defense Intelligence Agency
  - Defense Security Assistance Agency
  - Department of Defense Dependents Schools
  - National Security Agency/Central Security Service
- **Department of Education**
  - Office of International Education
  - Office of the Administrator of Education for Overseas Dependents
- **Department of Energy**
  - Office of International Energy Affairs

- Assistant Secretary for Defense Programs
- Assistant Secretary for Policy and Evaluation
- Economic Regulatory Administration
- Energy Information Administration
- Office of Energy Research
- **Department of Health and Human Services**
  - Office of International Health
  - Social Security Administration (Division of International
  - Operations and Office of International Policy)
  - National Institutes of Health (Fogarty International Center)
  - National Center for Health Statistics
    —Alcohol, Drug Abuse, and Mental Health Administration
    —Center for Disease Control
- **Department of Interior**
  - Office of Territorial and International Affairs
  - Bureau of Mines
  - U.S.Geological Survey
  - Bureau of Land Management
  - Ocean Mining Administration
  - U.S. Fish and Wildlife Service
  - National Park Service
  - Water and Power Resources Service
- **Department of Justice and Related Agencies**
  - Department of Justice
    —Antitrust Division
    —Civil Division
    —Criminal Division
    —Office of the Deputy Attorney General
    —Office of Intelligence Policy Review
    —Foreign Claims Settlement Commission of the United States
  - Drug Enforcement Administration (DEA)
    —Office of Intelligence
  - Federal Bureau of Investigation (FBI)
  - Immigration and Naturalization Service (INS)
- **Department of Labor**
  - Bureau of International Labor Affairs
  - Bureau of Labor Statistics
- **Department of State**
  - U.S. Foreign Service
  - All other offices
- **Department of Transportation**
  - Office of International Policy and Programs
  - Federal Aviation Administration (Office of International Aviation Affairs)
  - Federal Highway Administration

- Saint Lawrence Seaway Development Corporation
- U.S. Coast Guard (Office of Public and International Affairs)
■ **Department of Treasury**
  - Office of the Assistant Secretary for International Affairs
  - United States Customs Service
  - Office of International Tax Affairs
  - International Revenue Service (Office of International Operations; Foreign Tax Assistance Staff)
  - Office of the Comptroller of the Currency

Independent Agencies

Several independent agencies also are involved in international affairs. The major ones include:

■ **Central Intelligence Agency**
■ **Civil Aeronautics Board**
  - Bureau of International Affairs
■ **Consumer Product Safety Commission**
  - Office of International Affairs
■ **Environmental Protection Agency**
  - Office of International Activities
■ **Export-Import Bank of the United States**
■ **Federal Communications Commission**
  - Office of Science and Technology (International Staff)
  - Common Carrier Bureau (International Conference Staff)
  - International Facilities Office
■ **Federal Maritime Commission**
■ **Federal Reserve System**
  - Division of International Finance
  - Division of Banking Supervision and Regulation
  - Federal Open Market Committee
■ **General Services Administration**
  - National Archives and Records Service
■ **Inter-American Foundation**
■ **National Aeronautics and Space Administration**
  - Office of International Affairs
■ **National Science Foundation**
  - Division of International Programs
■ **Nuclear Regulatory Commission**
  - Office of International Programs
■ **Panama Canal Commission**
■ **Peace Corps**

- **Securities and Exchange Commission**
  - Corporate Finance Division
  - Enforcement Division
  - Market Regulation Division
- **Smithsonian Institution**
  - Office of International Activities
  - Office of Fellowships and Grants
  - Office of Museum Programs
  - International Exchange Service
  - Traveling Exhibition Service
  - Woodrow Wilson International Center for Scholars
- **U.S. Institute of Peace**
- **U.S. Arms Control and Disarmament Agency**
- **U.S. Information Agency**
- **U.S. International Development Cooperation Agency**
  - Agency for International Development
  - Overseas Private Investment Corporation
- **U.S. International Trade Commission**
- **U.S. Postal Service**
  - Office of International Postal Affairs

Commissions, Committees, Advisory Groups

A final group of Federal executive employers which hire international specialists are the various commissions, committees, and advisory groups established by the president or congress. Most of these groups are attached to particular departments or agencies. Some are permanent whereas others function for only one or two years. Examples of such groups include:

- Commission on the Ukraine Famine
- Committee for the Implementation of Textile Agreements
- Committee on Foreign Investment in the United States
  Japan-United States Friendship Commission
- National Advisory Council on International Monetary
  and Financial Policies
- U.S. National Commission for UNESCO (Department of State)

Your best strategy for getting a job with these groups is to monitor their formation through the *Congressional Record* and the *Federal Register*. As soon as you learn of the impending formation of a group, contact the individuals responsible for establishing the group. Schedule an appointment for an informational interview, and leave a copy of your resume with the individual you interviewed.

Overseas Staffs and Recruitment

Most executive agencies do not maintain overseas staffs. Agencies with overseas staffs sometimes recruit individuals locally, normally among staff spouses and talented expatriates, and through central personnel offices in Washington, DC. Overall, however, most recruitment for international jobs with Federal agencies is done in the United States. Indeed, given the Washington bias of Federal agencies, it is difficult to find employment with agencies if you are abroad, even though a vacancy is available for which you are highly qualified. Most agencies prefer recruiting individuals in the States and then transferring them to field sites.

The major agencies maintaining overseas staffs and conducting some in-country recruitment are:

- Department of Defense
- Department of State
- Peace Corps
- U.S. Agency for International Development
- U.S. Information Agency

Hiring Systems and Job Search Strategies

Hiring procedures and practices vary among executive agencies. Several agencies, for example, are exempted from the competitive service whereas others follow the Office of Personnel Management's (OPM) rules and regulations. Exempted services have their own hiring procedures. The **Department of State**, for example, follows the European pattern of a career and rank personnel service. Responsible for promoting U.S. foreign policy, the Foreign Service employs over 9,000 people as Foreign Service Officers and Specialists. Special recruitment and selection procedures define entry into the Foreign Service. Each December approximately 12,000 individuals sit for the written Foreign Service examination to gain entry into the Department of State (Foreign Service Officers), the U.S. Information Agency (Foreign Service Information Officers), and Department of Commerce (Foreign Service Commercial Officers).

Once selected, most Foreign Service Officers spend the rest of their career in the Foreign Service. Their "tour" involves being transferred to several of the 230 embassies and consulates the U.S. maintains throughout the world as well as moves from one type of position to another. Rather than being hired as specialists for a particular position, they are hired as international specialists who move through the ranks. The "ranks" consist of many positions requiring different types of skills and knowledge.

The **U.S. Agency for International Development** (USAID) is structured similarly to the Foreign Service. In fact, the majority of USAID positions are designated as Foreign Service positions. At the same time, nearly 40 percent of

USAID positions are civilian (GS positions and thus follow OPM procedures). USAID maintains two personnel offices—a civilian office and a Foreign Service office—which are located in Rosslyn, Virginia. If you want to work for USAID, you must decide which personnel system you want to enter. If your choice is Foreign Service, then your career will take a different pattern from that of the civilian-based civil service.

The **Peace Corps** is a good example of another type of personnel system. Peace Corps is one of the most unique agencies created in the Federal government. In many respects its volunteers are the "real" international workers. They learn local languages and work in the field with foreign counterparts. No other Federal employees work to the same extent at the field level and literally get their hands dirty in international development work. However, entry into the Peace Corps is extremely competitive today. Each year Peace Corps receives more than 13,500 applications for fewer than 3,500 volunteer positions. Once selected, the typical Peace Corps tour is two years; some volunteers extend an additional year. Altogether, there are approximately 6,000 volunteers working in 61 countries throughout the Third World.

Most Peace Corps staff positions are largely limited to individuals with Peace Corps volunteer experience. In addition, staff positions have a built-in time limit. To discourage the growth of a traditional, conservative, and entrenched bureaucracy, Congress placed a statutory time limit on employment with Peace Corps: staff members cannot work more than five consecutive years with the Agency. Consequently, Peace Corps members are hired for two and one-half year tours, which may be extended to a second tour for a total of five years of service. After the second tour, they must leave the Agency. Many staff members look for employment with other Federal agencies doing international development work. Indeed, the Department of State alone has 1,000 former Peace Corps volunteers and staff members on its staff. USAID has become one of the major recruiters and employers of former Peace Corps employees.

While some executive agencies may follow other recruitment patterns, most executive departments adhere to the competitive civil service system associated with the Office of Personnel Management. Positions are classified and announced, and candidates submit a formal application, the Standard Form 171 (SF-171), and supporting documents to agency personnel offices.

While you may use your resume in networking with agencies, the SF-171 is the critical document for opening the doors of agencies. Similar to writing a resume, the SF-171 needs to be written so it clearly communicates your qualifications to agency personnel. And like writing a resume, writing an outstanding SF-171 is an art which follows certain principles of effective writing for Federal agencies.

Employment with offices in the Executive Office of the President, independent agencies, committees, and commissions follow more independent hiring patterns. Most of these agencies and offices have their own internal hiring procedures. Therefore, it is best to directly contact their personnel offices to learn about vacancy announcements and the best procedures for applying for particular positions.

Knowing which Federal agencies perform international functions and hire international specialists is only the first of many steps involved in getting a Federal job with such agencies. You must go far beyond just names, addresses, and phone numbers. Above all, you will need a particular set of job search skills adapted to the Federal hiring process.

Keep in mind that both formal and informal hiring systems operate in the case of most Federal agencies. The formal system involves vacancy announcements and the submission of applications for specific positions. The informal system involves networking for information, advice, and referrals that hopefully lead to uncovering job vacancies as well as possibly being "sponsored" for positions or having positions "wired" around your qualifications. Your research and networking activities as outlined in Chapters Five and Seven will provide you with the necessary knowledge and contacts to gain entry into these agencies.

Useful Resources

You will find numerous resources available to help you navigate through what is often a confusing Federal government hiring process. These range from general job search books and manuals for completing and SF-171 to directories of agencies and biweekly listings of job vacancy announcements which include international jobs.

While most hiring decisions are decentralized to agencies, you still must follow the formal Federal hiring procedures outlined by OPM. These procedures —as well as the development and use of the SF-171 and informal job search strategies appropriate for Federal agencies—are outlined in our other three public employment books:

Find a Federal Job Fast!, Ron and Caryl Krannich (Woodbridge, VA: Impact Publications, 1992).

Almanac of American Government Jobs and Careers, Ron and Caryl Krannich (Woodbridge, VA Impact Publications, 1991).

The Complete Guide To Public Employment, Ron and Caryl Krannich (Woodbridge, VA: Impact Publications, 1990).

Two other books primarily examine the formal application process involved in finding a Federal job:

How To Get a Federal Job, David Waelde (Washington, DC: FEDHELP, 1989).

> *How To Get a Federal Job*, Krandall Kraus (New York: Facts on File, 1986).

For detailed information on how to create an effective SF-171, consult the following workbooks:

> *The Right SF-171 Writer,* Ron and Caryl Krannich (Manassas Park, VA: Impact Publications, 1993).

> *The 171 Reference Book*, Patricia B. Wood (Timonium, MD: Workbooks, Inc., 1991)

> *SF 171*, Pauline J. White (New York: Arco, 1989).

While many of these resources are difficult to find in bookstores and libraries, most of them are available through Impact Publications. Order information is available at the end of this book.

Your best sources of information for conducting research on Federal agencies with international positions will be several international job books and directories that primarily describe different types of Federal agencies. The key international job books include:

> *How To Find an Overseas Job With the U.S. Government*, Will Cantrell and Francine Modderno (Oakton, VA: Worldwise Books, 1992).

> *The Almanac of International Jobs and Careers*, Ron and Caryl Krannich (Woodbridge, VA: Impact Publications, 1990)

> *International Jobs*, Eric Kocher (Reading, MA: Addison-Wesley, 1989).

> *Careers In International Affairs* (Washington, DC: School of Foreign Service, Georgetown University, 1991).

> *Guide To Careers In World Affairs* (New York: Foreign Policy Association, 1993).

Several annual and biannual directories are also available for researching different Federal agencies:

> *The United States Government Manual* (Washington, DC: U.S. Government Printing Office, annual).

Federal Yellow Book (Washington, DC: Monitor Publishing Co., annual).

Washington Information Directory (Washington, DC: Congressional Quarterly, Inc., annual).

Federal Executive Directory (Washington, DC: Carroll Publishing Co., annual).

Federal Personnel Office Directory (Washington, DC: Federal Reports, annual).

Each of these books and directories provides names, addresses, and telephone numbers for locating the right offices and individuals you should contact for employment information.

One useful guide also provides information on where to find job vacancy resources, such as newspapers, magazines, newsletters, and job listing services: *The Government Job Finder*, Daniel Lauber (River Forest, IL: Planning/ Communications, 1992).

If you are interested in job vacancy announcements with the Federal government, two private firms publish biweekly listings of such announcements. Many of their listings include international jobs:

Federal Career Opportunities (Vienna, VA: Federal Research Service).

Federal Jobs Digest (Scarborough, NY: Break Through Publications).

Several of these and other useful government resources are available through Impact Publications.

CONGRESS

Both Congress and legislative agencies hire a variety of international specialists. Within Congress, international positions are found with congressional committee staffs and personal staffs of senators and representatives.

Committee Staffs

International positions on committee staffs are limited in number and are primarily found on the two most important committees dealing with international issues:

- Senate Foreign Relations Committee
- House Foreign Affairs Committee

Other committees and subcommittees in the House of Representatives also deal with international matters and thus hire individuals with some international background. The relevant committees include:

- Agriculture Committee
- Appropriations Committee
- Armed Services Committee
- Banking, Finance, and Urban Affairs Committee
- Energy and Commerce Committee
- Government Operations Committee
- Science and Technology Committee
- Ways and Means Committee

On the Senate side, several committees deal with similar international issues:

- Agriculture and Forestry Committee
- Appropriations Committee
- Armed Services Committee
- Banking, Housing, and Urban Affairs Committee Commerce Committee
- Finance Committee
- Government Affairs Committee

Both the House and Senate have various joint committees which also offer international employment opportunities. The major such committees include the Joint Economic Committee and the Joint Committee on Taxation.

Personal Staffs

Not all Senators and Representatives hire international specialists on their personal staffs. Those that do usually have major responsibilities on assigned committees and subcommittees which deal with international issues. Therefore, you need to first identify who sits on which international committee, and then contact their staffs for information on international positions. Most of these staff positions will involve conducting research, writing reports, and drafting legislation on committee-related matters.

Contact information on the various congressional committees and personal staffs can be found in *Congressional Yellow Book*, *Congressional Directory*, *Congressional Staffing Directory*, and *The American Almanac of Politics*. Follow the same strategies for finding an international job on these staffs as you would for finding any type of staff position in Congress. These strategies are detailed in our books on public employment, *Find a Federal Job Fast!* and *The Complete Guide To Public Employment.*

Legislative Agencies

Most legislative agencies also have international interests and thus hire international specialists. The major agencies and offices include:

- **Congressional Budget Office**
  - National Security and International Affairs Division
- **General Accounting Office**
  - International Division
- **Library of Congress**
  - Congressional Research Service
  - Office of Research Services (Office of the Director for Area Studies)
- **Office of Technology Assessment**

The *Directory of Federal Executives* provides the names and telephone numbers of key individuals to contact in each of these legislative agencies and offices.

STATE AND LOCAL GOVERNMENTS

International opportunities with state and local governments are both relatively unknown and widely overlooked among most international specialists. This is in part due to the expectation that only the Federal government engages in foreign policy and international affairs.

During the past two decades, state and city governments have increasingly become involved in international affairs. Many have their own foreign policies involving:

- Trade promotion
- Tourism
- Local economic development
- Immigration
- International shipping

Florida, for example, maintains a state tourism agency which attempts to promote travel to Florida among European tourists. Virginia Beach maintains sister city relationships and promotes foreign industrial investment in the city through their Department of Economic Development. In certain areas, regional economic development authorities, tourism boards, and port authorities perform international functions for several units of government.

State and local governments offer unique international opportunities. They combine local economic issues with international development activities. For individuals who want to be involved in international affairs but wish to avoid many of the negative aspects of international careers—such as living abroad and transfers—these positions may be ideal.

Finding an international job with state and local governments requires a great deal of research and initiative on your part. No directories or books outline state and local agencies with opportunities in international affairs. Hence, your best approach will be to identify which city or state governments you would like to work with and then research the organizations to find the offices involved in international affairs. Both the national and local branches of the World Affairs Council may be helpful in uncovering international positions with these governmental units.

Chapter Eleven

INTERNATIONAL ORGANIZATIONS

Numerous international organizations offer job opportunities for talented international specialists. Most of these organizations are either directly tied to the United Nations or function as regional military, political, economic, and social organizations. In most cases the United States is involved as a major bilateral or multilateral partner.

Since historically the United States has played a major role in developing international organizations and continues as a major funding source, many Americans have been employed with these groups. Yet, American participation in the day-to-day administration of international organizations is normally limited by specific hiring quotas imposed on all member nations related to population and financial contribution criteria. As a result, only certain positions requiring specific expertise will be open to American job seekers. In this sense, employment with many international organizations is very political in terms of both hiring for a position and retaining a job in competition with eager job seekers from the United States and other countries.

In this chapter we provide a brief overview of employment alternatives with numerous international organizations. Each organization has its own hiring system which you must understand in order to be effective in landing a job. Most important of all, each organization has a particular political environment which may or may not meet your criteria for a rewarding international job or career.

THE UNITED NATIONS

The United Nations is the largest single employer of international specialists. Its bureaucracy consists of nearly 50,000 individuals who work in over 600 duty stations throughout the world. Less than 10 percent of the UN civil servants are Americans.

The United Nations consists of a central organization and a loose collection of relatively autonomous specialized agencies and organizations. Given both the centralized and decentralized nature of the United Nations, all specialized agencies and related organizations recruit their own personnel. The United Nations, in effect, consists of more than 25 different hiring systems.

Organizations

The United Nations consists of six major organizational units and numerous specialized and autonomous agencies, standing committees, commissions, and other subsidiary bodies. The six principal organs are the:

- General Assembly
- Security Council
- Economic and Social Council
- Trusteeship Council
- International Court of Justice
- Secretariat

While job opportunities are available with all of these organs, the most numerous jobs are found with the Economic and Social Council and the UN Secretariat.

The **Economic and Social Council** is under the General Assembly. It coordinates the economic and social work of the United Nations and numerous specialized agencies, standing committees, commissions, and related organizations. The work of the Council involves international development, world trade, industrialization, natural resources, human rights, status of women, population, social welfare, science and technology, crime prevention, and other social and economic issues.

The Economic and Social Council is divided into a headquarters staff in New York City and five regional economic commissions:

- Economic Commission for Africa (Addis Ababa)
- Economic and Social Commission for Asia and the Pacific (Bangkok)
- Economic Commission for Europe (Geneva)
- Economic Commission for Latin America and the Caribbean (Santiago)
- Economic Commission for Western Asia (Baghdad)

Each Commission maintains a large staff of specialists. Furthermore, they promote the work of several standing committees and commissions which also have their own staffs. The Committee for Co-Ordination of Investigations of the Lower Mekong Basin (Mekong Committee), for example, was established in 1957. Under the Economic and Social Commission for Asia and the Pacific (ESCAP) and headquartered in Bangkok, this Committee has provided job opportunities for numerous consultants and full-time professionals. Indeed, some individuals have made a life-long career of working with the Mekong Committee.

Specialized or intergovernmental agencies are autonomous organizations linked to the United Nations by special intergovernmental agreements. In addition, they have their own membership, budgets, personnel systems, legislative and executive bodies, and secretariats. The International Atomic Energy Agency (IAEA), for example, consists of 35 member nations. It is administered by a professional staff of 619 and a general services staff of 941 which is headquartered in Vienna, Austria. The Economic and Social Council coordinates the work of these organizations with the United Nations as well as with each other. Altogether, there are 19 specialized agencies:

- Food and Agriculture Organization (FAO—Rome)
- General Agreement on Tariffs and Trade (GATT—Geneva)
- International Atomic Energy Agency (IAEA—Vienna)
- International Bank for Reconstruction and Development (IBRD or World Bank—Washington, DC)
- International Civil Aviation Organization (ICAO—Montreal)
- International Development Association (IDA—Washington, DC)
- International Finance Corporation (IFC—Washington, DC)
- International Fund for Agricultural Development (IFAD—Rome)
- International Labour Organization (ILO—Geneva)
- International Maritime Organization (IMO—London)
- International Monetary Fund (IMF—Washington, DC)
- International Telecommunication Union (ITU—Geneva)
- Multilateral Investment Guarantee Agency (MIGA—Washington, DC)
- U.N. Educational, Scientific and Cultural Organization (UNESCO—Paris)
- U.N. Industrial Development Organization (UNIDO—Vienna)
- Universal Postal Union (UPU—Berne, Switzerland)
- World Health Organization (WHO—Geneva)
- World Intellectual Property Organization (WIPO—Geneva)
- World Meteorological Organization (WMO—Geneva)

Several other major organizations also are attached to the Economic and Social Council as well as the Secretariat. These consist of:

- International Sea-Bed Authority (New York)
- Office of the United Nations Disaster Relief Co-Ordinator (UNDRO—Geneva)
- U.N. Centre for Human Settlements (HABITAT—Nairobi)
- U.N. Children's Fund (UNICEF—Geneva)
- U.N. Conference on Trade and Development (UNCTAD—New York)
- U.N. Development Programme (UNDP—New York)
- U.N. Environment Programme (UNEP—Nairobi)
- U.N. High Commissioner for Refugees (UNHCR—Geneva)
- U.N. Observer Missions and Peacekeeping Forces (New York)
- U.N. Population Fund (UNPF—New York)
- U.N. Relief and Works Agency for Palestine Refugees in the Near East (UNRWA—Vienna)
- World Food Council (WFC—Rome)
- World Food Programme (WFP—Rome)

The UN Secretariat employs nearly 3,000 international civil servants from 130 countries. Most are stationed at the United Nations headquarters in New York City. The Secretariat is the central "bureaucracy" in charge of carrying out the day-to-day work of the United Nations.

The largest UN agencies—those employing at least 1,500 individuals—consist of the following:

- Food and Agriculture Organization
- World Health Organization
- United Nations Development Program
- World Bank
- UNESCO
- International Labor Organization
- UNICEF
- International Monetary Fund

The United States is especially involved in the following United Nations organizations which are headquartered in various cities throughout the world:

- Food and Agricultural Organization (Rome)
- International Atomic Energy Agency (Vienna)
- International Bank for Reconstruction and Development or World Bank (Washington, DC)
- International Civil Aviation Organization (Montreal)
- International Finance Corporation (Washington, DC)
- International Monetary Fund (Washington, DC)
- International Telecommunication Union (Geneva)
- Universal Postal Union (Bern, Switzerland)

- World Health Organization (Geneva)
- World Meteorological Organization (Geneva)

Employment Alternatives

The United Nations and related specialized agencies and organizations hire all types of professionals and general service staff as full-time, permanent staff, technical assistance experts, and consultants. Major positions include engineers, lawyers, accountants, doctors, lawyers, researchers, translators, interpreters, demographers, guides, and typists. The UN also hires technical assistance experts who are then loaned to Third World governments. Except for general service staff positions, most UN jobs require highly educated and experienced professionals.

Many United Nations jobs are exciting. They involve traveling to interesting places, working with highly intelligent and competent professionals, and dealing with important international problems and issues. At the same time, many UN offices have acquired characteristics of Third World and Byzantine bureaucracies. They spend much of their time in meetings, which produce little or nothing except for a great deal of memos and reports requiring further meetings. Bureaucratic intrigue, power struggles, and maneuvers to take over others' positions characterize the daily work of some UN offices.

Competition for UN positions is keen for several reasons. UN jobs pay extremely well compared to comparable jobs in the U.S. Federal government or in any national government. Indeed, competition is most keen and the personnel process is most political among professionals from Third World countries—especially those from India, Pakistan, and Bangladesh—who cannot find comparable professions and pay elsewhere. For many of them, working for the United Nations, specialized agencies, or related organizations is extremely important to financing their lifestyles which frequently include plush homes, servants, private schools, and one or two Mercedes.

Qualifications and Positions

The United Nations describes its "typical recruit" as a 36-year old economist who has an advanced degree and is fluent in two of the official languages of the UN—Arabic, Chinese, English, French, Russian, or Spanish. For professional and technical positions, the United Nations places special emphasis on formal educational qualifications—the higher your degree the better—international experience, and language competency. Without these three in combination, you may be wasting your time applying for many UN positions. Translators or interpreters, of course, must demonstrate their competency by taking a qualifying examination.

The United Nations hires individuals for all types of positions. The major categories include the following positions: Administrative, Public Information,

Social Welfare, Demography and Population, Information Systems and Computers, Legal, Teachers, Political Affairs, Telecommunications, Economics, and Translators and Interpreters. The UN also offers several other types of positions for individuals interested in gaining some experience with the international organization: Summer Employment, UN Guides, Intern Programs, and UN Volunteers. Clerical and secretarial personnel are normally recruited from local residents where particular UN offices are located. Since the United States withdrew support from UNESCO, there are few job opportunities for Americans, especially teachers, in this agency.

Hiring Practices

The United Nations hires individuals for positions within the secretariats as well as its technical assistance programs. While many positions are full-time professional positions complete with generous salaries and retirement benefits, many other positions are short-term technical assistance positions that require the expertise of experts and consultants. The bias again is for individuals with post-graduate degrees, extensive international experience, and appropriate language competency. The United Nations in general hires few inexperienced people for entry-level positions, although politics within the United Nations is not adverse to hiring well connected individuals who appear to lack many of the so-called "prerequisite" educational, technical, experience, and language qualifications.

The hiring process is largely decentralized within the United Nations and among the specialized agencies and related organizations. Therefore, you must directly contact each agency for job vacancy information as well as network with your resume by conducting informational interviews. If, for example, you are interested in working for the UN Secretariat in New York City, contact the following offices for information on job vacancies:

United Nations
Recruitment Programs Section
Office of Personnel Services
New York, NY 10017

Most agencies and organizations will have a personnel office which issues job vacancy announcements. Bulletin boards outside personnel offices or cafeterias often include the latest vacancy announcements.

For technical assistance positions, you should contact the following office for information:

Technical Assistance Recruitment Service
Department of Technical Cooperation
United Nations
New York, NY 10017

The U.S. Department of State provides a recruitment and job referral service for individuals interested in working for the UN, specialized agencies, and related organizations. The Bureau of International Organization Affairs identifies qualified Americans who are then referred for UN assignments. Most candidates should have specialized and advanced academic degrees and several years of recent international experience. The categories of positions covered include: public information personnel; computer programmers; military personnel; administrative posts; legal posts; translators; interpreters; summer employment; clerical personnel; UN guides; intern programs; political affairs posts; telecommunication posts; economists; and UN volunteers. The Bureau maintains a computerized roster of qualified professional candidates whose backgrounds are matched against the qualifications specified in UN vacancy announcements. To get on this roster and be referred, send a detailed resume to:

> Office of UN Employment Information Assistance
> IO/EA, Rm. 3536
> Department of State
> Washington, DC 20520-6319
> Tel. 202/647-3396

You can write or call this office for information on the UN and the referral system. Ask for their *"Fact Sheet"* on employment with international organizations and "United Nations People." The *"Fact Sheet"* includes names and addresses of various UN agencies to which you can apply directly for vacancies. It also includes a useful list of U.S. counterpart agencies that work with the United Nations. These include:

- FAO: Foreign Agriculture Service (Department of Agriculture)

- IAEA: Office of International Affairs (Department of Energy)

- ICAO: Office of International Organization Aviation Affairs (Federal Aviation Administration)

- UPU: International Postal Affairs (U.S. Postal Service)

- WHO: Office of International Health (Public Health Service, Department of Health and Human Services)

- WMO: Office of International Affairs (National Oceanic and Atmospheric Administration)

The office's *"Fact Sheet"* also includes current contact information on some of the most popular international financial institutions as well as regional and Inter-

American organizations international job hunters seek information on: Inter-American Development Bank, International Monetary Fund, World Bank, Organization for Economic Cooperation and Development, and the Organization of American States.

Consequently, you may want to get on the State Department roster as well as apply directly to UN agencies and offices for positions.

The United Nations uses a special application form—the UN Personal History Form P-11 (UN P-11)—which is similar to the U.S. Federal government's SF-171. Be sure to complete this form and submit it along with a targeted resume for most UN positions.

Your most effective job search strategy will be to target particular agencies and organizations. Personnel offices will provide vacancy announcements and information on the formal hiring process, but you must make contact with the hiring personnel in the operating units. Do informational interviewing so you can uncover vacancies for which you may qualify. You will want to learn about the political environment of offices in order to avoid both wasting your time on positions which are wired and landing what may quickly become a terrible job!

Job Outlook

Many UN jobs are considered "plum" international jobs for those interested in pursuing an international career. This is one of very few organizations that enable one to pursue an international career up a single organizational hierarchy. While the climb up the hierarchy is different from the climb up any other organizational hierarchy—especially given political and nationality considerations in assignments and promotions—the UN can be a very satisfying and rewarding career for many international specialists.

However, the job outlook within the UN is not great these days. The United States, as well as many other nations, has increasingly put pressure on the United Nations to cut costs and implement internal administrative reforms. These pressures translate into more cost conscious personnel practices and leaner hiring for the decade ahead. Indeed, UNESCO and the World Bank have experienced major personnel cuts during the past five years. Cutbacks in other UN agencies are likely to continue over the next five years. As a result, competition for UN positions is very keen as individuals already working in the United Nations are the first to apply for vacancies. Given their inside "connections" and UN experience, they are in the best position to be "qualified" for such vacancies. Increasingly outsiders will have difficulty breaking into full-time professional UN positions. Part-time consulting positions, however, will continue to be a major avenue to other positions within the United Nations.

The long-term job outlook with the United Nations should be good to excellent. With the ending of the Cold War, the United Nations is likely to play an even greater role in international affairs. The United States and many other countries will place greater reliance on multilateral rather than bilateral arrangements for resolving international conflicts and promoting economic development. The United Nations will increasingly become the lead multilateral institution in international affairs. Employment prospects with the UN should increase accordingly.

MULTILATERAL AND BILATERAL ORGANIZATIONS

In addition to the United Nations, the United States participates in several other multilateral organizations which also provide job opportunities for enterprising job seekers. Most of these organizations are designed to promote regional security and economic and social development. The major multilateral organizations and corresponding headquarter locations are:

- African Development Bank (Abidjan, Ivory Coast)
- Asian Development Bank (Manila)
- Inter-American Defense Board (Washington, DC)
- Inter-American Development Bank (Washington, DC)
- Intergovernmental Committee for Migration (Geneva)
- International Finance Corporation (Washington, DC)
- International Telecommunication Union (Geneva)
- Organization of American States (Washington, DC)
- Organization for Economic Cooperation and Development (Paris)
- Pan American Health Organization (Washington, DC)
- South Pacific Commission (Noumea, New Caledonia)

The United States is also a member of several regional organizations as well as numerous subsidiary commissions, councils, and committees. Among its many affiliations are the:

- Colombo Plan for Cooperative Economic and Social Development in Asia and the Pacific
- Inter-American Indian Institute
- Inter-American Institute for Cooperation on Agriculture
- Inter-American Tropical Tuna Commission
- International Coffee Organization
- International Institute of Cotton
- International Sugar Organizations
- International Wheat Council
- Interparliamentary Union
- North Atlantic Ice Patrol
- North Atlantic Treaty Organization (NATO)
- North Atlantic Assembly
- Organization for Economic Cooperation and Development

- Pan American Health Organizations
- West African Rice Development Association
- World Tourism Organization

Other international organizations that hire international specialists include:

- Andean Group
- ANZUS
- Arab Bank for Economic Development in Africa (BADEA)
- Arab Fund for Economic and Social Development (AFESD)
- Arab Monetary Fund
- Association of Southeast Asian Nations (ASEAN)
- Bank for International Settlements (BIS)
- Benelux Economic Union
- Caribbean Community and Common Market (CARICOM)
- Central American Common Market (CACM)
- The Commonwealth
- Communaute Economique de l'Afrique de l'Ouest (CEAO)
- Conseil de l'Entente
- Co-operation Council for the Arab States of the Gulf
- Council for Mutual Economic Assistance (CMEA)
- Council of Arab Economic Unity
- Council of Europe
- Economic Community of West African States (ECOWAS)
- The European Communities
- European Free Trade Association (EFTA)
- The Franc Zone
- Inter-American Development Bank (IDB)
- International Bank for Economic Co-operation (IBEC)
- International Investment Bank
- International Olympic Committee
- Islamic Development Bank
- Latin American Integration Association (ALADI)
- League of Arab States
- Nordic Council
- Nordic Council of Ministers
- North Atlantic Treaty Organization (NATO)
- Organization Commune Africaine et Mauricienne (OCAM)
- Organization for Economic Co-operation and Development (OECD)
  —International Energy Agency
  —OECD Nuclear Energy Agency (NEA)
- Organization of African Unity (OAU)
- Organization of Arab Petroleum Exporting Countries (OAPEC)
- OPEC Fund for International Development
- South Pacific Forum

—South Pacific Bureau for Economic Co-operation (SPEC)
- Southern African Development Co-ordination Conference (SADCC)
- Western European Union (WEU)

While the U.S. Department of State can provide information on jobs with some of these regional organizations, you must contact the organizations directly for detailed job information. Keep in mind that U.S. participation on the staffs of these organizations will be limited and, in some cases, nonexistent. Furthermore, most regional organizations hire highly educated, skilled, and experienced professionals. Expect the hiring processes to be somewhat political in most cases.

USEFUL RESOURCES

Before contacting individuals in the international organizations for informational interviews, you should collect basic data on the organizations. Three directories in particular will give you important descriptions and contact information on all of these organizations as well as thousands of additional international organizations. Most libraries have the following annual directories for researching these organizations:

- *Yearbook of the United Nations*
- *Europa Year Book*
- *Yearbook of International Organizations*

The *Yearbook of the United Nations* provides detailed information on the operations of each UN agency. This invaluable directory is "must" reading for anyone interested in U.N. operations.

The *Europa Year Book* gives details on the United Nations as well as other political, economic, and commercial institutions throughout the world. This two-volume directory classifies international organizations into 21 categories:

- Agriculture, Food, Forestry, and Fisheries
- Aid and Development
- Arts and Culture
- Economics and Finance
- Education
- Government and Politics
- Industrial and Professional Relations
- Law
- Medicine and Health
- Posts and Telecommunications
- Press, Radio, and TV
- Religion
- Science

- Social Sciences and Humanities Studies
- Social Welfare
- Sports and Recreation
- Technology
- Tourism
- Trade and Industry
- Transport
- Youth and Students

The following types of information, for example, are found in the "Aid and Development" and "Government and Politics" sections of the *Europa Year Book*:

Committee for Co-ordination of Investigations of the Lower Mekong Basin: c/o ESCAP, United Nations Bldg, Rajadamnern Ave, Bangkok 10200, Thailand; aims to develop the resources of the lower Mekong basin, including hydroelectric power, irrigation, navigation, fisheries, and food production; contributions pledged by the end of 1983 amounted to US $520.5m., from member states, co-operating countries, and the UN and other international agencies. Mems: Laos, Thailand and Viet-Nam; 26 co-operating countries. Exec. Agent: Galal Magdi. International Union of Local Authorities: Wassenaarseweg 45, 2596 CG The Hague, Netherlands; tel. (070) 244032; f. 1913 to promote local government, improve local administration and encourage popular participation in public affairs. Functions include organization of conferences, seminars, and biennial international congress; servicing of specialized committees (municipal insurance, wholesale markets, European affairs, technical); research projects; comparative courses for local government officials, primarily from developing countries; development of intermunicipal relations to provide a link between local authorities of all countries; maintenance of a permanent office for the collection and distribution of information on municipal affairs. Members in over 65 countries. Pres. H. Koshnick (FRG); Sec.-Gen. J. G. Van Putten. Publs. *Local Government* (monthly newsletter), *Bibliographia* (bi-monthly), *Planning and Administration* (2 a year), preparatory reports and proceedings of conferences, reports of study groups.

The *Yearbook of International Organizations* compiles similar information on over 20,000 organizations. It provides annotated descriptions on all "international" organizations. These are organizations whose membership is comprised of at least 60 member nations. This directory includes all organs, specialized agencies, and related organizations of the United Nations; other international organizations; and individual country profiles of organizations. A typical entry in this directory appears as follows:

Society for International Development (SID) SG: Ponna Wignaraja, Palazzo Civilta del Lavoro, 1-00144 Roma, Italy. T. (06) 591 7897 - (06) 592 5506. C. SOCINTDEV Rome. Tx 612339 GBG for SID. North South Round Table Secretariat: Suite 501, 1717 Massachusetts Ave NW, Washington, DC 20036. USA. T. 234 8701 C. OVERCON United Nations Representative: Arthur Goldschmidt, 544 E. 86th Street, New York, NY 10028. Aims: Encourage, support and facilitate the creation at the local, national, regional, and international level of a sense of community among individuals and organizations committed to development; promote international dialogue, understanding and cooperation for social development and economic development that furthers the well-beings of all peoples and of a more equitable system of international relations; advance the science, processes and art of social and economic development through educational means including research, publication and discussion; provide support and services for national development constituencies which facilitate the foregoing. Structure: The form of the Chapter may vary from country to country, but each serves as an independent forum engaged in promoting the process of dialogue, and development education. International Secretariat in Rome since 1977, with a unit in Washington, DC. Languages: English, French, Spanish, Arabic. Staff: 7 full-time professional and administrative 2 part-time; 3 interns. Finance: Members' dues (income-rated). Contributions from private, public, international government, and non-governmental organizations.

You also should acquire annual reports from individual organizations. The World Bank, for example, publishes a comprehensive annual report on its organization, mission, and accomplishments which is required reading for anyone interested in working for this organization. In addition, the World Bank has a publications program which produces numerous special reports and books each year. You can get copies of these reports and publications by writing to or calling the Publications Division of the various organizations.

Most libraries also will have books about international organizations as well as magazines and journals published by different offices within the organization. Reference librarians can usually identify these publications for you.

Chapter Twelve

CONTRACTORS, CONSULTANTS, AND THE DEVELOPING WORLD

Although international organizations and U.S. government agencies have the greatest visibility in the international arena, numerous other organizations pursue public-related international interests. These peripheral institutions consist of consulting firms; trade and professional associations; nonprofit organizations; foundations; research organizations; and educational institutions. These organizations have international interests and interface in both the U.S. domestic and international arenas. This chapter as well as the next two chapters examine these organizations.

SPECIAL ROLES

Much of what gets done by government and international organizations is actually done through contractors and consultants. During the past 30 years more and more public services and programs have been contracted-out to private firms. The trend for the 1990s appears to be in the direction of even greater use of international consultants and contractors.

Consultants and contractors play important roles in providing services to government and business. They use consultants and contractors for several reasons:

- They require specialized information not available through their present staffs.

- They need special services and products only available from contractors and consultants.

- It is often more cost-effective to contract-out services than to increase the number of agency personnel to provide the services in-house.

- Many services are short-term and thus can be most quickly and effectively performed by outside consultants and contractors.

At the state and local government levels, contractors may provide sanitation services, road construction, health care, and building construction and maintenance. At the Federal level these firms run a variety of Federal programs, conduct numerous studies, and regularly supply agencies with every conceivable type of durable and nondurable goods from pencil sharpeners to submarines. At the international level, contractors and consultants are involved in building and maintaining U.S. facilities abroad, implementing the U.S. foreign aid program, and providing information on international developments.

> *Much of the work of government involves obligating funds and administering contracts rather than providing direct government services.*

Almost every job in the private sector will be performed in government. Ironically, these government jobs are often performed by private firms on contract with government agencies. Therefore, much of the work of government employees involves obligating funds and administering contracts rather than providing direct government services.

Contractor services are performed at the contractor's or agency's site. In many cases, an agency will provide office space for a contractor's staff which then performs services in offices adjacent to agency personnel. The extreme example of this type of relationship is found in the U.S. Department of Energy where over 80 percent of its personnel are actually private contractors.

THE PROCUREMENT PROCESS

The work of contractors and consultants centers around the **procurement process**. Procurement is the process by which government acquires goods and services. Well defined rules and regulations govern the process by which agencies can contract-out various services.

The Federal government strictly regulates the procurement process through a set of general regulations:

- Federal Acquisition Regulations (FAR)

- Competition in Contracting Act of 1984 (CICA)

In addition, each agency develops more detailed regulations based upon each section of the FAR and in line with the CICA. Altogether, over $400 billion a year flows from the Federal government to the private sector through this process.

One major result of the Federal procurement process has been to create competition among consulting and contracting firms. For example, all goods and services amounting to $25,000 or more must be procured through competitive bidding or negotiation processes. This normally takes the form of sealed bids for equipment or negotiations with agency personnel for services. Once a procurement need is identified and defined by agency personnel, contractors are identified and the procurement process follows specific rules and procedures. If a service is for less than $25,000, contracting officials must contact at least three firms for competitive bids. If the amount for small purchases is more than $25,000, then the officials must issue a Request for Proposal (RFP). An announcement must be published in the *Commerce Business Daily (CBD)* for at least 30 days. During that time firms request copies of the solicitation which outlines the Statement of Work and evaluation criteria for judging proposals. Firms normally have 30 days to develop and submit detailed proposals. Once proposals are received and reviewed by contracting officers and technical personnel, an award is made to the firm receiving the highest evaluation on both technical and cost criteria. This may take anywhere from one to three months after the closing date for submitting proposals.

While all Federal agencies are supposed to follow these rules for ensuring competition, informal systems also operate to limit competition. Many agencies prefer working with a single contractor and thus they "wire" RFPs to favor one particular contractor. This is done by specifying in both the Statement of Work and the evaluation criteria various requirements which only one firm is likely to meet.

HIRING STRUCTURE

It is extremely important to understand this procurement process if you are interested in working for international consulting and contracting firms. The process creates a job market situation which is very fluid, unstable, and unpredictable. A typical organizational structure looks something like this:

TYPICAL STRUCTURE OF SMALL AND
FLEXIBLE CONSULTING FIRM

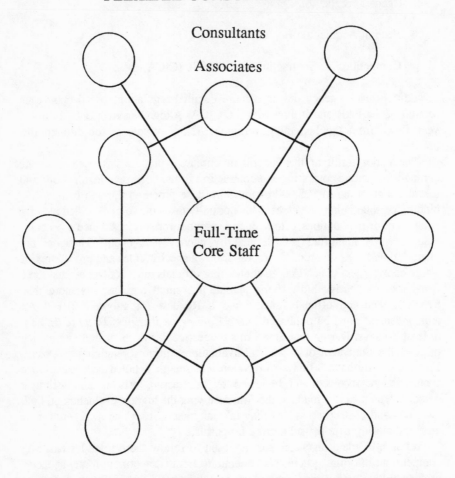

Consultants

Associates

Full-Time
Core Staff

Many firms keep a small **core staff** which is employed full-time to respond to RFPs and manage a lean organizational infrastructure. As contracts are won, they hire two types of additional personnel—often on a consulting basis—for implementing the contract. **Associates** normally work closely with the core staff on several projects; these individuals are relatively loyal to the firm and are given a disproportionate amount of contract work as individuals or subcontractors. **Consultants** are less closely linked to the firm; they have specific skills not found with the core staff or associates, and they tend to freelance with several such firms. Therefore, many positions with these firms are short-term positions tied to specific contracts, ranging from one month to one or more years. Most contracts are for one year with options to renew contracts up to two to three years before resubmitting them for open competition.

Many positions with these firms are short-term positions tied to specific contracts, ranging from one month to one or more years.

Given this structure, you must consider whether you want a full-time organization position or a contract-specific position as either an associate or consultant. An organization position may be more stable and predictable, but not necessarily so. For example, most contracting and consulting firms are small organizations employing fewer than 50 individuals. Many specialize in a particular government function or public policy area and work primarily with one or two government agencies. A few firms straddle the public and private sectors by doing contract work for both government and business. Many international consulting firms, for example, only work in the fields of health care, population planning, or rural development. Others specialize in educational development and human resource management. Given the highly competitive nature of their work, many of these firms find they must quickly staff-up and staff-down depending on which contracts they receive. If they receive a large contract, they may need to more than double or triple their staff overnight. If they lose a large contract, everyone except the president may go off the payroll and, instead, work on a daily consulting basis. For many small firms, contracting work is a feast or famine business.

On the other hand, large firms with several large contracts—especially defense contractors—will maintain a relatively large permanent staff. They normally can afford to do this, because their overhead and profits are greater on larger contracts. Furthermore, procurement officials find it difficult to estimate and monitor the costs of large contracts. But recent revelations about alleged contracting abuses by noted Department of Defense contractors as well as numerous contractors doing business with the Department of Housing and Urban Development and highly publicized cases of graft and corruption in the U.S. Agency for International Development (USAID) have created a new element of instability among contractors. Some contractors violated one of the most important unwritten rules of the contracting business—do not get your contracting practices, however legal or illegal, exposed in the news media and thus endanger the careers of agency personnel. Many firms involved in the scandal-ridden Housing and Urban Development (HUD) contracting practices of the late 1980s also took several politicians with them. Contracting abuses within the USAID system—major or minor—often become publicized because of the high public visibility and intense congressional oversight centering on this agency.

CONTRACTORS AND CONSULTANTS IN THE FOREIGN AID SYSTEM

Several contractors and consulting firms are organized to acquire contracts with Federal agencies and international organizations. These include huge firms such as Coopers and Lybrand, which does contract work with both public and private institutions and maintains an international staff of 30,000 in 97 countries; medium-sized firms with staffs of 10 to 50 individuals; and one or two-person firms which primarily rely on short-term contracts with a single agency or office. These firms provide every conceivable service from constructing roads and dams to dispensing food and condoms in Third World countries.

The contracting and consulting business is widespread throughout the international arena. However, its exact dimensions are difficult to measure since much of the work of contractors and consultants is not visible to the public. Government agencies may have responsibility for administering foreign aid programs, but much of what they take credit for is done by contractors. Many agencies primarily obligate funds which are, in turn, dispensed to contractors and consultants who actually get the work done. The agency, in turn, primarily becomes involved in dispensing funds, monitoring contractors, and evaluating contract performance.

The World Bank, United Nations, and several Federal agencies are the major funding sources for these contracting and consulting firms. Federal agencies most frequently using international contractors are the U.S. Agency for International Development, Department of Agriculture, Department of State, Department of Defense, and the Central Intelligence Agency.

Take, for example, the U.S. Agency for International Development. This is a good case for getting a sense of how the government procurement process operates in the international arena and how it affects the operation of contractors and consultants as well as several nonprofit or nongovernmental (NGOs) organizations discussed in the next chapter. USAID is one of the largest dispensers of government contracts to large, small, and minority consulting firms. Since USAID is primarily organized to obligate funds for development projects in Third World countries, numerous consulting firms in the United States and abroad are recipients of USAID funding. The contracts deal with every conceivable type of service and project. USAID, for example, classifies all contractors according to 21 activity categories:

- Accounting and Financial Management
- Agriculture
- Architecture and Engineering
- Auditing
- Development Information/Evaluation
- Development Management
- Disaster Assistance
- Education
- Energy
- Environmental/Natural Resources
- Foreign Language Instruction
- Health (Planning and Delivery)
- Housing and Urban Development
- Macroeconomic Analysis
- Management Assistance/Skills
- Management Consulting Services
- Nutrition and Multisectoral Development
- Printing Services
- Procurement Services
- Records Management
- Rural/Regional Income Generation

A USAID contracting officer is assigned to each category. This individual issues solicitations, negotiates, and regularly communicates with the firms doing work under USAID contracts.

USAID does business with nearly 2,000 contractors in the United States and abroad. While many job opportunities are available with U.S. firms, additional opportunities are available with firms located in Third World countries which receive "Host Country Contracts." As part of USAID's emphasis on decentralization, capacity building, and private sector initiatives, more and more USAID contracts are earmarked for consulting firms in Third World countries. Since many of these firms lack basic capabilities to develop proposals and implement projects, some will hire experienced Americans to help them get and manage USAID contracts. The contracting officer attached to each USAID mission should have a list of local firms, which usually will be available upon request.

USAID publishes a wealth of information on U.S. and European-based firms which receive contracts as well as have special relationships with the Agency. Indeed, of all Federal agencies, this one is a job hunters paradise. The *Current Technical Services Contracts and Grants* directory, for example, is issued by the Procurement Support Division of USAID's Office of Procurement. This lengthy document identifies most firms receiving contracts and grants from USAID each fiscal year. It includes a statistical summary, a regional directory, and a state and country listing of contractors and grantees. Each contract is identified by contract number, contract name, contract term, dollar amount, contract description, and address of contractor. If you conduct some basic analysis of this document, you will acquire some very useful information for your job search. For example, in the period October 1, 1990 to September 30, 1991, USAID awarded the following number of contracts by region and total dollar amounts:

Area	No. of countries	No. of contracts	Amount in dollars
Worldwide	—	595	$2,085,771,030
Asia	17	493	957,123,967
Latin America	22	626	940,755,583
Africa	41	493	766,506,769
Near East	10	155	507,498,082
Europe	16	113	397,300,520
United States	—	216	356,902,874
South Pacific	7	14	18,203,755
TOTAL	**114**	**2,705**	**$6,030,062,580**

Firms headquartered in eight states received the largest number and dollar value of USAID contracts and grants:

Location of Firms	Total Amount
District of Columbia	$1,691,950,762
New York	$654,650,802
Virginia	$422,202,107
Massachusetts	$422,190,357
Maryland	$360,513,319
North Carolina	$193,944,077
California	$172,436,355
Connecticut	$140,080,576

Hundreds of firms are located throughout the United States—not just in these eight states. Not surprising, firms in and around Washington, DC—the so-called "Beltway Bandits"—received the largest number of USAID contracts, totaling nearly $2.5 billion. In fact, from 1984 to 1992 the total dollars pouring into contractors and consultants in the Washington Metropolitan area nearly tripled (from $809,806,103 to $2,474,666,188) whereas most other areas in the country experienced about a 60 percent increase. The Washington Metropolitan area remained the central area for these firms which continued to receive the lion's share of USAID funding. Not surprising, this area remains a job hunter's paradise for those interested in doing international contracting and consulting work.

A useful feature of this key USAID document is the index. It identifies which firms received the largest number of contracts and grants during the fiscal year. For example, during Fiscal Year 1991 nearly 1500 foundations, universities, contracting firms, and nonprofit organizations received USAID contracts and grants. Of these, 33 organizations received 10 or more contracts or grants:

USAID CONTRACTORS/GRANTEES RECEIVING 10 OR MORE CONTRACTS

Firms/ Organizations	Number of Contracts/ Grants Awarded
▪ Abt Associates, Inc.	30
▪ Academy for Educational Development	24
▪ Adventist Development and Relief Agency International	14
▪ Africare, Inc.	18
▪ Agricultural Cooperative Development International	12
▪ Asia Foundation	13
▪ Camp Dresser and McKee International	10
▪ Catholic Relief Services (CRS)	22
▪ Chemonics International Consulting Division	19
▪ Cooperative for American Relief Everywhere, Inc. (CARE)	41
▪ Coopers and Lybrand	13
▪ Development Alternatives, Inc.	20
▪ Futures Group	18
▪ Helen Keller International, Inc.	11
▪ Institute of International Education	10
▪ International Executive Service Corps	23

- International Resources Group, Ltd.   10
- International Sciences and
  Technology Institute, Inc.   12
- John Snow Public Health Group, Inc.   13
- Louis Berger International, Inc.   12
- Management Systems for Health   17
- Management Systems International   11
- Nathan, Robert, Associates, Inc.   15
- People to People Health Foundation, Inc.   12
- Population Services International   10
- Price Waterhouse   26
- Private Agencies Collaborating Together   12
- Research Triangle Institute   10
- Save the Children Foundation   23
- University Research Corporation   10
- Winrock International   15
- World Vision Relief and Development   13
- United Nations Children's Fund   13

While most firms compete with each other in receiving individual company contacts, an increasing number of contractors receive joint contracts. The major firms joining together in such cooperative efforts include:

- Checchi and Co./Louis Berger International (5 contracts)
- Development Alternatives, Inc./International Science and Technology Institute (6 contracts)
- Development Alternatives, Inc./Nathan Associates, Inc. (5 contracts)
- Development Associates, Inc./Development Alternatives, Inc. (5 contracts)
- Robert Nathan Associates, Inc./Duke University/Louis Berger International/Mid-American International Agricultural Consortium (4 contracts)
- World Wildlife Fund/Conservation Foundation (8 contracts)

Most of these contractors are major firms involved in Third World development projects. They constitute an important network for those interested in working for such types of firms.

Contracting firms, including nonprofit NGOs and universities, receiving $10 million or more in USAID contracts include the following:

CONTRACTORS RECEIVING $10 MILLION
OR MORE IN USAID CONTRACTS, 1991

Contractor	Amount Awarded
▪ A.T. International	$24,873,462
▪ Abt Associates, Inc.	24,611,245
▪ Academy for Educational Development	182,744,998
▪ African-American Labor Center	32,463,868
▪ African-American Institute	60,119,061
▪ Africare, Inc.	17,918,011
▪ Agricultural Cooperative Development International	21,484,011
▪ Aguirre International, Inc.	29,152,780
▪ American AG International, Inc.	12,908,200
▪ American Institute for Free Labor Development	15,486,269
▪ American Mideast Educational and Training Services	56,151,175
▪ American Near East Refugee Aid, Inc.	11,043,766
▪ Ansell, Inc.	29,881,248
▪ Appropriate Technology International	10,947,527
▪ Asian American Free Labor Institute	16,228,600
▪ Association for Voluntary Surgical Contraception	48,994,108
▪ Association in Rural Development	19,674,224
▪ Berger, Louis, International, Inc.	37,812,049
▪ Black and Veatch International/ James M. Montgomery Assoc.	29,238,000
▪ Camp, Dresser and McKee International, Inc.	44,672,876
▪ Catholic Relief Services	42,787,203
▪ Center for Human Services	10,693,624
▪ CH2M Hill International	10,422,022
▪ Chemonics International	49,966,974
▪ Clark University	14,120,608
▪ Consortium for International Development	40,205,209
▪ Construction Control Services Corp.	17,373,248
▪ Cooperative for American Relief Everywhere, Inc. (CARE)	36,755,515
▪ Coopers and Lybrand	18,444,685
▪ Creative Associates International, Inc.	10,125,992
▪ Credit Union National Association	20,827,931

- Czech and Slovak American Enterprise   15,000,000
- Deloitte and Touche   14,739,054
- Development Alternatives Inc.   40,104,863
- Development Associates Inc.   33,639,930
- Development Associates/Nathan Associates   11,769,662
- EBASCO Services, Inc.   10,200,000
- Eastern Virginia Medical School   31,407,000
- Educational Development Center, Inc.   13,306,322
- Executive Resource Associates   49,096,094
- Family Health International   117,908,937
- Florida International University   10,708,302
- Florida State University   13,614,196
- Futures Group   61,122,036
- Georgetown University   117,311,055
- Hagler, Bailly and Co., Inc.   12,008,543
- Harvard University   28,883,237
- Harza Engineering Company   21,943,328
- Hungarian-American Enterprise Fund   36,462,250
- Institute for Contemporary Studies   10,325,516
- Institute for Resource Development, Inc.   21,425,542
- Institution of International Education   50,614,403
- International Executive Service Corps   32,296,590
- International Food Policy Research Institute   11,057,168
- International Planned Parenthood Federation   36,775,118
- International Science and
    Technology Institute, Inc.   32,494,726
- JHPIEGO Corporation   37,654,593
- John Snow Public Health Group, Inc.   102,597,711
- Johns Hopkins University   113,867,315
- Labat Anderson, Inc.   11,154,053
- Management Sciences for Health   73,557,130
- Matrix International Logistics   10,538,000
- Medcalf and Eddy International   14,538,891
- Medical Service Consultants, Inc.   16,431,623
- Michigan State University   34,777,800
- Midamerica International Agricultural Consortium 16,010,000
- Morrison Knudsen Engineers, Inc.   23,841,449
- National Academy of Sciences   14,193,260
- National Academy of Sciences/
    National Research Council   37,682,702
- National Association of the
    Partners of the Americas, Inc.   25,570,694
- National Capital Administrative Services   17,010,532
- National Endowment for Democracy   22,230,700

- National Rural Electric Cooperative Association   28,537,805
- North Carolina State University   19,555,392
- Overseas Bechtel, Inc.   10,135,506
- Partners for International Education and Training   86,856,390
- Pathfinder Fund   88,745,614
- People-to-People Health Foundation, Inc.   76,980,735
- Planned Parenthood Federation of America   98,627,591
- Polish-American Enterprise Fund, Inc.   137,692,050
- Population Council   46,293,154
- Population Services International   30,077,589
- Pragma Corporation   23,117,032
- Price Waterhouse   25,575,537
- Private Agencies Collaborating Together   25,795,971
- Program for Appropriate Technology in Health   16,433,954
- Project Concern International   11,788,800
- Purdue University   13,639,956
- Ronco Consulting Corporation   17,617,050
- Save the Children Federation   70,919,004
- Scientex Corporation   20,033,603
- Technoserve, Inc.   14,705,058
- Trustees of the American University of Beirut   22,846,828
- Tulane University   14,140,498
- United Nations Children's Fund   15,116,000
- University of Florida   11,829,856
- University of Hawaii   18,996,743
- University of Idaho   11,663,956
- University of Illinois   14,235,320
- University of Kentucky   11,800,988
- University of Maryland   11,460,411
- University of Michigan   11,958,339
- University of Nebraska   26,099,000
- University of North Carolina   11,692,049
- University of Rhode Island   10,899,232
- University of Wisconsin-Madison   17,822,594
- University Research Corporation   24,784,912
- Volunteers in Overseas Cooperative Assistance   14,049,811
- Volunteers in Technical Assistance   18,117,759
- Wilbur Smith and Associates   22,871,232
- Winrock International   39,615,285
- World Resources Institute   12,091,293
- World Vision Relief and Development, Inc.   23,451,235
- World Wildlife Fund/Conservation Foundation   16,560,812

The names and addresses of these and other organizations, as well as hundreds of individuals who also receive USAID contracts and grants, are included in the section entitled "State/Country Listing of Contractor/Grantee Addresses" of the *Current Technical Service Contracts and Grants* directory. This document is required reading for anyone interested in identifying firms doing international contracting and consulting work. You can get a free copy of this document by requesting it through the Support Division of USAID's Office of Procurement, Procurement Support Division (Tel. 703/875-1270). If you are interested in contracts and grants awarded to colleges and university, be sure to ask for a copy of the current edition of the *AID-Financed University Contracts, Grants, and Cooperative Agreements* directory.

Another useful USAID document is required reading: *Functional Report: Current Indefinite Quantity Contracts (IQCs).* Issued on a quarterly basis, this document identifies all firms which have a "special" relationship with USAID. The Indefinite Quantity Contract, or IQC, is a unique contracting mechanism which enables USAID to acquire short-term technical services—normally for 120 days or less—by issuing a "work order" to firms which qualify as eligible for IQCs. In other words, the IQC limits competition to a few USAID approved firms. This special contracting mechanism and agency-contractor relationship ostensibly saves USAID time and avoids lengthy and sometimes difficult negotiation procedures. At the same time, the IQC is highly valued by many firms. These are bread-and-butter contracts which regularly pay salaries and overhead and keep full-time staffs and associates employed especially during periods between large contracts. If you contact firms with IQC status, you may find they have work in your skill and interest areas.

The IQC report identifies every firm which has this special relationship with USAID for the particular quarter. In addition, it classifies firms according to the 21 contracting categories, identifies the number of delivery orders and their dollar value, and includes contact information—name, address, and phone number of the firm. The November 1991 report identified the following firms with IQC status that also were awarded IQCs for the period 1988 through 1994:

Accounting/ **Financial Management:**	▪ DAC International, Inc. ▪ Price Waterhouse ▪ Radan Systems, Inc.
Agriculture:	▪ Winrock International ▪ Chemonics International ▪ International Resources Groups ▪ Agricultural Development Consultants ▪ Tropical Research and Development, Inc.
Architecture and **Engineering Services:**	▪ Harza Engineering Co. ▪ Deleuw Cather International

Auditing:	■ Price Waterhouse
	■ Deloitte and Touche
	■ KPMG Peat Marwick
Development Information and Evaluation:	■ Management Systems International
	■ Academy of Educational Development
	■ TVT Associates
	■ Devres, Inc.
Development Management:	■ International Science and Technology
	■ Agricultural Cooperative Development
	■ Datex, Inc.
Disaster Assistance:	■ Jianas Brothers Packaging Co.
	■ Protective Plastics, Inc.
Education:	■ Academy for Educational Development
	■ Education Development Center
	■ Meridian House International
Energy:	■ International Resources Group, Ltd.
	■ RCG/Hagler, Bailly, Inc.
	■ Resources Management Associates
Environmental/ Natural Resources:	■ Chemonics International Consulting Division
	■ International Resources Group, Ltd.
	■ Tropical Research and Development/KBN
Foreign Language Instruction:	■ International Center for Language Studies
	■ CACI, Inc.—Federal
	■ Language Learning Enterprises
Health (Planning and Delivery):	■ Devres, Inc.
	■ John Snow Public Health Group, Inc.
	■ Research Triangle Institute
Housing & Urban Development:	■ Nathan Associates, Inc.
	■ Abt Associates, Inc.
	■ The Urban Institute
	■ Research Triangle Institute
	■ Planning and Development Collaborative
Macroeconomic Analysis:	■ Nathan Associates, Inc.
	■ Development Alternatives, Inc.

Management Assistance/Skills:	■ Sheladia Associates, Inc.
Management Consulting Services:	■ Coopers and Lybrand ■ Deloitte and Touche ■ KPMG Peat Marwick ■ Management Systems International, Inc. ■ Thunder and Associates
Nutrition and Multisectoral Development:	■ Casals and Associates, Inc. ■ Pragma Corporation
Printing Services:	■ Classic Press, Inc. ■ Goodway Graphics of Virginia, Inc. ■ Technigraphix
Records Management:	■ TASCOnsultation Associates, Inc.
Rural/Regional Income Generation:	■ Chemonics International Consulting Division ■ Development Alternatives, Inc. ■ Devres, Inc.

This document is available in the main USAID library in Rosslyn, Virginia or by calling, writing, or dropping into the USAID Office of Procurement. The USAID library is located and open as follows:

USAID Library
SA18
Rosslyn Plaza
Rosslyn, VA 20523
Tel. 703/875-4818
Hours: 10am—4pm, Monday thru Friday

The Office of Procurement is located near the library in the Gannett Building:

Office of Procurement
Procurement Support Division
Agency for International Development
1100 Wilson, 14th Floor
Rosslyn, VA 20523
Tel. 703/875-1270
Open: 7am to 7pm (reception area), Monday thru Friday

While most government publications are available through the U.S. Government Printing Office, USAID's publications are handled through an in-house documentation center. These and other useful USAID publications, most of which are also found in the USAID Library, can be purchased through the USAID Document Information Handling Facility:

AID/DIHF
7222 47th St., Suite 100
Chevy Chase, MD 20815
Tel. 301/951-7191

You will normally need a document number to order the publication. You can get this number by calling the USAID Library (703/875-4818).

USAID is the only agency we know which compiles such comprehensive and informative documents on contractors. Other agencies either do not organize this data or will not release it unless pressured to do so through a Freedom of Information request.

Information on most USAID-affiliated firms—names, addresses, telephone numbers, and annotated descriptions—is found in a few international job books and directories of consultants:

- *The Almanac of International Jobs and Careers*
- *Careers In International Affairs*
- *Guide To Careers In World Affairs*
- *The Consultants and Consulting Organizations Directory*
- *Directory of Consultant Members*
- *Directory of Management Consultants*
- *Who's Who In Consulting*

The most comprehensive directory to USAID-funded organizations is *Internet Profiles* (Network for International Technical Assistance, P.O. Box 3245, Chapel Hill, NC 27515). This is the "bible" for locating all types of organizations involved in development assistance. It is available in a few specialized libraries. It also ca be ordered directly from the publisher for $500. Call (919/968-8324) for details.

You also may want to monitor firms receiving Federal government contracts by regularly reviewing the "Contract Awards" section of the *Commerce Business Daily* as well as the *Federal Register*.

Several minority firms also receive contracts with Federal agencies, but they are less visible to the public. Known as "8(a) firms," these ostensibly disadvantaged businesses qualify for noncompetitive contracts. DAC International, Development Assistance Corporation, Dimpex Associates, Metrotec, Research Management Corporation, Global Exchange, TEM Associates, Energy Systems Engineering, Pragma Corporation, International Development and Energy

Associates, Lambet Company, and American Manufacturers Export Group, for example, are 8(a) firms working with USAID. Agencies can reserve certain projects and activities for 8(a) firms. Indeed, many prefer using this contracting mechanism, because it expedites agency spending without requiring a lengthy competitive procurement process for obligating funds. Since agencies keep lists of these firms, contact their contracting office for the names of the 8(a) firms they are using for noncompetitive contracts. The contracting office may or may not willingly release this information unless requested through the Freedom of Information Act. These firms can provide excellent job opportunities, because they often take on projects for which they lack sufficient full-time expertise. They may need additional qualified professionals to plan and implement projects.

International consulting firms should be approached by using networking techniques as outlined in Chapter Seven: conduct your research; call for information; arrange informational interviews; get your resume in their hands and files; and follow-up with telephone calls, letters, and personal visits. As we noted earlier in our discussion of resumes and letters (Chapter Six), be sure to get your resume in the resume banks of contracting and consulting firms. Many of these firms welcome unsolicited resumes, because they often must quickly staff projects. They frequently turn to their in-house resume banks to locate qualified individuals. If a position requires relocating abroad, the more exotic your skills and the quicker you can relocate, the better your chances of landing a job with these firms. Many firms are always looking for individuals with a combination of technical skills and a willingness to relocate abroad for two or three years.

PERSONAL SERVICES CONTRACTS

If you are interested in doing independent consulting, your best strategy will be to network with government employees who are responsible for contracting-out services. In many cases, agencies prefer giving certain work to individuals rather than incurring the overhead costs involved with contracting-out to an established firm. In addition, agencies can avoid lengthy competitive procedures and maintain closer control when they contract directly with individuals for amounts less than $10,000 or use a special category of contracts—the Personal Services Contract (PSC)—for larger amounts. Many individuals have been able to create consulting jobs for themselves by proposing to agency personnel new projects requiring their expertise.

You should be aware of this category of contracts frequently used in international consulting: Personal Service Contracts. These contracts are convenient ways for an agency to acquire specific expertise as well as additional personnel without disturbing personnel ceilings or increasing the agency payroll. Individuals are hired on one to three year contracts to perform specific services within the agency. Normally these positions are announced in the *Commerce Business*

Daily (CBD) and appear similar to classified employment ads. The following announcement appeared in the *CBD*:

> **HONDURAS: PROGRAM OPERATIONS SPECIALIST.** The USAID/H is accepting CV's (curriculum vitae) and private data from qualified individuals to fill the position of program operations specialist. The position involves assisting the USAID in the analysis, planning, budgeting, monitoring, and implementation of US economic assistance program in Honduras. These programs include economic support funds, development assistance, housing guarantees, and PL 480 Titles I, II, and III. Qualifications include a master's degree in business administration, economics, or a similar discipline. Fluency in Spanish/English at R3, S2 IAW the Foreign Service Institute's standards. Have considerable and proven USAID program office experience relating to the programming, monitoring, reporting, and implementation of the aid program, and a thorough knowledge of aid goals and major programs including NBCCA recommendations. No formal sol will be issued. CV's and biodata from individuals only will be accepted. The contractual relationship will be personal services (PSC) between the USG and the selected individual. Interested applicants should submit CV and salary history NLT mid-Dec. (The Agency for International Development, Contracting Officer, c/o American Embassy, Teguigalpa, Honduras, or USAID Honduras APO Miami, FL 34022)

Notice that like many other international employers, AID requests a Curriculum Vita (CV) rather than a resume. The curriculum vita will place heavy emphasis on educational background, publications, and professional activities. A one to two-page resume normally associated with job-hunting in the United States would be inappropriate for such a position, although we recommend attaching a summary resume to such a curriculum vita (see Chapter Six).

While agencies are required to announce their intent to conclude a Personal Services Contract, often the positions are "wired" for individuals who already have worked for the agency—especially a former employee who has retired or started a consulting business—or who helped develop a project for the agency and thus created his or her own full-time consulting position with the agency.

USEFUL RESOURCES

Several useful information sources are available for locating opportunities with various contracting and consulting firms. The single most comprehensive source of names, addresses, phone numbers, and annotated descriptions of firms is found in *The Consultants and Consulting Organizations Directory* and *Who's Who in Consulting* (Detroit: Gale Research Company). Most libraries have current editions of the three-volume *Directory*. It lists over 3,000 consulting firms according to the following categories:

1. Agriculture, Forestry, and Landscaping
2. Architecture and Interior Design
3. Arts and Entertainment
4. Business and Finance
5. Data Processing, Telecommunications, and Information Services
6. Education and Personal Development
7. Engineering, Science, and Technology
8. Environment
9. Health, Medicine, and Safety
10. Human Resources
11. Management
12. Manufacturing/Industrial/Transportation Operations
13. Marketing and Sales
14. Social Issues and Concerns

Since these volumes include all types of consulting firms, regardless of their public or private orientation as well as domestic or international operations, you will need to read through the various annotated descriptions to find which firms are primarily involved in international contract work. Although this is the best directory of such firms, keep in mind it does not include all contracting and consulting firms—only those willing to reveal information on their operations to Gale Research Company. Many firms do not want to publicize their operations through this or other public information resource directories. Consequently, you will have to locate these firms through other resources and investigative efforts.

One of the most useful resources for identifying international contracting and consulting firms doing business with the Federal government is the *Commerce Business Daily (CBD)*, which is available in most major libraries. Issued five days a week, this Department of Commerce publication lists information on all upcoming competitive contracts for $10,000 or more as well as contracts awarded to particular firms for the amounts of $25,000 or more. You should pay particular attention to the "Contract Awards" section. This section identifies which firms received contracts for what amounts. A good job search strategy is to continuously monitor who receives contracts and contact the firm when you see an award made in your area of expertise or interest. But you must do this immediately upon seeing the announcement since there is a lag time between when a contract is awarded and when it is announced in the *CBD*.

We suggest this *CBD* job search strategy because typically firms operate in the following manner. The firm submits a proposal complete with a management structure, job descriptions, and resumes. But once they receive the award, the proposed staff changes due to the unavailability of some individuals proposed. At this time, the contractor must find new personnel and get them approved for the contract. In other words, the contractor now has a personnel problem or vacancy which must be filled immediately. If your qualifications and timing are right, you may find a job very quickly with such a firm. At the same time, you will make an important contact which could lead to having your resume included in other proposals. Most contractors are happy to receive resumes since they are continuously in need of personnel to propose for as well as staff new projects. As noted earlier, many contractors maintain in-house resume or talent banks which they continuously refer to when dealing with their personnel needs. Staffing-up is always a problem employers prefer to solve before it becomes a major project implementation issue with clients.

You should also monitor the section of the *CBD* dealing with impending contracts. Once you become familiar with various specialty areas within the consulting business, you can nearly predict which firms will submit proposals for which projects. Knowing this, you can call a firm and mention your interest and availability in being included in their proposal. They may even offer you a short-term contract to help write the proposal should you have such interests and skills. In some cases, individuals manage to get included in two or more proposals for the same contract, thus better ensuring they will get the work once the contract is awarded. Some firms have no problems with your inclusion in competitors' proposals while others frown on such opportunism. But in the contracting game, where competition is heavy, the basic goal is to get the contract and cash flowing.

Another source of information on contractors is the contracts procurement, or acquisitions office in each agency. Some offices, such as the Agency for International Development, gladly provide you with a listing of firms doing contract work with their agency. Others are less organized and willing to provide such information. Also, ask the officials **which** contractors are doing **what** and **whom** you might contact. Sometimes these individuals are very open with such information and will make several useful suggestions. On the other hand, agency officials may guard this information as private and confidential, even though it is public information. In this instance, you may consider formally requesting the information through the Freedom of Information Act.

You will find that some firms largely specialize in one function in a single agency whereas other firms do contract work in one or many functional areas with several agencies. For example, if you are interested in working for a firm in the field of energy or environmental protection, you should contact the Contracts Office at the Department of Energy or Environmental Protection Agency for a list of contractors. Once you have this information, you will know whom to contact. The firms working with these agencies also may be doing similar work in other agencies and in private industry. Call the firms and let them know you are interested in working for them. Try to set up an appointment for an interview. Make sure you get your resume in their file. Indeed, many firms refer to this file when they need personnel for new projects. While they may not have a vacancy at the time you contact them, they very well may submit a proposal which results in a position for you.

Many international contracting and consulting firms also periodically place employment ads in either the classified or business sections of major newspapers, especially the Sunday editions of the *Washington Post* and *The New York Times*. You should monitor these sections of the newspaper. However, don't expect to get a job by responding to these ads. Many firms periodically place such ads in order to increase the number of resumes for their files. Sometimes they are in the process of bidding on a project, so they advertise for resumes to put in a particular proposal. If you manage to get your resume in the proposal and the firm wins the contract, you have a job. But more often than not, such ads are "fishing expeditions" with no particular vacancy available at the time of the ad. They want to build their stock of resumes for certain skill areas in the event they need to quickly respond to an RFP.

PROFESSIONAL POSITIONS

Most international contracting and consulting firms hire individuals with strong analytical, communication, and technical skills along with language and area skills and extensive international work experience. Given the nature of consulting work, consultants are hired as problem-solvers. They must quickly analyze situations, devise plans of action, and often implement projects. Such activities require a great deal of analytical skill and the ability to communicate to clients both orally and in writing. Projects continuously require flows of paper—workplans, monthly reports, memos, evaluations, studies—between the consultants and clients. If you are both a good and fast writer, stress these facts to potential employers. They especially need smart, quick thinking, fast writers.

While most firms hire general support staff positions for word processors, receptionists, secretaries, and accountants, most continuously seek technical specialists. Defense contractors and construction firms hire a disproportionate number of engineers, systems analysts, and computer specialists. Rural development firms hire a disproportionate number of agronomists and agricultural marketing specialists. Research firms hire policy analysts with skills unique to specific programs and agencies. Other firms need specialists in a variety of areas. If you survey the *Commerce Business Daily* notices, you will quickly get a sense of which technical specialties are in demand.

It is much easier to break into an international contracting and consulting firm if you have previous government experience in a specialty area involving contractors. Your special knowledge and contacts with agency personnel will make you very marketable among firms working in your area. Indeed, much of the revolving door with government involves employees leaving an agency and working for the same contractor they previously worked with from within the agency. These individuals become key contact people and informants for the firm. Furthermore, since agency personnel usually think they are "unique"—

believing outsiders can't possibly understand their problems, situations, and needs —they prefer working with one of their own who can speak their agency "language."

> ### *The best skill to have is an ability to work with agency personnel who are suspicious of outsiders and who feel their agency is unique.*

Educational qualifications also are important with international contracting and consulting firms. They prefer individuals with MAs and PhDs because government places heavy emphasis on educational qualifications of contractors' personnel when awarding contracts. After all, agency personnel working with contracts tend to be well educated—many have MAs and PhDs. When it comes to educational background, they prefer working with consultants who are at least their equal or have higher educations. As the very minimum, a BA degree is expected but an MA or PhD is much preferred. As noted earlier, this is in line with the general emphasis within the international job market on educational qualifications. Education has a much different meaning in terms of "qualifications" in other cultures. The American egalitarian emphasis on "job performance skills" is not widely embraced throughout the world.

But how do you break into the international contracting and consulting game if you don't have experience, technical skills, or advanced degrees? If you have strong analytical and writing skills, along with basic foreign language and area skills as well as some international experience, you should be able to land a position through sheer persistence. These firms continuously need such skills. Often they find their technical personnel with government experience cannot write. Therefore, they must have on their staff individuals who can write and edit. If you get into a firm based on your analytical and writing skills, you may be able to quickly pick up the technical aspects of the work and in time be able to work directly with clients on projects. In the meantime, you will probably stay in the background providing support for technical personnel.

This is a very basic and typical pattern of how individuals break into the government consulting business and become specialists in a short time even though they lack experience as a government employee. In the long run, the best skill to have is an ability to work with agency personnel who are suspicious of outsiders and who feel their agency is unique. They respond best to firms they feel recognize their uniqueness, respond to their problems, and can be trusted. Responsiveness and trust are perhaps the most important elements in developing and maintaining a good contractor-client relationship. On-the-job experience in interacting with clients is the basic requirement for becoming an effective consultant. Education and previous government experience will not be enough.

INDEPENDENT CONSULTANTS
AND THE NETWORKING GAME

If you are thinking of starting your own independent international consulting business on either a part-time or full-time basis, you should talk to consultants who have taken this road. They can provide you with useful tips on avoiding the pitfalls of independence as well as suggest useful strategies for becoming successful. You might also read a few of the ever increasing number of how-to books on entering the consulting business. Among the best titles are:

- *The International Consultant*
- *The Consultant's Kit: Establishing and Operating Your Successful Consulting Business*
- *Consultants Handbook*
- *Cashing In On the Consulting Boom*
- *Consulting: The Complete Guide To a Profitable Career*
- *How To Become a Successful Consultant*
- *How To Succeed As an Independent Consultant*
- *Marketing Your Consulting and Professional Services*

If you are especially interested in the Federal contracting process, you should consult Barry McVay's two primers that detail the Federal contracting process:

- *Getting Started in Federal Contracting: A Guide Through the Federal Procurement Maze*
- *Proposals That Win Federal Contracts*

Most of these titles can be ordered directly from Impact Publications.

If you wish to monitor Federal contracts of more than $25,000, you may want to subscribe to the *Commerce Business Daily*. This daily publication is available on an annual subscription basis from the Superintendent of Documents, U.S. Government Printing Office, Washington, DC 20402 ($261 for first class mail or $208 for second class mail).

Several professional networks can provide information on consulting job opportunities. Many consultants belong to professional organizations in their specialty areas. These organizations often list job vacancies with consulting firms. Within many of these associations, consultants form their own interest groups or sections to focus on various aspects of consulting work. For example, the American Psychological Association has a Division of Consulting Psychologists. Many local chapters of the American Society of Training and Development have a Consultants' Section. These groups regularly meet to exchange ideas and promote their interests and themselves. Some associations specialize in consulting. For example, several professionals have formed their own professional organizations:

- Academy of Health Care Consultants (Chicago)
- American Association of Hospital Consultants (Arlington, VA)
- American Consulting Engineers Council (Washington, DC)
- American Society of Agricultural Consultants (McLean, VA)
- Association of Management Consultants (Milwaukee)
- Institute of Management Consultants (New York City)
- National Association of Public Employer Negotiators and Administrators (Chicago)
- National Council of Professional Services Firm (Washington, DC)

Several other organizations publish directories of consultants and consulting organizations as well as newsletters in various specialized fields. If you are interested in management consulting, for example, you may want to contact Consulting News, an organization which publishes two newsletters (*Consultant News* and *Executive Recruiter News*) and two directories (*Directory of Executive Recruiters* and *Key European Search Firms and Their U.S. Links*): Consultants News, Templeton Road, Fitzwilliam, NH 03447 or call 603/585-2200 or 603/585-6544.

Chapter Thirteen

NONPROFIT ORGANIZATIONS AND VOLUNTEER OPPORTUNITIES

Numerous nonprofit and volunteer organizations offer excellent opportunities to break into as well as pursue long-term careers in the international job market. Similar to many contracting and consulting firms, nonprofit and volunteer organizations operating in the international arena are disproportionately involved in social and economic development efforts in Third World countries.

Nonprofit and volunteer organizations are the true missionaries in today's world. They feed the hungry, care for women and children, promote improved health care standards, provide needed medical assistance and education, improve sanitation, evacuate and resettle refugees, develop rural water and sanitation systems, promote family planning and pre-natal care, develop rural lending institutions and cooperatives, assist in marketing crops, and promote community development efforts. They are the major catalysts for change in much of the developing world. They rely heavily on funding from government agencies, especially USAID, and foundations as well as from their own fund raising efforts.

If you are interested in pursuing a cause or making a difference in the lives of others, you should seriously consider working for a non-profit organization. While most of these organizations pay medium to low salaries, they do provide unique and extremely rewarding opportunities to get involved in development that are largely absent in other types of organizations except for perhaps the U.S. Peace Corps and specialized agencies of the United Nations.

THE ORGANIZATIONS

The nonprofit category of international organizations includes organizations frequently referred to as Nongovernmental Organizations (NGO's) or Private Voluntary Organizations (PVO's) which are primarily oriented toward promoting a particular international issue or cause. In contrast to more than 100,000 nonprofit organizations operating within the United States, international nonprofits are fewer in number and operate almost solely in the international arena. They span a broad spectrum of issues and causes:

foreign affairs	relief
education	human rights
energy	religion
economic development	rural development
population planning	cultural exchange
food	water resources
social welfare	housing
health	community development
children and youth	

---

*Nonprofit and volunteer organizations
are the true missionaries
in today's world.*

Examples of different types of nonprofit organizations and their diverse missions abound throughout the international arena. Most of these organizations cluster around important health, agricultural, social welfare, and disaster issues that are inadequately dealt with in most poor countries: medical services, population planning, agricultural productivity, community development, employment generation, refugee resettlement, and natural disaster relief. Nonprofit organizations such as the International Voluntary Service, Catholic Relief Service, and CARE provide similar development services as the U.S. Peace Corps. The Population Council's involvement in family planning and health issues affects all other development issues in Third World countries. The World Affairs Councils function to increase the awareness of Americans concerning international issues. The Council for International Exchange of Scholars (Fulbright-Hays) and Meridian House International focus on promoting educational and cultural exchanges.

The major nonprofit international organizations which hire international specialists for headquarter and field locations and have full-time staffs of at least 20 and an annual budget exceeding $5 million include:

- Africare
- Agricultural Cooperative Development International
- American Friends Service Committee
- American Institute for Free Labor Development
- American Jewish Joint Distribution Committee
- Association for Voluntary Sterilization
- Cooperative for American Relief Everywhere, Inc. (CARE)
- Catholic Medical Mission Board
- Catholic Relief Services
- Christian Children's Fund, Inc.
- Church World Service
- Direct Relief International
- Family Planning International Assistance
- Food for the Hungry
- Foster Parents Plan International
- Heifer Project International
- Holt International Children's Services
- The Institute of Cultural Affairs
- Interchurch Medical Assistance, Inc.
- International Eye Foundation
- International Executive Service Corps
- International Human Assistance Programs, Inc.
- International Planned Parenthood Federation
- International Rescue Committee
- Lutheran World Relief
- MAP International
- Mennonite Economic Development Associates, Inc.
- Overseas Education Fund
- Partnership for Productivity International
- Pathfinder Fund
- People to People Health Foundation, Inc.
- Population Council
- Salvation Army
- Save the Children Federation, Inc.
- United Methodist Committee on Relief
- Volunteers in Technical Assistance (VITA)
- World Concern
- World Relief
- World Vision International

Many of these nonprofit organizations, including religious-affiliated organizations, are major recipients of USAID contracts. They work closely with the USAID bureaucracy as well as many private contracting firms and universities that are also major recipients of USAID funding. As such, they play an important role in the peripheral network of organizations involved in U.S. foreign policy efforts. From October 1990 to September 1991, for example, the following U.S.nonprofit organizations, or NGOs, were major recipients of USAID funding:

Non-Governmental Organization	Total dollars awarded
■ Adventist Development and Relief Agency International	$6,383,863
■ Africare, Inc.	$17,918,011
■ Catholic Relief Services	$42,787,203
■ Cooperative for American Relief Everywhere, Inc. (CARE)	$36,755,515
■ Helen Keller International	$9,293,177
■ Pathfinder Fund	$88,745,614
■ People-to-People Health Foundation, Inc.	$76,980,735
■ Planned Parenthood Federation of America	$98,627,591
■ Population Council	$46,293,154
■ Population Services International	$30,077,589
■ Private Agencies Collaborating Together	$25,795,971
■ Save the Children Foundation	$70,919,004
■ Volunteers in Technical Assistance	$18,117,759
■ World Vision Relief and Development, Inc.	$16,560,812

However, many other nonprofit organizations are not linked to the government in this manner. Organizations such as **Oxfam America**, a noted self-help development and disaster relief organization operating in Africa, Asia, Latin America, and the Caribbean, the **Pearl S. Buck Foundation** that works with Amerasian children, and numerous religious organizations doing development-related missionary work abroad have their own funding sources.

Most of these nonprofit organizations are headquartered in the United States—primarily Washington, DC, New York City, and a few other east coast cities—but have field operations in many countries throughout Latin America, Africa, and Asia. Most of the job opportunities will be in the field and thus require individuals with certain technical and linguistic skills along with some international experience.

VOLUNTEER OPPORTUNITIES

You will also find numerous volunteer groups operating in Third World countries. Many of these groups, such as Amigos de las Americas (5618 Star Lane, Houston, TX 77057, Tel. 800/231-7796) and Volunteers for Peace (43 Tiffany Road, Belmont, VT 05730, Tel. 802/259-2759), offer students and others opportunities to work on development projects in Third World countries. Many groups require you to pay for your own transportation, food, and housing—which are often minimal—but they do provide excellent opportunities to get international experience without joining the U.S. Peace Corps or some other type of organization. If you lack international experience and want to "test the waters" to see if this type of international lifestyle is for you, consider joining a volunteer group for three to six months that would put you in a work situation abroad. You will acquire valuable experience and learn a great deal about the Third World and the network of government agencies, nonprofit organizations, and contracting firms operating abroad—as well as yourself.

USEFUL RESOURCES

When conducting research on international nonprofit organizations, you should examine several directories that identify who's who in the international nonprofit arena:

- *Encyclopedia of Associations*
- *Yearbook of International Organizations*
- *USAID Current Technical Service Contracts and Grants*

The first two publications are found in the reference section of most major libraries. The third item is produced by USAID. Information on getting access to this document is provided in Chapter Twelve.

USAID also publishes two useful directories on nonprofit organizations:

Voluntary Foreign Aid Programs (Washington, DC: USAID, Food for Peace and Voluntary Assistance Bureau, Private Voluntary Cooperation Office, Tel. 703/235-1689 to receive a copy).

Directory of Development Resources (Washington, DC: USAID, Bureau of Science and Technology; Tel. 301/9517191 for order information from AID/DIHF).

Although somewhat dated, these directories will be available at the USAID Library in Rosslyn, Virginia (SA18, Rosslyn Plaza, Tel. 703/875-4818) as well as many other libraries.

Several books on international jobs and careers identify and discuss numerous nonprofit organizations offering job opportunities:

- *The Almanac of International Jobs and Careers*
- *The Overseas List*
- *International Jobs*
- *Careers In International Affairs*
- *Guide To Careers In World Affairs*
- *International Careers*
- *The Nonprofit's Job Finder*

Our forthcoming *Jobs and Careers With Nonprofit Organizations* will also include useful contact information on such organizations.

A few other books focus solely on finding jobs with nonprofit organizations regardless of their domestic or international settings. Some of these books may be useful:

- *Careers in the Nonprofit Sector*
- *Doing Well by Doing Good*
- *Goodworks: A Guide to Social Change Careers*
- *Great Careers: The Fourth of July Guide to Careers, Internships, and Volunteer Opportunities in the Nonprofit Sector*
- *Profitable Careers in Nonprofit*

Several other books and directories focus specifically on nonprofit international organizations. These include:

The Development Directory: Published by Editorial PKG, 108 Neck Road, Madison, CT 00443, Tel. 203/421-3497.

Internet Profiles: Published by Network for International Technical Assistance, P.O. Box 3245, Chapel Hill, NC 27515, Tel. 919/968-8324. This is the "bible" for locating organizations involved in development assistance. Provides detailed information on all development-oriented organizations. Since this directory costs $500, you may want to check with a major library to see if they have it in their reference section.

Interaction Member Profiles: Published by American Council for Voluntary International Action, 200 Park Avenue South, New York, NY 10003.

US Non-Profit Organizations in Development Assistance Abroad (TAICH Directory): Published in 1983 by the Council of Volunteer Agencies for Foreign Service, 200 Park Avenue South, New York, NY

10003. Includes 535 nonprofits. One of the best of the directories, it is now out-of-print but available in many large libraries.

Overseas Development Network (ODN) Opportunities Catalog: Published by the Overseas Development Network in Cambridge, MA. Describes 52 development organizations offering internships, research, and employment opportunities for students. To join ODN, write or call: Overseas Development Network, P.O. Box 1430, Cambridge, MA 02238, Tel. 617868-3002. For correspondence, write or call: SIDO, ODN Clearinghouse Project, Box 2306, Stanford, CA 94305, Tel. 415/4979262.

Technical Assistance Programs of US Non-Profit Organizations: Published by the American Council of Voluntary Agencies for Foreign Service, New York City, NY.

Several organizations provide clearinghouse, job listing, and placement services for individuals interested in working for nonprofit international organizations. Among these are:

InterAction: American Council For Voluntary International Action (200 Park Avenue S., New York, NY 10003, Tel. 212/777-8210 or 1815 H Street, NW, Washington, DC 20006, Tel. 202/822-8429: Consisting of a coalition of over 100 U.S. private and voluntary international organizations, InterAction provides information and advice on employment with nonprofit international organizations. This is one of the best international networks available.

CODEL (Coordination in Development, 79 Madison Ave., New York, NY 10016, Tel. 212/685-2030): Clearinghouse for over 40 church-related agencies working abroad.

PACT (Private Agencies Collaborating Together, 777 U.N. Plaza, New York, NY 10017, Tel. 212/697-6222): Consortium of 19 nonprofit agencies working abroad.

The International Service Agencies: (6000 Executive Blvd., Suite 608, Rockville, MD 29852, Tel. 800/638-8079). A federation of 37 American service organizations involved in disaster relief as well as agricultural development, education, job training, medical care, and refugee assistance.

Intercristo, The Career and Human Resources Specialists (19303 Fremont Avenue North, Seattle, WA 98133, Tel. 800/251-7740 or 206/546-7330): This is a Christian placement network which focuses on job opportunities in mission and ministry organizations, many of which are overseas.

If you are in the field of international health, you are fortunate to have a career-aware professional organization to assist you in locating health organizations and job opportunities. The National Council for International Health (NCIH) promotes international health through numerous educational services and publishes the *International Health News, Directory of Health Agencies,* and *U.S. Based Agencies Involved in International Health.* It also publishes job listings: *Monthly Job Vacancy Bulletin.* For information on these publications and their job related services, contact:

> National Council for International Health
> 1701 K Street, NW, Suite 600
> Washington, DC 20036
> Tel. 202/833-5900

If you are interested in international volunteer opportunities, including internships, you will find several useful directories and books to assist you in locating organizations whose missions most meet your interests and needs:

- *Alternatives to the Peace Corps: Gaining Third World Experience*
- *Career Opportunities in International Development in Washington, DC*
- *The Directory of International Internships*
- *Directory of Overseas Summer Jobs*
- *Directory of Volunteer Opportunities*
- *The Directory of Work and Study in Developing Countries*
- *The International Directory of Voluntary Work*
- *The International Directory of Youth Internships*
- *International Internships and Volunteer Programs*
- *Invest Yourself: The Catalogue of Volunteer Opportunities*
- *Jobs Abroad: Over 3,000 Vacancies of Interest to Christians*
- *U.S. Voluntary Organizations and World Affairs*
- *Volunteer! The Comprehensive Guide to Voluntary Service in the U.S. and Abroad*
- *Volunteer Vacations*
- *VolunteerWork*
- *Work, Study, Travel Abroad*
- *Work Your Way Around the World*
- *Working Holidays*

Several professional organizations provide assistance for individuals seeking information on employment with nonprofit organizations. The Society for

Nonprofit Organizations, for example, is the only national society organized to promote nonprofit organizations. Its more than 5,000 member organizations constitute an important professional network of nonprofit executives and directors. The Society publishes a bimonthly journal (*The Nonprofit World*, $59 annual subscription) and regularly conducts workshops, provides technical assistance, and publishes resources for strengthening nonprofit organizations. The Society also distributes a *Resource Center Catalog* that includes some books on careers in nonprofit organizations. You can contact this organization at the following address and phone number:

> Society For Nonprofit Organizations
> 6314 Odana Rd., Suite 1
> Madison, WI 53719
> Tel. 608/274-9777

However, do not call this organization for information on jobs or for acquiring a directory of its members. They have neither. What they will do is refer you to their catalog as well as a job network organized for nonprofit organizations—*Access*.

The Taft Group, one of the nation's leading information and professional service firms for nonprofit organizations, provides numerous resources and services for individuals seeking employment with these organizations. The Taft Group provides executive search services for individuals seeking positions in development marketing and public relations. If you are interested in executive level positions, you may want to subscribe to their newsletter, *The Nonprofit Executive*, which provides the latest information on executive level developments. However, keep in mind that this organization, as well as the Society for Nonprofit Organizations, is oriented toward all nonprofit organizations which are primarily U.S. domestic organizations. International nonprofit organizations make up only a small percentage of their organizational scope. You can contact this organization by writing or calling:

> The Taft Group
> 12300 Twinbrook Pkwy., Suite 450
> Rockville, MD 20852
> Tel. 301/816-0210

Other organizations can provide information on other types of international experiences, including sponsoring internships and volunteer experiences, that can be useful for developing international skills and experiences. A sample of the many such organizations available include:

The Experiment in International Living: Conducts numerous programs in international education, training, and technical assistance, including homestay programs where participants live with families abroad while learning about the local culture. Contact: The Experiment in International Living, Kipling Road, Brattleboro, VT 05302, Tel. 802/257-7751.

Association Internationale des Etudiants en Sciences Economiques et Commerciales (AIESEC). This international management organization provides students with training opportunities in international business. Most positions are internships with businesses abroad for periods ranging from 2 to 18 months. Contact: Public Relations Director, AIESEC-U.S., Inc., 14 West 23rd Street, New York, NY 10010, Tel. 212/206-1888.

International Association for the Exchange of Students for Technical Experience (IAESTE). Provides students with technical backgrounds opportunities to work abroad for 2-3 month periods. Contact: IAESTE Trainee Program, c/o Association for International Practical Training, Park View Boulevard, 10480 Little Patuxent Parkway, Columbia, MD 21044, Tel. 301/997-2200.

Volunteers for Peace, Inc. Operates a program that places individuals in work camps at home and abroad. Much of the work involves construction, agricultural, and environmental programs. Contact: Volunteers for Peace, Inc., Tiffany Road, Belmont, VT 05730, Tel. 802/259-2759.

Major job listing information services that provide biweekly or monthly information on job vacancies with nonprofit organizations include:

Community Jobs: The Employment Newspaper For the Non-Profit Sector: A "must" resource for anyone looking for a job with nonprofits. This 40-page monthly newspaper is filled with job hunting tips as well as nearly 400 job listings for individuals interested in working in the nonprofit sector. Each issue includes some listings for international nonprofit organizations. Individuals can subscribe by sending $29 for 3 issues or $39 for 6 issues to: Access: Networking in the Public Interest, 50 Beacon Street, Boston, MA 02108, Tel. 617/720-5627.

International Employment Gazette: One of the newest and most comprehensive bi-weekly publications listing more than 400 vacancies in each issue. Includes many jobs in construction and business but also with nonprofit organizations. Offers a custom-designed International Placement Network service for individuals. Contact: International Employment Gazette, 1525 Wade Hampton Blvd., Greenville, SC 29609, Tel. 800/882-9188. $35 for 6 issues; $55 for 12 issues; $95 for 24 issues (1 year).

International Jobs Bulletin: A biweekly publication listing information on hundreds of organizations offering job vacancies overseas. Contact: University Placement Center, Southern Illinois University, Carbondale, IL 62901-4703. $25 for 20 issues.

International Employment Hotline: Monthly listing of job vacancies available worldwide in government, consulting firms, nonprofit organizations, educational institutions, and business. Includes informative articles on the problems, pitfalls, and promises of finding an international job, including useful job search tips. Contact: International Employment Hotline, P.O. Box 3030, Oakton, VA 22124, Tel. 703/620-1972. $36 for 12 issues.

Job Opportunities Bulletin: A bimonthly listing of job vacancies available for individuals interested in the field of international development. Includes many NGOs, consulting firms, and educational institutions funded by USAID. Contact: TransCentury Recruitment Center, 1724 Kalorama Rd., NW, Washington, DC 20009, Tel. 202/328-4400. $25.00 (US/Canada/Mexico) or $40.00 (all other locations) for airmail. This organization also offers weekly international job search workshops.

Monthly Job Vacancy Bulletin: A monthly job listing bulletin published by the National Council for International Health, 1701 K St., NW, Suite 600, Washington, DC 20006, Tel. 202/833-5900. Includes jobs for health care professionals only.

Options: Published by Project Concern, P.O. Box 85322, San Diego, CA 92138, Tel. 619/279-9690. Includes jobs for health care professionals in the U.S., East Asia, the Pacific, Latin America, and Africa.

PDRC Placement Hotline: Published by the School for International Training, Kipling Road, Brattleboro, VT 03302, Tel. 257-7751, Ext. 258.

Monday Developments: Published by Interaction, 1815 H St., NW, Washington, DC 20006, Tel. 202/822-8429.

Modern Language Association Job Information Lists: Published four times a year. 62 Fifth Avenue, New York, NY 10011.

If you are a *Returned Peace Corps Volunteer*, you will want to use the job services available through the Returned Volunteer Services office: Peace Corps, 1990 K Street, NW, Room 8428, Washington, DC 20526, Tel. 202/254-8326 or 1-800/424-8580, Ext. 284. Please do not contact this office unless you are a returned volunteer. This already over-worked office can only provide information and services to its former volunteers and staff members—both old and recently separated. If you left Peace Corps 20 years ago, you can still use this service. It has an excellent library of international resources as well as numerous job listings relevant to its volunteers. It also publishes a biweekly job listing bulletin called *HOTLINE: A Bulletin of Opportunities for Returned Peace Corps Volunteers*. You should also request a copy of *International Careers*, a useful directory summarizing major international employers relevant to the interests and skills of ex-Peace Corps Volunteers. It may well be worth your time and effort to visit this center. After all, Washington, DC is located in the heart of hundreds of organizations offering international job opportunities for those interested in pursuing jobs and careers with nonprofit organizations as well as with consulting firms and educational organizations relevant to the Peace Corps experience. Better still, many of these organizations are staffed by individuals who are part of the growing "old boy/girl network" of ex-Peace Corps volunteers who look favorably toward individuals with Peace Corps experience. Better still, many nonprofit organizations, consulting firms, and educational organizations automatically contact this office when they have impending vacancies.

JOB SEARCH STRATEGIES

Use the same strategies for landing a job with an international nonprofit organization as you would for any other nongovernmental organization. This essentially involves networking, informational interviewing, and moving your face, name, and resume among key people associated with these organizations at both the staff and board levels—the subjects of Chapters Six and Seven. Success in landing such a job will take time, tenacity, and a positive attitude. Your best location for literally "hitting the streets" and "pounding the pavement" for nonprofit organizations will be Washington, DC and to a lesser extent New York City.

At the same time you will encounter numerous contracting firms and educational organizations that are part of a closely knit network of international development organizations. You may discover that many of these other organizations offer similar job opportunities as the nonprofit organizations. Consequently, we recommend conducting a job search that is **inclusive** of these other counterpart network organizations. All of the books and directories outlined thus far will go a long way in helping you focus your job search on specific organizations for networking, informational interviews, and submitting applications for job vacancies.

Many of the nonprofit international organizations will be organized with headquarters in the United States, especially New York City and Washington, DC, and field operations in developing countries. While most nonprofits hire through headquarters, many also hire individuals in the field. If you are already in the field and neither have the time nor money to travel to Washington, DC or New York City to conduct an intensive job search, make sure you develop contacts with field representatives in your area. Nonprofit organizations tend to be very field oriented and thus many useful job contacts can be made at the field level. Your research on each organization will determine how, where, and with whom to best target your job search within each organization.

Chapter Fourteen

ASSOCIATIONS, FOUNDATIONS, RESEARCH, AND EDUCATIONAL ORGANIZATIONS

Several other types of public-oriented organizations also provide numerous international job opportunities. These organizations are part of an important network that pursues similar public goals. In contrast to the consulting firms and nonprofit organizations that primarily function within Third World countries, the organizations in this chapter play important roles in both developed and developing countries. If, for example, you are more interested in working in Western Europe than in Africa or Latin America, the associations, foundations, research, and educational organizations outlined in this chapter may provide you with some interesting job and career options.

TRADE AND PROFESSIONAL ASSOCIATIONS

Trade and professional associations are particular types of organizations involved in pursuing public goals. Since most associations promote the interests of their members by influencing government policies, they become involved in the political process. In this sense, they are public organizations maintaining close relationships with elected representative and government agencies.

National trade and professional organizations consist of various types of organizations such as trade associations, labor unions, and professional, scientific, and technical societies. While no exact statistics are compiled on the number of such organizations, best estimates put the number at approximately 40,000 associations in the United States. The largest number operate at the state and local levels. More than 100,000—many of which are chapters of parent organizations—function at the state level alone. Approximately 7,000 are national associations with numerous affiliated regional groups and local chapters. More than 200 organizations function as association management firms involved in managing the affairs of over 500 national associations and nearly 1000 local and regional associations.

The largest concentration of associations is in the Washington, DC Metro area. Approximately 2,500 associations, or 32 percent of all associations, are headquartered in Washington, DC; 18 percent in Chicago; and 16 percent in New York City. The remaining 34 percent are located in other cities throughout the United States, especially in San Francisco, Los Angeles, Cleveland, and Philadelphia.

Many of the major trade and professional associations in the United States have international affiliations or are organized primarily as international associations to promote members' interests among international organizations and national governments.

There are literally thousands of international trade and professional associations. For example, under the key word "International" the *Encyclopedia of Associations* lists over 3,300 such associations; the key word "World" generates another 675 international associations. The major international trade and professional associations include:

U.S.-Based Trade and Professional Associations

- Aerospace Industries Associations of America
- Aircraft Owners and Pilots Association
- Airline Pilots Association International
- American Bankers Association
- American Chemical Society
- American Insurance Association
- American Iron and Steel Institute
- American Management Association
- American Paper Institute
- American Petroleum Institute
- American Plywood Association
- American Political Science Association
- American Society of International Law
- Chamber of Commerce of the United States
- Electronic Industries Association
- Foreign Credit Insurance Association
- International Studies Association
- Motor Vehicle Manufacturers Association of the U.S., Inc.
- National Association of Manufacturers
- National Education Association of the United States

- National Foreign Trade Council
- National Geographic Society

Trade Unions

- AFL-CIO
- Aluminum Workers International Union
- Amalgamated Clothing and Textile Workers Union
- Communications Workers of America
- International Association of Machinists and Aerospace Workers
- United Automobile, Aerospace and Agricultural Implementation
- Workers International Union
- United Food and Commercial Workers International Union
- United Mine Workers
- United Steelworkers

International Trade and Professional Organizations

- International Air Transport Association
- International Chamber of Commerce
- International Co-Operative Alliance
- Council of the Americas
- Foreign Policy Association
- National Association of Foreign Student Affairs
- National Council for U.S.-China Trade
- Transafrica
- Young President's Organization

Most of these organizations offer job opportunities with their headquarter's staff. The positions involve everything from public relations, communications, and research to organizing annual meetings and lobbying legislatures.

Detailed information on these and other international trade and professional associations is found in the following directories:

- *Encyclopedia of Associations*
- *Europa Year Book*
- *National Trade and Professional Associations of the U.S.*
- *Yearbook of International Organizations*

These directories provide the necessary names, addresses, telephone numbers, and annotated descriptions to get you started in the proper direction for locating job opportunities with these associations.

You may also want to monitor vacancy announcements and use the job placement services of the two major professional organizations for association executives:

- American Society of Association Executives (ASAE)
- Greater Washington Society of Association Executives (GWSAE)

The American Society of Association Executives is the largest professional association of association executives. It maintains a Washington staff of 110 individuals who assist 17,000 members. ASAE publishes a magazine, maintains a resume referral system, and provides executive search services for all types of positions—not just executive level ones. ASAE also publishes a useful annual directory of its members: *Who's Who in Association Management.* The directory comes free with membership, which can cost anywhere from $125 to $255 a year, depending on your affiliate status. You can also purchase the directory separately by sending $80 ($75 + $5 for postage) to the above address. You can contact them at:

American Society of Association Executives
1575 Eye St., NW
Washington, DC 20005
Tel. 202/727-2750 (Referral Services)
     202/626-2742 (Information)

The Greater Washington Society of Association Executives provides similar services. It publishes an annual association salary survey as well as a directory of their 3,100 members—*GWSAE Directory.* Nonmembers can purchase the directory for $90 ($85 plus $5 postage); members receive it free. Annual membership dues range from $100 to $245, depending on your affiliation. Contact them at:

Greater Washington Society of Association Executives
1426 21st St., NW, Suite 200
Washington, DC 20036-5901
Tel. 202/429-9370

The U.S. Chamber of Commerce also can provide job assistance. Included among its over 185,000 members are nearly 1,100 trade and professional associations that belong to this organization. One useful service of the Chamber is its Referral service which is organized especially for trade and professional associations. This is a free job referral service for professionals. They collect resumes and forward them to associations in need of specific personnel. You should pick up their application form at the reception desk (just ask for the Association Referral Service application form), complete it, and send it to the

Association Department so you can get into their resume data bank. For information on this and other Chamber of Commerce services, contact:

U.S. Chamber of Commerce
1615 H St., NW
Washington, DC 20062
Tel. 202/659-6000 (Information)
202/463-5560 (Association Department which
operates the Referral Service)

The U.S. Chamber of Commerce is also a potential source of employment. It presently has a staff of 1,100 and an annual operating budget of over $5 million. It publishes a booklet on working abroad: *Employment Abroad: Facts and Fallacies*.

Two organizations publish useful newspapers and maintain job services for associations. *Association Trends*, a weekly newspaper ($65 for 52 weekly issues), also maintains a job referral service. This publication goes to 7,000 associations throughout the United States and abroad with a readership of nearly 25,000. You want to pay particular attention to two sections in this newspaper: *"Executive Changes"* and *"Moves and Changes."* The newspaper reports on who leaves which association and thus identifies potential job vacancies. The *"Moves and Changes"* section identifies associations moving office locations from one city to another. Normally, these associations have immediate staffing needs since many of their employees will not move with the association. *Trends* also maintains a *"Free Resume"* service. For $52 and 10 copies of your resume, they will place a 30-word classified ad for the job you want in their Washington, New York, of Chicago editions for three consecutive weekly issues. When associations respond to your ad, *Trends* sends them a copy of your resume. The association then contacts you directly for more information or schedules you for an interview. Your only cost for this service is the $52 and 10 resumes. *Trends* will keep your file active for three months. You can get information on this publication and service by writing or calling:

Association Trends
4948 St. Elmo Ave., #306
Bethesda, MD 20814
Tel. 301/652-8666

The United States Association Executive also publishes a weekly newspaper which includes a classified section with association job listings. You will want to monitor various sections relevant to your job search, especially "Executive Changes", "Classifieds", and various calendars of meetings. A one-year, 60-issue subscription to this newspaper costs $75. For further information, contact:

United States Association Executive
4341 Montgomery Avenue
Bethesda, MD 20814
Tel. 301/951-1881

FOUNDATIONS AND
RESEARCH ORGANIZATIONS

Several foundations and research organizations either focus solely on the international arena or maintain an international division or section. You will need to consult the *Foundation Directory* and the *Research Center Directory* to identify the appropriate organizations.

Foundations vary in their approach to the international arena. Some foundations operate similarly to nonprofit development assistance organizations by maintaining full-time staffs at both headquarter and field locations. Other foundations primarily dispense grants to nonprofit organizations engaged in international development. The major foundations primarily funding international development include:

- Carnegie Corporation of New York
- China Medical Board of New York
- Edna McConnell Clark Foundation
- Ford Foundation
- W. K. Kellogg Foundation
- Lilly Endowment, Inc.
- Rockefeller Brothers Fund
- Rockefeller Foundation

Research organizations focusing on public international issues include several types of organizations. Some research organizations are special research units of universities or are part of graduate degree programs. Some research organizations function as think tanks for addressing major international economic and political issues. Several consulting firms also conduct research as a major part of their work. Some of the major research firms conducting international research include:

- American Enterprise Institute
- The Aspen Institute
- The Brookings Institute
- Carnegie Endowment for International Peace
- Center for Strategic and International Studies
- The Chicago Council on Foreign Relations
- The Conference Board
- Council on Foreign Relations

- East-West Center
- Economic Growth Center
- Economic Strategy Institute
- Government Research Corporation
- The Heritage Foundation
- The Hoover Institution
- Hudson Institute
- Institute For Policy Studies
- Institute of War and Peace Studies
- International Development Research Centre
- International Institute of Economics
- International Management and Development Institute
- Rand Corporation
- SRI (Stanford Research Institute) International

A few major domestic research organizations, such as the Urban Institute and Cato Institute, occasionally do some international research.

Four of these international-related "think tanks" should experience major growth throughout the 1990s and thus offer excellent job opportunities for those with the proper mix of international research skills:

- World Resource Institute
- Economic Strategy Institute
- International Institute of Economics
- Brookings Institute

Each of these foundations and research organizations have staff positions for highly skilled specialists. When seeking employment with these organizations, use the same job search strategies we outline in Chapters Five, Six, and Seven for other types of international organizations—research, networking, and informational interviewing.

EDUCATIONAL ORGANIZATIONS

Educational institutions have always been a major avenue for acquiring international experience as well as for pursuing education-related jobs and careers. One of the best ways to break into the international arena is through an educational program. Numerous colleges and universities offer area studies programs as well as internships and semester abroad programs which enable students to acquire first hand experience in living and studying abroad. Some programs even involve working abroad as part of an internship experience.

If you are interested in participating in an international education program that also provides a semester abroad, internship, or work experience, you should contact the following organizations for detailed information of how to identify and participate in such programs:

Council On International Educational Exchange (CIEE): 205 E. 42nd St., New York, NY 10017.

The Institute of International Education (IIE): 809 United Nations Plaza, New York, NY 10017.

National Association For Foreign Student Affairs (NAFSA): 1860 19th St., NW, Washington, DC 20009.

School For International Training: The Experiment In International Living, Kipling Road, Brattleboro, VT 05301-0676.

YWCA Intern Abroad Programme International: YMCA of Metropolitan Washington, 1711 Rhode Island Ave., NW, Washington, DC 20036.

YMCA International Camp Counsellors Program/Abroad: 236 East 47th St., New York, NY 10017.

American Friends Service Committee: 1501 Cherry Street, Philadelphia, PA 19102, Tel. 215/295-7000.

Amigos de Las Americas: 5618 Star Lane, Houston, TX 77057, Tel. 800/231-7796.

Association For the Advancement of International Education: Rm. 200 Norman Hall, College of Education, University of Florida, Gainesville, FL 32611.

American Institute For Foreign Study: Greenwich Avenue, Greenwich, CT 06830, Tel. 800/727-2437 or 203/869-9090.

Each group offers a variety of publications and services to assist you in identifying the best program for your particular interests.

Numerous books and resource guides can provide you with a wealth of information on how to locate the right educational program or related work experience abroad. One of our favorite resources is the bimonthly magazine *Transitions Abroad: The Guide To Learning, Living, and Working Overseas* ($18 for 6 issues—subscribe by contacting Transitions Abroad, Dept. TRA, Box 3000, Denville, NJ 07834; it's also available through Impact Publications by completing the order form at the end of this book). This publication is filled with practical information on educational, travel, and work programs abroad. Be sure to examine the special July/August issue entitled *Educational Travel Directory* which is the annual roundup of the year's best international resources.

Other excellent resources on educational, work, and travel abroad programs include:

- *The ABC's of Study In Japan*
- *Academic Year Abroad*
- *China Bound: A Guide To Academic Life and Work In the PRC*
- *Directory of International Internships*
- *Directory of Programs In Soviet and East European Studies*
- *Directory of Work and Study In Developing Countries*
- *The ECIS Directory of International Schools*
- *Fellowship Guide To Western Europe*
- *Fellowships, Scholarships, and Related Opportunities In International Education*
- *Guide To Educational Programs In the Third World*
- *Guide To Living, Studying, and Working In the People's Republic of China*
- *Higher Education In the European Community: Student Handbook*
- *Higher Education In the United Kingdom*
- *International Directory For Youth Internships With the United Nations, Its Specialized Agencies, and Nongovernmental Organizations*
- *International Educational Travel Planner*
- *International Handbook of Universities*
- *The International Scholarship Book*
- *International Work Camps Directory*
- *Learning Vacations*
- *Management Study Abroad*
- *The New Global Yellow Pages*
- *New Guide To Study Abroad*
- *Schools Abroad of Interest To Americans*
- *Social Science Research Council Fellowships and Grants*
- *Student Travel Catalog*
- *Study and Research Opportunities In the Middle East and North Africa*
- *Study Abroad*
- *Study Holidays*
- *Studying In India*
- *Study In the United Kingdom and Ireland*
- *Taking Off: Extraordinary Ways To Spend Your First Year Out of College*
- *Teaching Abroad*

- *The Teenager's Guide To Study, Travel, and Adventure Abroad*
- *Third World Resource Directory: A Guide To Organizations and Publications*
- *Vacation Study Abroad*
- *Work, Study, Travel Abroad*
- *The Young American's Scholarship Guide To Travel and Learning Abroad*

Several embassies and consulates also provide pamphlets and booklets which outline education opportunities in their countries.

Many educators are interested in pursuing international careers either as teachers and instructors in the United States and abroad or as members of educational groups involved in developing educational institutions abroad. Elementary and secondary teachers interested in teaching abroad are well advised to contact the following organizations for assistance in locating teaching jobs abroad:

The Association of American Schools in South American Teacher Search (AASSA): 6972 NW 50th St., Miami, FL 33166, Tel. 305/594-3936.

Educational Career Services, Ohio State University: 110 Arps Hall, 1945 N. High St., Columbus, OH 43201, Tel. 614/292-2741.

English Educational Services International (EEIS) Newsletter: 139 Massachusetts Ave., Boston, MA 02115

ESOL Placement Service: The Center for Applied Linguistics, 3520 Prospect Street NW, Washington, DC 20007.

European Council of International Schools (ECIS): 21B Lavant St., Petersfield Hampshire, GU32 3EW England, Tel. 011/44-730-68244.

International Educators Cooperative (IEC): 212 Alcott Rd., E., Falmouth, MA 02536, Tel. 508/540-8173.

International Schools Services (ISS): P.O. Box 5910, 15 Roszel Rd., Princeton, NJ 08543, Tel. 609/452-0990.

Overseas Academic Opportunities: 949 E. 29th St., 2nd Floor, Brooklyn, NY 11210.

Overseas Employment Information For Teachers: Department of State, Washington, DC 20520.

Overseas Placement Service for Educators, University of Northern Iowa: Students Services Center #19, Cedar Falls, IA 50614, Tel. 319/273-2061.

Overseas Recruiting Fair Placement Office, Queen's University: Faculty of Education, Kingston, Ontario K7L 3N6, Tel. 613/545-6222.

Overseas Schools Services: 446 Louise St., Farmville, VA 23901, Tel. 804/392-6445.

Register For International Service In Education: Institute of International Education, 809 United Nations Plaza, New York, NY 10017.

Teachers Overseas Recruitment Center (TORC): National Teacher Placement Bureau, P.O. Box 609027, Cleveland, OH 44109, Tel. 216/741-3771.

TESOL Bulletin: Teaching English to Speakers of Other Languages (TESOL), 1600 Cameron St., Suite 300, Alexandria, VA 22314.

We especially like *The International Educator* which is published by The Overseas Schools Assistance Corporation (P.O. Box 103, West Bridgewater, MA 02379, Tel. 508/580-1880, $25 a year for 4 issues). This quarterly tabloid covers international education developments as well as includes numerous job vacancies in each issue.

If you are interested in university positions, contact the following organization for information on the Fulbright Program:

Council For International Exchange of Scholars: 11 Dupont Circle, Suite 300, Washington, DC 20036, Tel. 202/939-5400.

You will find many other publications purporting to provide information on teaching opportunities abroad. However, many of these publications are basically a rip-off which provide nothing more than names and addresses of international schools you can acquire free from your public library or the Department of Defense.

If you are interested in working for a Department of Defense school abroad, you should write or call for a free copy of a list of nearly 270 DOD schools:

Office of Overseas Dependents Schools
Department of Defense
2461 Eisenhower Ave.
Alexandria, VA 22331
Tel. 202/325-0885

Beware of advertisements that offer to sell you the same list for $10 per country! Also keep in mind that during the next three years several DOD schools are closing or cutting back on personnel in response to the downsizing of American military personnel in both Europe and Asia.

The Department of State also assists more than 100 international schools abroad. For information on teaching opportunities with these schools, contact:

Office of Overseas Schools
Room 234, SA-6
Department of State
Washington, DC 20520
Tel. 703/235-9600

Several American corporations also operate schools abroad for American dependents. Contact the following corporations for information on their schools:

Arabian American Oil Company
1345 Avenue of the Americas
New York, NY 10105

Exxon
1251 Avenue of the Americas
New York, NY 10020

Firestone Tire and Rubber Company
Akron, OH 44317

Orinoco Mining Company
525 William Penn Place
Pittsburgh, PA 15230

Texaco, Inc.
1345 Avenue of the Americas
New York, NY 10105

United Brands Company
Prudential Center
Boston, MA 02199

The Panama Canal Company also offers teaching positions in their schools. Write to the following address for information on opportunities and application procedures:

Panama Canal Company
Division of Schools
Box 2012
Balboa Heights
Canal Zone, PANAMA

Other useful sources of information on overseas teaching positions include:

Information and Reference Division
Institute of International Education
809 United Nations Plaza
New York, NY 10017

Teacher Exchange Section
U.S. Department of Education
Washington, DC 20202

Office of Personnel and Training
U.S. Information Agency
1776 Pennsylvania Ave., NW
Washington, DC 20547

Individuals can also find numerous opportunities relating to teaching English abroad. For a country-by-country examination of such opportunities, Susan Griffith's *Teaching English Abroad* (Princeton, NJ: Peterson's, 1991) is one of the best resources for finding teaching positions abroad. While written from a British perspective, the book includes valuable information for anyone interested in international teaching positions. Some books focus on a single country. If, for example, you are interested in teaching English in Japan, you should consult John Wharton's *Jobs In Japan* (Denver, CO: The Global Press, 1991) or Terra Brockman's *The Job Hunter's Guide To Japan* (1991).

Other books of interest to teachers include:

- *The ECIS Directory of International Schools*
- *The Educators' Passport To International Jobs*
- *The ISS Directory of Overseas Schools*
- *How To Teach Abroad*
- *Overseas American-Sponsored Elementary and Secondary Schools Assisted By the U.S. Department of State*
- *Schools Abroad of Interest to Americans*
- *Teaching Abroad*
- *Teaching In Private American and International Schools Overseas*
- *Teaching Opportunities In the Middle East and North Africa*
- *Teaching Overseas: The Caribbean and Latin American Area*

If you teach at the university level, you may find opportunities to teach and conduct research abroad through your present institution, through a regional international consortium, or through such programs as the Fulbright Program (Council For International Exchange of Scholars). You should also monitor the job vacancy announcements appearing in *The Chronicle of Higher Education* as well as in professional journals and newsletters of your academic discipline. Occasionally overseas university vacancy announcements appear in *The New York Times, Washington Post, Wall Street Journal, National Business Employment Weekly*, and a few other major newspapers. Major international magazines, such as *The Far Eastern Economic Review* and *The Economist*, regularly list university vacancy announcements.

Numerous teaching opportunities are also available by directly applying to local schools in each country without the assistance of a U.S.-based organization or with a U.S.-sponsored school. While salaries may appear inadequate in many local schools, such teaching positions do offer an opportunity to gain experience in living and working abroad.

Foundations are major funding sources for educators who are involved in research abroad. Educators normally submit research proposals to foundations willing to fund certain types of projects in various regions and countries. The Ford Foundation and Rockefeller Foundations have been particularly active in promoting research abroad. If you are interested in receiving foundation support for your international research, begin by consulting the *Foundation Directory* for information on the various foundations that may fund projects in your area of interest. Your university and college library or research and development office should be able to provide you with additional assistance.

Chapter Fifteen

BUSINESS AND THE TRAVEL INDUSTRY

The international changes taking place in the early 1990s have significant implications for new international jobs in the decade ahead. While government, international organizations, contracting firms, nonprofit organizations, associations, foundations, and educational institutions will continue to provide numerous international job and career opportunities, business and the travel industry especially will be riding high throughout the latter half of the 1990s. These industries are likely to create the largest number of new international jobs and careers in the coming decade.

Indeed, the network of public institutions that have primarily focused on solving the development problems of Third World countries during the past four decades have in recent years recognized the importance of promoting greater foreign investment and entrepreneurship in developing countries. Ironically, many of these ostensibly "public institutions" may play key roles in the expansion of foreign investment as well as in developing local entrepreneurial skills for an increasingly interdependent world economy due to the developing linkages with strong private sectors among countries. Countries that fail to curtail as well as trim their bulging and often parasitic public bureaucracies and, at the same time, expand and strengthen their private sectors will be left out of the international economic mainstreams of the 1990s. Where business goes in the 1990s so too will many new international jobs and careers—and opportunities for you.

Business and the travel industry go hand in hand. As more countries become developed through an expanding and strong private sector of manufacturing and service industries, so too does the travel industry. Hotels, airlines, restaurants, and travel and tourist services expand in response to increased business activity as well as to public sector efforts to develop and position a country's travel industry through foreign investment and local private initiatives.

INTERNATIONAL BUSINESS

Opportunities in international business cover a wide range of organizations and jobs. They include jobs with such traditional organizations as banks, oil and chemical companies, manufacturers, importers, and exporters. Positions involve everything from political risk analysis to sourcing for new products and management, sales, and marketing positions.

Breaking In

Breaking into international business requires experience within particular industries—moreso than the knowledge of foreign languages, area studies, or international experience. Most large corporations, for example, assign employees to foreign operations as one step in a promotion hierarchy that requires key personnel to have foreign experience prior to advancing to other positions within the company. Many well established companies have few overseas assignments because they have already developed talented local staffs that have the requisite skills to function locally. An ideal company would be one just starting to develop overseas operations. During their initial stage of developing a new market and establishing a local base of operations, they normally send expatriates abroad. As more and more companies expand their operations abroad or broaden the scope of operations into new countries, numerous opportunities should be available for working abroad. Many of the positions will involve marketing, sales, finance, and sourcing for new parts and products. Consequently, your best opportunities in international business may be with small companies just starting to enter the international business arena or expanding into new locations. Many large corporations with established operations abroad will be closed to individuals seeking entry-level international positions.

Many small international companies look for individuals with management and marketing skills who also enjoy working abroad. Many of these positions may be in international sales and involve working from a home base in New York, London, Rome, Singapore, Hong Kong, or Tokyo. Breaking into these firms requires having the right kinds of "connections" to people who make the hiring decisions. It involves networking within the international business community. One of the best ways to get such connections is to know people who already work in the international business community. You might, for example, attend a semester abroad program in Europe, Asia, or Latin America which involves studying the local international business community. Alternatively, you might acquire an internship with an international business that puts you in the heart of the international business community where you develop numerous contacts with individuals in many different businesses. The people may later become your ticket to gaining entry to many international businesses.

Several of the organizations and programs outlined in the educational section of Chapter Fourteen should help you in making connections to the international business community. You should also consider taking international business-related courses in college as well as such bread-and-butter business courses as accounting, finance, and marketing along with one or two foreign languages. If you are a business major, you should consider participating in an international business internship or other international work-related business experience. Three of the best such programs are:

Association Internationale des Etudiants en Sciences Economiques et Commerciales (AIESEC): Public Relations Director, AIESEC-U.S., Inc., 14 West 23rd Street, New York, NY 10010, Tel. 212/206-1888.

Association For International Practical Training (AIPT): American City Building, Suite 217, Columbia, MD 21044, Tel. 301/997-2200.

U.S. Student Travel Service (USSTS): 801 2nd Avenue, New York, NY 10017, Tel. 212/867-8770.

In the case of AIESEC, you will need to be involved in a local AIESEC chapter in order to participate in this student operated program. Check first to see if your college or university has a chapter. If not, you might want to contact AIESEC for information on establishing a chapter.

Several companies, such as Chase Manhattan Bank, Salomon Brothers, IBM, Monsanto, United Technologies, General Electric, and Allied-Signal, have established summer internship programs in a variety of business areas. You will have to apply directly to these companies for application information. For information on these and other international internship opportunities, see Will Cantrell's and Francine Moderno's *International Internships and Volunteer Programs* (Oakton, VA: Worldwise Books, 1992). This book can be ordered directly from the publisher by sending $20.95 ($18.95 plus $2.00 shipping) to Worldwise Books, P.O. Box 3030, Oakton, VA 22124.

You might also consider creating your own internship by contacting companies directly and selling them on the idea of letting you work for them as an unpaid or low paid intern. This form of volunteerism within the business community may be well received by some small companies that basically receive an offer they can't refuse!

Not all international business opportunities are with U.S.-based multinational corporations or small businesses. Don't neglect foreign-based businesses that may be interested in American management and marketing skills—two major American business strengths that are highly sought in many countries. Many foreign companies interested in breaking into the American, European, or Asian markets may be interested in your international business skills or your general management and marketing expertise. Again, you learn about these companies through the process of networking within particular countries and selling your skills to potential foreign employers.

Know Your Business

Numerous types of businesses offer a large variety of international job and career opportunities:

- Commercial and investment banking
- Marketing
- Management
- Finance
- Accounting
- Consulting
- News media and broadcasting
- Entertainment (motion pictures, video, games)
- Telecommunications
- Architectural and engineering services
- Construction
- Transportation
- Aerospace
- Shipping
- Insurance
- Publishing and printing
- Retailing and trading
- Sourcing for parts/products
- Mining
- Natural resource production (mining, petroleum, natural gas)
- Manufacturing product lines (food, beverages, chemicals, paper, wood products, fiber, pharmaceuticals, computers, electronics, cosmetics, sporting goods, toys, musical instruments, industrial and farm equipment, apparel, appliances, tobacco, plastics, rubber, motor vehicles, military hardware)

Corporate United States plays a major role in world trade. Thousands of American businesses operate abroad and thousands more will be entering the international arena in the coming decade. Indeed, of the 500 largest world traders, 157—or 31.4 percent of the total—are U.S. corporations; Japan follows next with 150 companies. Collectively, European countries have the largest number of companies in the top 500—161. The U.S. barely remains dominant at present with seven of the 20 largest world traders being U.S. corporations:

20 LARGEST WORLD TRADERS

Rank	Company	Industry	Sales (billions)
1	General Motors (USA)	Auto	$126.9
2	Ford Motor (USA)	Auto	92.5
3	IBM (USA)	Data	62.7
4	Toyota Motor Corp. (Japan)	Auto	58.3
5	Hitachi Ltd. (Japan)	Elec	46.3
6	Philip Morris (USA)	Bev	44.8
7	General Electric (USA)	Elec	41.0
8	Matsushita Elect. (Japan)	Appl	39.8
9	Daimler-Benz (Germany)	Auto	39.3
10	Du Pont (USA)	Chem	35.5
11	Chrysler (USA)	Auto	34.9
12	Nissan Motor (Japan)	Auto	34.8
13	Siemens (Germany)	Elec	32.7
14	Fiat (Italy)	Auto	32.5
15	Volkswagen (Germany)	Auto	31.7
16	Unilevel NV (Netherlands)	Food	29.4
17	Unilever PLC (UK)	Food	27.9
18	Toshiba (Japan)	Auto	27.5
19	Philips (Netherlands)	Appl	26.6
20	Honda Motor (Japan)	Auto	25.2

SOURCE: *World Trade*, April/May 1990

Other large international companies included in the top 500 are leaders in aerospace, steel, beverage, photo, paper, computer, construction, machinery, health, textile, energy, and building materials industries. All of these multinational companies offer numerous international job and career opportunities at home and abroad regardless of one's nationality.

Useful Resources

Descriptions of many firms offering international job opportunities for these different types of businesses and industries, including important contact information, are found in the following international job and career books:

- *The Almanac of International Jobs and Careers*
- *Careers In International Affairs*
- *Guide To Careers In World Affairs*

- *How To Get a Job In Europe*
- *How To Get a Job In the Pacific Rim*
- *International Jobs*
- *Passport To Overseas Employment*
- *Worldwide Jobs* 1993

However, it is best that you conduct your own research for identifying the many thousands of businesses offering international job and career opportunities. Your best approach will be to initially consult the many business directories available in your local library. Three of the most useful directories are:

Directory of American Firms Operating In Foreign Countries (World Trade Academy Press, 50 E. 42nd St., Suite 509, New York, NY 10017). This three-volume, 2,500+ page directory is invaluable for locating the more than 3,200 U.S. companies operating in more than 120 countries. Provides information on the products/service lines of each company as well as identifies the countries in which they operate. Includes employment statistics and contact information.

Hoover's Handbook of World Business and *Hoover's Handbook of American Business* (Austin, TX: Reference Press, 1992). These two directories identify hundreds of major corporations in the U.S. and abroad. Each is filled with facts, statistics, corporate histories, and profiles with contact information.

You can find these directories in most major libraries.

Other useful business directories for researching businesses with international operations include:

- *The International Corporate 1,000*
- *The Multinational Marketing and Employment Directory*
- *Directory of Foreign Firms Operating in the U.S.*
- *Directory of Japanese Firms and Offices in the U.S.*
- *American Register of Exporters and Importers*
- *Dun and Bradstreet Exporter's Encyclopedia*
- *American Encyclopedia of International Information*
- *Trade Directories of the World*
- *Jane's Major Companies of Europe*
- *Principal International Business*
- *Fortune 500: Top 50 Exporters*
- *International Bankers Directory*
- *Who's Who in Banking*
- *Major Companies of Europe*
- *Directory of U.S. Firms Operating in Latin America*

- *Dun & Bradstreet's Middle Market Directory*
- *Dun & Bradstreet's Million Dollar Directory*
- *Standard & Poor's Industrial Index*
- *Standard & Poor's Register of Corporations, Directors and Executives*
- *How to Find Information About Companies*
- *Moody's Industrial Manual*
- *Thomas' Register of American Manufacturers*

Several other useful business directories are identified on pages 102-103 in our discussion of library research.

Many embassies also have special directories on international companies operating in their country. If you are interested in a particular country, you might call the embassy to find out if they have such a directory or information. Better still, many embassies maintain libraries which are primarily oriented toward business and commerce. They stock the library with numerous business and city telephone directories as well as magazines, newsletters, and reports that have a wealth of information on their local business community. If you are in Washington, DC, you should definitely plan to visit some of these libraries. They will give you the in-depth information you need on particular businesses rather than just general descriptive and contact information found in the international job books and directories. However, call ahead of time to find out if the embassy of your choice has such a library as well as inquire if and when you can use it.

THE TRAVEL INDUSTRY

We examine the travel industry as a separate category for international job and career opportunities for one major reason: many individuals are motivated to seek international jobs because of their initial international travel experiences. However, they frequently discover after landing an international job that working abroad is not the same as traveling abroad. In many cases, they would be much happier if they sought a job that enabled them to frequently travel abroad, which may or may not be through a job with government, international organizations, nonprofit organizations, contracting firms, associations, foundations, research organizations, educational institutions, or businesses. Better still, they may particularly enjoy working in an industry that enables them to pursue their passion—travel to exciting and exotic locations.

The international travel industry is one of the biggest and fastest growing industries in the world. It will be even bigger in the decade ahead as it is predicted to out-perform all other industries. As international business expands and more and more people travel abroad, the travel industry will be undergoing major expansion in the decade ahead. It will offer some of the most exciting job and career opportunities for people who love to travel and work at interesting jobs at the same time.

The travel industry is much more than the stereotypical travel agent arranging tickets, tours, and hotels for tour groups and anxious tourists. A highly segmented industry, it involves a network of airlines, hotels, resorts, cruise lines, restaurants, wholesalers, incentive groups, retail tour agents, car rental and catering firms, meeting planners, corporate travel divisions, educators, journalists, travel writers, and a host of related organizations and jobs centered on the business of moving and managing people from one location to another. It's a challenging, exciting, and highly entrepreneurial industry with many people reporting a high degree of job satisfaction and claiming to have found *"the best job in the world"*—and with all the perks to prove it! Public relations officers in major hotels, for example, continuously meet and entertain international celebrities, work closely with the local international business community, and participate in numerous community activities—a worklife many still can't believe they "fell into" in the travel industry.

While many of the businesses, such as major airlines and major hotel chains, are huge corporations, most travel-related businesses appear big but are actually small and highly entrepreneurial. They appear big because they are connected to one another through efficient communication and marketing systems which places everyone within a mutually interdependent network of business transactions. It's the type of business where there is a high degree of competition as well as a high degree of mutual cooperation.

If your major motivation for seeking an international job is your desire to travel and see and experience new places and if you seek challenges, like to do different things, and have a sense of entrepreneurship, you should seriously investigate the variety of job and career opportunities available in the travel industry. In contrast to many other international jobs that require a great deal of education, foreign language expertise, and international experience, the international travel business is more oriented to individuals demonstrating entrepreneurship and job performance skills relevant to the particular industry. In other words, it is much easier to break into this field than into many other international fields. Many individuals without college degrees are able to pursue successful careers in this industry.

Like any other industry, the travel industry has its positives and negatives. Depending on which segment of the industry you enter, you will find few high paying jobs. In fact, individuals in these industries make about 20 to 30 percent less than people in other industries, including government. However, they do get special travel benefits and perks not available in other industries, and a high degree of job satisfaction tends to be widespread throughout the industry. Many people in the industry do not travel as much as they originally thought they would or they travel too much to the point where traveling is no longer as exciting as it once was. At the same time, given the highly segmented and interdependent nature of the industry, careers in travel may involve working for several segments within the industry. For example, you may start working on a cruise line and then later work for a hotel or resort chain and finally move into the incentive travel business or airlines. This mobility amongst segments within the industry leads to interesting career changes and work environments.

A Highly Segmented Industry

The travel industry is the ultimate example of a highly segmented yet integrated industry where entrepreneurship plays a key role in the continuing vitality and expansion of the industry as well as the career mobility of individuals within the industry. It's an industry organized to move about $300 billion spent on travel by Americans each year. It employs over 6 million people who work in over 500,000 businesses, from the small mom and pop corner travel agency to large corporate hotels and airlines. Huge franchised travel agencies such as Ask Mr. Foster and incentive travel groups such as E. F. McDonald and Maritz offer thousands of job opportunities in the travel industry. When linked to travel industries in other countries—including airlines, hotels, tour companies, ground operators, and incentive groups—this is a very global industry with a great deal of movement of employees among countries and segments of the industry.

The major segments or sub-industries and players within the travel industry include planners, operators, suppliers, promoters, and supporters:

- travel agencies and operators
- corporate travel managers
- tour operators
- incentive travel companies
- convention and meeting planners
- airlines
- cruise lines
- rail services
- car rentals
- bus lines
- accommodations and lodging industry
- advertising agencies
- research and marketing groups
- travel writers and photographers
- publishing and journalism
- computer support services
- education and training
- public relations
- travel clubs
- tourist sites and attractions
- airport and aviation management groups
- government tourist promotion offices
- culture and arts promotion groups

Not surprising, the travel industry employs numerous types of workers from computer specialists to marketing researchers and artists. While many people in this industry do little traveling, others may do a great deal of traveling as part of their day-to-day work. In addition, many people are involved in exciting international work environments.

Breaking In

There are no hard and fast rules on how to break into the travel industry. The bad news is that it is a highly competitive industry given its glamorous reputation and numerous job seekers who want to break into the industry. The good news is that it is a rapidly expanding industry that offers many opportunities for individuals with the right combination of motivations, skills, abilities, interests, and drive. The good news also is that you don't need a great deal of education and training to make it in this industry. The skills you need are specific to each segment within the industry, and they are best acquired on the job. Therefore, what you need most of all is an entry-level job that will enable you to acquire skills and contacts that will enable you to later move within the larger industry.

While more than 200 colleges and universities offer travel programs and several travel schools offer courses of study that ostensibly lead to travel careers, the industry has yet to recognize such formal educational mechanisms as necessary prerequisites for entry into and advancement within the industry. Nonetheless, many of these programs and schools can assist you in specialized areas within the industry. Furthermore, they are more likely to assist you through their network of contacts within the industry than by imparting specific classroom knowledge and skills relevant to the industry.

If you are interested in attending a travel school, many of which offer six month to one-year full-time courses of study, some of the best known and respected ones include: Ask Mr. Foster Travel Academy, Associated Schools, Wilma Boyd Career Schools, Colorado School of Travel, Conlin-Hallissey Travel School, Echols Travel School, Institute of Certified Travel Agents, Intensive Trainers, International Aviation and Travel Academy, International Travel Institute, International Travel Training Courses, Mundus Institute of Travel, The New York School of Travel, Southeastern Academy, Travel Career School of Minnesota, Travel Education Center, and Travel Trade School.

If you are interested in the hotel industry, Cornell University's School of Hotel Administration has a fine reputation. Other universities offering special degree programs in travel include: Adelphi University, Clemson University, Florida International University, George Washington University, Metropolitan State College (Denver), Michigan State University, National College (Rapid City), New School for Social Research, Parks College of St. Louis University, Quinsigamond Community College, Rochester Institute of Technology, Santa Ana College, University of Hawaii, University of Nevada, University of New Haven, University of New Orleans, and University of Notre Dame.

You will also find several internship opportunities available with businesses in the travel industry. An internship can be an important way to acquire specialized experience and develop contacts within the industry.

Your best strategy for breaking into the travel industry will be to network among individuals within the travel industry. Make contacts, conduct informational interviews, and locate job vacancies that best fit your interests, skills, and abilities. Most entry-level positions will be based in the United States and hopefully provide opportunities to travel and work abroad.

Useful Resources

You will find numerous resources available to assist you with a job search within the travel industry from general job and career books to directories and publications of professional associations. A good starting point is to consult the following books:

Flying High In Travel, Karen Rubin (New York: Wiley & Sons)

Jobs For People Who Love Travel, Ron and Caryl Krannich (Manassas Park, VA: Impact Publications)

Travel and Hospitality Career Directory, Ronald W. Fry, ed. (Detroit, MI: Gale Research)

Internships In Airlines, Cruise Lines, Hotels and Motels, Resorts, and Travel Agencies, Ronald W. Fry, ed. (Detroit, MI: Gale Research).

These books are available through Impact Publications (see order form at the end of this book). You will also find a few other career books that deal with specific segments of the industry, such as careers as a travel agent, airline pilot, travel writer, or in hotel management and cruise lines. Many of these books should be available in your local library and a few bookstores.

You should also begin reading several of the trade publications and following developments within the professional travel associations. Magazines such as *Travel Digest, Travel Weekly, Hotel and Resort Industry, Meetings and Conventions, Successful Meetings,* and *Tour and Travel News* will keep you abreast of developments in the travel industry. Professional associations such as the Institute of Certified Travel Agents, International Association of Convention and Visitors Bureaus, Meeting Planners Inter-National, and the Society of Incentive Travel Executives provide information on their organization and membership. Contact information on these and other travel industry publications, associations, and companies is provided in the *Travel and Hospitality Career Directory*.

Chapter Sixteen

STARTING YOUR OWN INTERNATIONAL BUSINESS

Working for someone else in the international arena is not for everyone. Indeed, given the problems of finding employment in many "favorite countries," due to legal restrictions and few opportunities as well as the overall unpredictability and instability of many international jobs, working for someone else has numerous limitations. Once established, most U.S. companies with operations abroad, for example, offer few job opportunities for Americans, because they prefer developing local staffs rather than relocating personal abroad. Contractors working in Third World development increasingly find themselves working in some of the world's least attractive places. Many initially got involved in this type of work because they enjoyed the particular countries in which they worked. In contrast to such jobs 10 or 15 years ago, international work in these new countries is no longer as much fun as it used to be in the countries which are now Newly Industrialized Countries (NICs) and which are primarily expanding their private sectors through foreign investment and trade.

BE YOUR OWN BOSS

One way around these problems is to create your own employment with you being the employer. Indeed, why not hire yourself by creating a job for you in your favorite countries? Why don't you make the decisions when, where, and with whom you want to work internationally during the next 10 to 20 years? Why not avoid the hassles of finding an international job on someone else's payroll and then having to repeat the process again in another two or three years?

For some people the best of all worlds is to have the freedom to travel and work wherever and whenever they want and make a good living at the same time. Given the increased emphasis on business, economics, global trade, and travel in the international arena, the 1990s should be an unprecedented decade for starting small international businesses, especially import/export, consulting, travel, and sourcing businesses. The climate is right for such a move. After all, with the ending of the Cold War and increased emphasis on solving national development problems through economic expansion, more and more countries are eager to develop trade relations and encourage foreign investment and joint ventures. Whether you are just starting out or changing jobs and careers within the international arena, you may well discover that going into an international business for yourself may be the most exciting and rewarding approach to the international job market.

During the past few years we have met more and more people who have decided to either break into the international arena or change international jobs and careers by starting their own businesses. Some of these people decide to open a small shop which sells imported arts, crafts, antiques, and home furnishings. Others become wholesalers of jewelry and other products for retail stores offering imported products or function as traders and brokers for other businesses. Some become consultants or agents for U.S. businesses interested in expanding trade abroad. And still others start their own travel business with emphasis on international travel. All quickly become involved in major business activities—purchasing, marketing, trade activities, shipping, and administration.

In most cases the primary motivation to start an international business or expand domestic operations into the international arena is to make a living at something they enjoy and periodically travel abroad to countries that most interest them. What these people often discover is that it is much easier and more rewarding to work abroad via your own business than working for someone else. They make three or four trips abroad each year to places they most enjoy.

GETTING STARTED

Going into business is not for everyone. While you will have opportunities to travel abroad and the freedom to pick and choose where you want to work, sustaining a business long-term involves a great deal more than travel. You first of all need to be entrepreneurial and secondly willing to deal with the details of managing a business. This means commitment, hard work, and a willingness to do things you don't necessarily enjoy doing all of the time. You may need to simultaneously be an accountant, marketer, salesperson, administrator, planner, purchasing agent, travel planner, and shipper. If you are primarily interested in import/export business, you need to process two key skills for success—sales and marketing. In addition, you must develop a base of suppliers and customers. To be successful, all of these activities take time, money, and persistence.

While nearly 600,000 new businesses are started each year in the United States, grim business statistics also discourage would-be entrepreneurs: another 400,000 to 500,000 businesses fail; 50 percent fail within the first 38 months; and nearly 90 percent fail within 10 years. Unfortunately, starting your own business is a risky business; the statistical odds are against anyone becoming a successful entrepreneur.

Nonetheless, owning your business is a viable international job and career alternative to working for someone else—if you approach business intelligently. Many people fail because they lack the necessary ingredients for success.

LEARN TO TAKE RISKS

You will find few challenges riskier than starting your own business. At the same time, you may experience your greatest professional satisfaction in running your own business. If done right, an international business can become the perfect solution to the international job and career question.

Starting a business means taking risks. First, you will probably go into debt and realize little income during the first two years you are building your business, even though you had grandiose visions of becoming an overnight success. You may be under-capitalized or have overhead costs higher than anticipated. It takes time to develop a regular group of suppliers and clients. What profits you do realize are normally plowed back into the business in order to expand operations and guarantee larger future profits. Second, business is often a trial and error process in which it is difficult to predict or ensure outcomes. Due to unforeseen circumstances beyond your control, you may fail even though you work hard and make intelligent planning, investment, and management decisions. Third, you could go bankrupt and lose more than just your investments of time and money.

At the same time, owning your own business can be tremendously satisfying. It is the ultimate of independence. Being your own boss means you are in control, and no one can fire you. You are rewarded in direct proportion to your productivity. Your salary is not limited by a boss, nor are your accomplishments credited to others. Unless you decide otherwise, you are not wedded to an 8 to 5 work routine or an annual two-week vacation. Depending on how successful your business becomes, you may be able to retire young and pursue other interests. You can turn what you truly enjoy doing, such as hobbies, into a profitable, rewarding, and fun career.

But such self-indulgence and gratification has costs. You will probably need at least $20,000 to $40,000 of start-up capital, or perhaps much more depending upon the type of business you enter. No one will be sending you a paycheck every two weeks so you can regularly pay your bills. You may work 12 and 14 hour days, seven days a week, and have no vacation during the first few years. And you may become heavily indebted, experience frequent cash flow problems, and eventually have creditors descend on you.

Why, then, start your own business? If you talk to people who have worked for others and then started their own businesses, they will tell you similar stories. They got tired of drawing a salary while making someone else rich. they got bored with their work and hated the 8 to 5 routine. Some were victims of organizational politics. On a more positive note, many started businesses because they had a great idea they wanted to pursue or they wanted the challenge of independently accomplishing their own goals.

There are few things that are more self-actualizing than running your own business. But you must have realistic expectations as well as a motivational pattern which is conducive to taking risks and being an entrepreneur. In Chapter Five you should have identified your motivational patterns and skills. If you like security, predictability, and stability, you probably are a candidate for a position where someone hands you a paycheck. If you read and believe in the get-rich-quick book which tries to minimize your risks and uncertainty with *"positive thinking"*, you probably have been ripped-off by an enterprising author who is getting rich writing books for naive people!

POSSESS THE RIGHT
STRENGTHS FOR SUCCESS

How can you become self-employed and successful at the same time? No one has a magical success formula for the budding entrepreneur—only advice. We do know why many businesses fail, and we can identify some basic characteristics for success. Poor planning, management, and decision-making lie at the heart of most business failures. Many people go into business without doing sufficient market research; they under-capitalize; they select a poor location; they incur extremely high and debilitating overhead costs; they lack commitment for the long-term; they are unwilling to sacrifice; they can't read or count; and they lack interpersonal and salesmanship skills.

On the positive side, studies continue to identify something called *"drive"*, or the need to achieve, as a key characteristic of successful entrepreneurs. According to Kellogg (*Fast Track*, McGraw-Hill), and others, young achievers and successful entrepreneurs possess similar characteristics:

> *"A high energy level, restless, a willingness to work hard*
> *and take risks, a desire to escape from insecurity."*

Successful business people combine certain motivations, skills, and circumstances. Contrary to popular myths, you don't need to be rich or have an MBA or business experience to get started. If you are willing to gamble and are a self-starter, self-confident, or organizer, and you like people, you may be on the right track for business success. These characteristics along with drive, thinking ability, human relations, communication, technical knowledge, hard work, persistence, and good luck are essential ingredients for business success.

If these are among your strengths, as identified in Chapter Five, you may be a good candidate for starting your own business with a high probability of success. If you feel you have recurring weaknesses in certain areas, you may want to consider finding a business partner who has particular complementary strengths for running a business.

KNOW YOURSELF

There are many different ways to get started in business. You can buy into a franchise which can initially cost you $20,000 to $500,000. Advertisements n the *Wall Street Journal* are a good source for hundreds of franchise opportunities from flipping hamburgers to selling animals. You can join someone else's business on a full-time or part-time basis as a partner or employee in order to get some direct business experience. You can try your hand at a direct-sales business such as Amway, Shaklee, or Avon. You can buy someone else's business or you can start your own business from scratch.

Your decision on how to get started in business should be based upon the data you generated on your skills and goals in Chapter Five. Do not go into business for negative reasons—get fired, hate your present job, or can't find work. Unfortunately, many people go into business with totally unrealistic expectations as well as with little understanding of their own goals, skills, and motivations and how small businesses operate. For example, while it is nice to import clothes and accessories from Hong Kong and work around pretty clothes, owning a dress shop requires handling inventory and personnel as well as paying the rent and doing bookkeeping. Getting all those pretty dresses on the rack is hard work! Many people also don't understand how the business world works. It requires a great deal of interpersonal skill to develop and expand personal networks of creditors, suppliers, clients, colleagues, and competitors.

Therefore, you should do two things before you decide to go into business. First, thoroughly explore your goals and motivations. The questions are familiar:

- What do you want to go?
- What do you do well?
- What do you enjoy doing?

Second, research different types of businesses in order to better understand advantages, disadvantages, procedures, processes, and possible problems. Talk to business persons about their work. Try to learn as much as possible about the reality before you invest your time and money in your own venture. Surprisingly, few people do this. Many people leap into a business that they think will be great and then later learn it was neither right for them nor did they have realistic expectations of what was involved. Indeed, many people would like to get into the import/export business. Perhaps they were traveling abroad and found a particular product they thought would sell well back home. All of a sudden they have great expectations of turning this little discovery into a profitable business. However, reality strikes them once they have to address such nuts-and-bolts business issues of suppliers, export permits, shipping arrangements, duties, markets, buyers, advertising, and distribution. Failure to address such issues in concrete "who does what, where, and when" terms is precisely why so many businesses fail each year and why the import/export business is filled with numerous dreamers who have difficult turning an idea into a profitable reality.

You should approach business opportunities the same way you approach the job market: do research, develop networks, and conduct informational and referral interviews. Most business people, including your competition, will be happy to share their experiences with you and assist you with advice and referrals. Such research is absolutely invaluable. If you fail to do it initially, you will pay later on by making the same mistakes that millions of others have made in starting their own businesses in isolation of others. Don't be high on motivation but low on knowledge and skills, for "positive thinking" and "thinking big" are not substitutes for doing the work!

LOOK FOR NEW OPPORTUNITIES

Most business people will tell you similar stories of the reality of running your own business. Do your market research, spend long hours, plan, and be persistent. They also will give you advice on what businesses to avoid and what business routines you should be prepared to handle.

Numerous international products and services are excellent candidates for a business. Many developing countries, for example, offer excellent quality arts, crafts, and home furnishings that appeal to American buyers either through direct-mail or in small shops and department stores. Indeed, some enterprising individuals have been able to develop businesses as wholesalers and suppliers of such products to mail-order houses and major department stores. They regularly make trips to Africa, Asia, and Latin America seeking products and suppliers for major buyers back home. Others operate their own "international" arts, crafts, antique, home decorative, clothing, or gift shop and periodically make trips abroad to purchase new products as well as work with their suppliers on designs and quality control. Some develop specialty travel businesses that focus primarily on adventure travel to Third World countries.

Whatever your choices, try to select a product or service that you enjoy working with and which has a readily identifiable market.

PREPARE THE BASICS

You also need to consider several other factors before starting a business. Since a business requires financing, locating, planning, developing suppliers and customer relations, and meeting legal requirements, be prepared to address these questions:

1. **How can I best finance the business?** Take out a personal or business loan with a bank? Go into a partnership in order to share the risks and costs? Get a loan from the Small Business Administration?

2. **How much financing do I need?** Many businesses fail because they are under-capitalized. Others fail because of over-spending on rent, furnishings, inventory, personnel, and advertising.

3. **Where is my market?** Just in this community, region, or nationwide, or internationally? Mail-order businesses enable you to expand your market nationwide whereas retail and service businesses tend to be confined to particular neighborhoods or communities.

4. **Who are my suppliers?** How many must I work with? What about credit arrangements? Who handles export and import permits? What about quality control? Can they deliver in a timely and correct manner?

5. **Where is the best location for the business?** Do you need to open a store or operate out of your home? If you need a store or office, is it conveniently located for your clientele? "Location is everything" still best summarizes the success of many businesses.

6. **How should the business be legally structured?** Sole proprietorship, partnership, or corporation? Each has certain tax and liability advantages and disadvantages.

7. **What licenses and permits do I need?** These consist of local business licenses and permits, federal employee identification numbers, state sales tax number, state occupational licenses, federal licenses and permits, and special state and local regulations which vary from state to state and from community to community. What type of insurance do I need? Fire, theft, liability, workers' compensation, auto, disability?

8. **How many employees do I need?** Can I do without personnel initially until the business expands? Should I use part-time and temporary help?

9. **What business name should I use?** If incorporated, is anyone else using the name? If a trade name, is it registered?

10. **What accounting system should I use?** Cash or accrual? Can I handle the books or do I need a part-time or full-time accountant?

11. **Do I need a lawyer?** What type of lawyer? What legal work can I do myself?

12. **How do I develop a business plan?** A business plan should include a definition of the business, a marketing strategy, operational policies, purchasing plans, financial statements, and capital raising plans.

GET USEFUL ADVICE

If you decide to go into business, make sure you choose the right business for your particular skills, abilities, motivation, and interests. A good starting point is Douglas Gray's *The Entrepreneur's Complete Self-Assessment Guide* (Bellingham, WA: Self-Counsel Press). This book provides you with useful exercises for assessing your suitability for becoming an entrepreneur. For a good overview of the many decisions you must make in establishing a small business, see Bernard Kamaroff's *Small-Time Operators* (Laytonville, CA: Bell Springs Publishing). This book provides you with all the basic information you need for starting your own business, including ledger sheets for setting up your books. Albert Lowry's *How To Become Financially Successful By Owning Your Own Business* (New York: Simon and Schuster) also outlines the basics for both small-time and big-time operators.

Several other books provide similar how-to advice for the neophyte entrepreneur:

Avoiding the Pitfalls of Starting Your Own Business, Jeffrey P. Davidson (New York: Shapolsky Publishers, Inc.)

The Entrepreneur's Guide To Starting a Successful Business, James W. Holloran (Blue Ridge Summit, PA: TAB Books)

Going Into Business For Yourself: New Beginnings After 50, Ina Lee Selden (Washington, DC: American Association of Retired Persons)

How To Run a Small Business, The J. K. Lasser Tax Institute (New York: St. Martin's Press)

Starting On a Shoestring: Building a Business Without a Bankroll, Arnold S. Goldstein (New York: Wiley and Sons)

The Federal government will help you with several publications available through the Small Business Administration: 1441 L Street, NW, Washington DC 20416, Tel. 800/368-5855. SBA field offices are located in 85 cities. The Consumer Information Center publishes a free booklet entitled *More Than a Dream: Running Your Own Business*: Dept. 616J, Pueblo, Colorado 81009. The Internal Revenue Service sponsors several one-day tax workshops for small businesses. Your local chamber of commerce also can give you useful information.

A great deal of information is also available on specific international businesses. Several books, for example, address the major issues involved in operating an import or export business:

Building an Import/Export Business, Kenneth D. Weiss (New York: Wiley and Sons)

The Export Trading Company Guidebook (Washington, DC: International Trade Administration, U.S. Department of Commerce)

Exportise: An International Trade Source Book for Smaller Company Executives (Boston, MA: The Small Business Foundation of America)

How To Be an Importer and Pay For Your World Travel, Mary Green and Stanley Gillmar (Berkeley, CA: Ten Speed Press)

Importing Into the United States (Washington, DC: United States Customs Service, Department of Treasury)

Your Own Import-Export Business, Carl A. Nelson (Chula Vista, CA: Global Business and Trade)

Magazines such as *Global Trade Executive* and *World Trade* as well as regional business publications such as *The Far Eastern Economic Review* are well worth reading in order to keep abreast of current international business developments.

Several organizations provide assistance for importers and exporters. The *American Association of Importers and Exporters* (11 West 42nd St., New York, NY 10036, Tel. 212/944-2230), for example, assists its members with numerous services. Many state and local organizations also provide assistance in the form of regular meetings and seminars focusing on international trade. You may also want to attend international trade fairs where you will have an opportunity to inspect products, attend useful seminars, and network with fellow international business people.

CONTINUE SUCCESS

The factors for operating a successful business are similar to the 20 principles we outlined in Chapter Three for conducting a successful job search. Once your initial start-up problems are solved, you must organize, plan, implement, and manage in relation to your goals. Many people lack these abilities as well as the drive to sustain a business long-term. Some people are good at initially starting a business, but they are unable to follow-through in managing day-to-day routines once the business is established. And others have the ability to start, manage, and expand businesses successfully.

Be careful about business success. Many business people become obsessed with their work, put in 12 and 14 hour days continuously, and spend seven day weeks to make the business successful. Unwilling to delegate, they try to do too much and thus become a prisoner to the business. The proverbial "tail wagging the dog" is a common phenomenon in small businesses. For some people, this lifestyle feeds their ego and makes them happy. For others, the 8 to 5 routine of working for someone else on salary may look very attractive. Similar to landing an international job, you must be prepared to change your lifestyle when embarking on your own business. Your major limitation will be yourself. So think it over carefully, do your research, and plan, organize, implement, and manage for success. The thrill of independence and success is hard to beat!

Chapter Seventeen

TURN YOUR
GOALS INTO REALITIES

Understanding without action is a waste of time. And buying a how-to book without implementing it is a waste of money. Many people read how-to books, attend how-to seminars, and do nothing other than read more books, attend more seminars, and engage in more wishful thinking. While these activities become forms of therapy for some individuals, they should lead to positive actions for you. If with your new understanding of international employment you still want an international job, you must take action to land an international position that is right for you.

From the very beginning of this book we stressed the importance of both understanding how the international job market operates and developing appropriate job search strategies linked to specific organizations for getting the job you want. We make no assumptions nor claim any magic is contained in this book. Rather, we have attempted to assemble useful information to help individuals realistically approach an international job search. Individual chapters examined international trends, myths, and specific job search skills such as writing resumes and conducting informational interviews, as well as outlined specific structures and opportunities among government agencies, international organizations, contracting firms, nonprofit organizations, associations, research firms, foundations, educational institutions, and businesses. We have done our part in getting you to the implementation stage. What happens next is your responsibility.

Assuming you have a firm understanding of each job search step and how to relate them to each international organization, what do you do next? The next steps involve **hard work**. Just how motivated are you to seek an international job? Our experience is that individuals need to be sufficiently **motivated** to make the first move and do it properly. If you go about your job search half-heartedly —you just want to "test the international waters"—to see what's out there— don't expect to be successful. You must be committed to achieving specific goals. Make the decision to properly develop and implement your job search and be prepared to work hard in achieving your goals.

Understanding without action is a waste of time. And buying a how-to book without implementing it is a waste of money.

Once you've convinced yourself to take the necessary steps to find a job or change and advance your career, you need to find the **time** to properly implement your job search. This requires setting aside specific blocks of time for identifying your motivated skills, developing your resume, writing letters, making telephone calls, and conducting the necessary research and networking required for success. This whole process takes time. If you are a busy person, like most people, you simply must make the time. Practice your own versions of time management or cutback management. Get better organized, give some things up, or cut back on all your activities. If, for example, you can set aside one hour each day to devote to your job search, you will spend seven hours a week or 28 hours a month on your search. However, you should and can find more time than this for these activities.

Time and again we find successful job hunters are ones who routinize a job search schedule and keep at it. They make contact after contact, conduct numerous informational interviews, submit many applications and resumes, and keep repeating these activities in spite of encountering rejections. They learn that success is just a few more "nos" and informational interviews away!

You may find it useful to commit yourself in writing to achieving job search success. This is a very useful way to get both motivated and directed for action. Start by completing the following job search contract and keep it near you—in your briefcase or on your desk.

─── JOB SEARCH CONTRACT ───

1. I will begin my job search on _____.
2. I will involve <u>(individual/group)</u> with my job search.
3. I will complete my skills identification step by ___.
4. I will complete my objective statement by ____.
5. I will complete my resume by ____.
6. Each week I will:
   make ____ new job contacts.
   conduct ____ informational interviews.
   follow-up on ____ referrals.
7. My first job interview will take place during the
   week of ____.
8. I will begin my new international job on ____.
9. I will manage my time so that I can successfully
   complete my job search and find a high quality job.

   Signature: _____
   Date: _____

In addition, you should complete weekly performance reports. These reports identify what you actually accomplished rather than what your good intentions tell you to do. Make copies of the performance and planning report form on page 297 and use one each week to track your actual progress and to plan your activities for the next week.

If you fail to meet these written commitments, issue yourself a revised and updated contract. But if you do this three or more times, we strongly suggest you stop kidding yourself about your motivation and commitment to find an international job. Start over again, but this time consult a professional career counselor who can provide you with the necessary structure to make progress in finding a job.

A professional may not be cheap, but if paying for help gets you on the right track and results in the job you want, it's money well spent. Do not be "penny wise but pound foolish" with your future. If you must seek professional advice, be sure you are an informed consumer according to our "shopping" advice in Chapter Four. By all means avoid the many hucksters who prey on highly motivated international job seekers with promises of job placements in exchange for exorbitant upfront fees. And don't confuse these so-called "helpers" with professional career counselors who are trained to assist you with the most critical step in the job search process—self assessment.

WEEKLY JOB SEARCH PERFORMANCE AND PLANNING REPORT

1. The week of: _____.
2. This week I:
   - wrote ___ job search letters.
   - sent ___ resumes and ___ letters to potential employers.
   - completed ___ applications.
   - made ___ job search telephone calls.
   - completed ___ hours of job research.
   - set up ___ appointments for informational interviews.
   - conducted ___ informational interviews.
   - received ___ invitations to a job interview.
   - followed up on ___ contacts and ___ referrals.
3. Next week I will:
   - write ___ job search letters.
   - send ___ resumes and ___ letters to potential employers.
   - complete ___ applications.
   - make ___ job search telephone calls.
   - complete ___ hours of job research.
   - set up ___ appointments for informational interviews.
   - conduct ___ informational interviews.
     follow up on ___ contacts and ___ referrals.
4. Summary of progress this week in reference to my Job Search Contract commitments:

   _____

   _____

   _____

   _____

The international job market as outlined in this book is a fascinating employment arena. It attracts all types of people with different skills and motivations. It encompasses a large variety of jobs located in some of the world's most exciting and exotic places. If you plan your international job search according to the advice outlined in the first half of this book and then take action that links your job search to the organizations and opportunities outlined in the second half of the book as well as in our companion directory, *The Almanac of International Jobs and Careers*, you should be successful in landing an international job you want. Above all, take the time to sail through this job market with a plan of action that links your qualifications to the needs of employers.

INDEX

CAREER RESOURCES

Contact Impact Publications to receive a free copy of their latest comprehensive and annotated catalog of over 1,000 career resources (books, subscriptions, training programs, videos, audiocassettes, computer software).

The following career resources, many of which are mentioned in previous chapters, are available directly from Impact Publications. Complete the following form or list the titles, include postage (see formula at the end), enclose payment, and send your order to:

IMPACT PUBLICATIONS
9104-N Manassas Drive
Manassas Park, VA 22111
Tel. 703/361-7300
FAX 703/335-9486

Orders from individuals must be prepaid by check, moneyorder, Visa or MasterCard number. We accept telephone and FAX orders with a Visa or MasterCard number.

Qty.	TITLES	Price	TOTAL

INTERNATIONAL & OVERSEAS JOBS

Qty.	TITLES	Price	TOTAL
___	Almanac of International Jobs and Careers	$14.95	___
___	Building an Import/Export Business	$14.95	___
___	Careers in International Affairs	$15.00	___
___	Complete Guide To International Jobs & Careers	$13.95	___
___	Directory of Jobs and Careers Abroad	$14.95	___
___	Directory of Overseas Summer Jobs	$14.95	___
___	Education Travel Directory	$5.95	___
___	Guide To Careers in World Affairs	$13.95	___
___	Hoover's Handbook of World Business	$21.95	___
___	How To Get a Job in Europe	$15.95	___
___	How To Get a Job in the Pacific Rim	$17.95	___
___	How To Live and Work in Australia	$12.95	___
___	How To Live and Work in Great Britain	$12.95	___
___	International Business Woman of the 1990's	$19.95	___
___	International Careers	$10.95	___
___	International Consultant	$22.95	___
___	International Directory of Voluntary Work	$13.95	___

___	International Jobs	$12.95	___
___	ISS Directory of Overseas Schools	$29.95	___
___	Job Hunter's Guide To Japan	$12.95	___
___	Key European Search Firms & Their U.S. Links	$39.95	___
___	Making It Abroad	$14.95	___
___	Overseas List	$14.95	___
___	Passport To Overseas Employment	$14.95	___
___	Teaching English Abroad	$13.95	___
___	Work Your Way Around the World	$16.95	___
___	Work, Study, Travel Abroad	$12.95	___
___	Worldwide Jobs 1993	$19.95	___

TRAVEL JOBS & CAREERS

___	Flying High in Travel	$16.95	___
___	How To Get a Job With a Cruise Line	$12.95	___
___	Internships: Travel and Hospitality Industries	$11.95	___
___	Jobs For People Who Love Travel	$12.95	___
___	Travel and Hospitality Career Directory	$19.95	___

PUBLIC EMPLOYMENT & WASHINGTON, DC

___	The 171 Reference Book	$18.95	___
___	ACWA: Administrative Careers With America	$15.00	___
___	Almanac of American Government Jobs and Careers	$14.95	___
___	Book of U.S. Government Jobs	$15.95	___
___	Complete Guide To Public Employment	$15.95	___
___	Federal Jobs For College Graduates	$15.00	___
___	Find a Federal Job Fast!	$9.95	___
___	Government Job Finder	$14.95	___
___	How To Get a Federal Job	$15.00	___
___	How To Get a Job in Washington, DC	$15.95	___
___	Jobs in Washington, DC	$11.95	___
___	The Right SF-171 Writer	$14.95	___
___	Washington, DC Job Bank	$12.95	___

JOBS WITH NONPROFIT ORGANIZATIONS

___	Good Works	$18.00	___
___	Jobs and Careers With Nonprofit Organizations	$12.95	___
___	Nonprofits' Job Finder	$14.95	___
___	Profitable Careers in Nonprofit	$12.95	___

CONTRACTING & CONSULTING OPPORTUNITIES

___	Getting Started in Federal Contracting	$21.95	___
___	International Consultant	$19.95	___
___	Proposals That Win Federal Contracts	$24.95	___

COMPUTER SOFTWARE

___	INSTANT Job Winning Letters	$39.95	___
___	Quick & Easy 171's	$49.95	___

JOB LISTINGS & VACANCY ANNOUNCEMENTS

___ Federal Career Opportunities (6 issues)	$38.00	_____
___ Federal Jobs Digest (6 issues)	$29.00	_____
___ The International Educator (4 issues)	$25.00	_____
___ International Employment Gazette (6 issues)	$35.00	_____
___ International Employment Hotline (12 issues)	$39.00	_____

KEY DIRECTORIES

___ American Almanac of Jobs and Salaries	$15.95	_____
___ Dictionary of Occupational Titles	$39.95	_____
___ Directory of Executive Recruiters (annual)	$39.95	_____
___ Directory of Outplacement Firms	$69.95	_____
___ Directory of Special Programs For Minority Group Members	$31.95	_____
___ Encyclopedia of Careers and Vocational Guidance	$129.95	_____
___ Enhanced Guide For Occupational Exploration	$29.95	_____
___ Internships 1992 (annual)	$27.95	_____
___ Job Hunter's Sourcebook	$49.95	_____
___ Jobs 1992 (annual)	$15.95	_____
___ Jobs Rated Almanac	$14.95	_____
___ National Trade and Professional Associations	$69.95	_____
___ Minority Organizations	$50.00	_____
___ National Job Bank	$229.95	_____
___ Occupational Outlook Handbook	$22.95	_____
___ Professional Careers Sourcebook	$79.95	_____
___ Washington (annual)	$55.95	_____

JOB SEARCH STRATEGIES & TACTICS

___ Careering and Re-Careering For the 1990s	$12.95	_____
___ Complete Job Search Handbook	$11.95	_____
___ Go Hire Yourself an Employer	$9.95	_____
___ Graduating To the 9-5 World	$11.95	_____
___ Joyce Lain Kennedy's Career Book	$29.95	_____
___ Professional's Job Finder	$15.95	_____
___ Right Place at the Right Time	$11.95	_____
___ Super Job Search	$22.95	_____

SKILLS, TESTING, & SELF-ASSESSMENT

___ Discover the Right Job For You!	$11.95	_____
___ Discover What You're Best At	$10.95	_____
___ New Quick Job Hunting Map	$3.95	_____
___ Three Boxes of Life	$14.95	_____
___ What Color Is Your Parachute	$12.95	_____
___ Where Do I Go From Here With My Life?	$10.95	_____

RESUMES, LETTERS, & NETWORKING

___ Dynamite Cover Letters	$9.95	_____
___ Dynamite Resumes	$9.95	_____
___ Great Connections	$11.95	_____

___ High Impact Resumes and Letters	$12.95	___
___ How To Work a Room	$9.95	___
___ Job Search Letters That Get Results	$12.95	___
___ Network Your Way To Job and Career Success	$11.95	___
___ Perfect Resume	$10.95	___
___ Resume Catalog	$15.95	___
___ Sure-Hire Resumes	$14.95	___
___ Your First Resume	$10.95	___

DRESS, APPEARANCE, IMAGE, & ETIQUETTE

___ Dressing Smart	$19.95	___
___ John Molloy's New Dress For Success	$10.95	___
___ Miss Manners' Guide To the Turn-of-the Millennium	$24.95	___
___ Professional Image	$10.95	___
___ Professional Presence	$21.95	___
___ Women's Dress For Success	$8.95	___

INTERVIEWS & SALARY NEGOTIATIONS

___ Dynamite Answers To Interview Questions	$9.95	___
___ How To Get Interviews From Job Ads	$16.95	___
___ Interview For Success	$11.95	___
___ Knock 'Em Dead With Great Answers To Interview Questions	$19.95	___
___ Listening: The Forgotten Skill	$12.95	___
___ Salary Success	$11.95	___

MILITARY

___ Beyond the Uniform	$12.95	___
___ Does Your Resume Wear Combat Boots?	$7.95	___
___ Job Search: Marketing Your Military Experience	$14.95	___
___ Re-Entry	$13.95	___
___ Retiring From the Military	$22.95	___
___ Transition To Civilian Life	$15.95	___

SUBTOTAL ___

Virginia residents add 4½% sales tax ___

POSTAGE/HANDLING ($3.00 for first title and 75¢ for each additional book) $3.00

Number of additional titles x 75¢ ----------------- ___

TOTAL ENCLOSED ------------------- ___